THE METAPHYSICS
OF EXPERIENCE

THE METAPHYSICS OF EXPERIENCE

A COMPANION TO WHITEHEAD'S

PROCESS AND REALITY

ELIZABETH M. KRAUS

New York
FORDHAM UNIVERSITY PRESS
1979

Printed in the United States of America

TO

L. A. D.

FOR LOVE,
UNDERSTANDING,
AND ENCOURAGEMENT

ACKNOWLEDGMENTS

The author is indebted to many people through whose assistance this *Companion* has reached completion. To thank them all would be impossible, but I would be remiss if I should fail to extend my gratitude to Professor Quentin Lauer, S.J., and Professor Leonard C. Feldstein, both of Fordham University, to Professor Robert C. Neville of the State University of New York at Stony Brook, and to Professor Lewis S. Ford of Old Dominion University, all of whom read the manuscript and provided me with the kind of insightful and scholarly criticism needed to sharpen one's thought. I would also like to thank Rev. Paul Kelly, assistant professor of philosophy at Wadhams Hall, for his invaluable help in the proofreading of both the manuscript and the galley proofs and in the preparation of the index.

NOTE

This volume should be read in conjunction with *Process and Reality*. As a comparison of the tables of contents of both works will reveal, the author has deliberately paralleled the structure of PR chapter by chapter in order to facilitate concurrent study. For optimum advantage, a section of the *Companion* should be read, followed by a reading of the corresponding chapter of PR. Thus the reader can move step by step through both works.

ABBREVIATIONS

Citations of Whitehead's works appear, for the most part, as listed here.

AE   *The Aims of Education*. New York: Mentor Books, n.d.

AI   *Adventures of Ideas*. New York: Free Press, 1967.

CN   *The Concept of Nature*. Cambridge: Cambridge University Press, 1964.

ESP   *Essays in Science and Philosophy*. New York: Greenwood, 1968.

FR   *The Function of Reason*. Boston: Beacon, 1966.

IM   *An Introduction to Mathematics*. New York: Holt, 1911.

IS   *The Interpretation of Science*. Ed. A. H. Johnson. Indianapolis & New York: Bobbs-Merrill, 1961.

MT   *Modes of Thought*. New York: Capricorn, 1958.

PNK   *An Enquiry Concerning the Principles of Natural Knowledge*. Cambridge: Cambridge University Press, 1925.

PRel   *The Principle of Relativity*. Cambridge: Cambridge University Press, 1922.

PR   *Process and Reality*. New York: Harper Torchbooks, 1960.

RM   *Religion in the Making*. Cleveland & New York: World, 1960.

SMW   *Science and the Modern World*. New York: Macmillan, 1925.

S   *Symbolism: Its Meaning and Effect*. New York: Capricorn, 1959.

This *Companion* was already in press when the Corrected Edition of PR, edd. D. R. Griffin and D. W. Sherburne (New York: Free Press, 1978), was published, and thus the new edition could not be cited.

CONTENTS

Preface   xi

Introduction   1

    I · The Nature of Process Philosophy   1
    II · The First Formulation   3
    III · The Language Problem   5
    IV · The Language of Feeling   9

1 *Science and the Modern World* as a Romantic Version
    of *Process and Reality*   11
    I · The Rhythms of Growth   11
    II · Scientific Materialism and the Fallacy of Simple Location   12
    III · Prehension as the Basis of Induction   17
    IV · The Actual Occasion as a Space–Time Quantum   21
    V · The Literary Experience   26
    VI · Eternal Objects   29
    VII · Creativity   36
    VIII · God   38

2 The Speculative Scheme (PR, Part I)   41
    I · The Nature of Speculative Philosophy   41
    II · The Categoreal Scheme and Derivative Notions   46

3 Discussions and Applications (PR, Part II)   55
    I · Givenness   55
    II · The Extensive Continuum   58
    III · Order, Society, Organisms, and Environment   60
    IV · The Modal Theory of Perception   69
        a. Perception in the Mode of Causal Efficacy   72
        b. Perception in the Mode of Presentational Immediacy   76
        c. Perception in the Mode of Symbolic Reference   80
    V · Prolegomenon to a Theory of Judgment: Propositions   87
    VI · The Theory of Judgment   94
    VII · Process: On Overview   98

4 The Structure of a Concrescence (PR, Part III)   101
    I · The Nature of Genetic Analysis   101
    II · The Nature of Feelings in General   102
    III · The Primary Feelings   108

IV · Propositions and Feelings   112
v · Comparative Feelings   117

5 The Theory of Extension (PR, Part IV)   127
    I · Coordinate Division   127
    II · Extensive Connection   133
    III · Flat Loci   141
    IV · Strains   149
    v · Measurement   154

6 God and the World (PR, Part V)   159
    I · God the Redeemer   159
    II · Concluding Meditations   169

Bibliography   175

Indices   177

PREFACE

Process and Reality undoubtedly ranks as one of the most difficult works in philosophical literature, second only to Kant's *Critique of Pure Reason* and Hegel's *Logic*. At the same time, it presents a philosophic schema capable (*a*) of interpreting and grounding twentieth-century advances in the physical, biological, psychological, and social sciences while avoiding crude reductionism, crass determinism, or neo-Positivism; (*b*) of taking the phenomenon of religion into account; and (*c*) of admitting the aesthetic as a valid element in human experience. Yet the unquestionable value of the work is shrouded by its inaccessibility to all save those few Whiteheadians willing to follow the tortuous path through the text, a path made incessantly circular by the continued necessity to retrace one's steps again and again in search of clarification. This *Companion* does not profess to make the journey easy, for to present a *"Process and Reality* without tears" would be to explain the work by explaining it away. There is not, nor can there be, a popularization of PR. The subtleties and intricacies of the work are essential to a genuine grasp of Whitehead's metaphysics. This *Companion* offers itself rather as a Sherpa guide to PR: to assist the serious student in grasping the meaning of the text and to prevent falls into misinterpretation.

The most obvious difficulty with PR lies in the language itself: the exasperatingly technical and strange vocabulary Whitehead was compelled to create as a vehicle for his thought. Ideally speaking, a translation of the technical jargon into more experiential terms would be the most valuable option for a PR commentary to follow; in the concrete, this is impossible. Such an attempt would render the commentary as hopelessly complex as the original and quadruple its length. The only remaining option is the careful use of explanatory metaphor to enable the reader to make the imaginative leap toward meaning which Whitehead calls for.

The obscurities and inconsistencies scattered throughout PR constitute an additional difficulty, one which has spawned a generation of Whiteheadian scholars with varying interpretations. Wherever possible, this *Companion* will sidestep interpretative disputes, since its goal is to explore PR rather than to go beyond it.[1] It will also sidestep the multiplicity of secondary sources available to the serious student of Whitehead because its intent is different. Most Whitehead analyses concentrate either on presenting a broad overview of Whitehead's philosophical system (as in the

---

[1] However, exploration entails both selection and interpretation, neither of which activities can be performed without at the same time revealing the perspective and consequent valuations of the explorer. The author's biases will become apparent as the *Companion* unfolds. Wherever these are conscious and result in non-traditional readings of the text, they will be noted, and a summary defense mounted in an accompanying note.

excellent works of Christian, Johnson, Leclerc, Lowe, Mays, Sherburne, et al.) or on detailed renderings of particular aspects—the sorts of studies found in scholarly journals. This work aims at an in-depth treatment of PR, a treatment which attempts to do justice both to the general contours and to the intricate detail of the philosophy of organism laid out in Whitehead's *magnum opus*.

A more serious difficulty lies in the circularity of the fundamental elements of the metaphysical scheme. Whitehead does not present a graded series of concepts through which one can move in linear fashion; rather, the comprehension of each entails the prior comprehension of the others. The reader must leap into the speculative circle, realizing that understanding will come like James's drops of perception—all at once or not at all. This *Companion* aims at obviating the latter possibility.

In the attempt to translate that aim into reality, this study will take the following format. The introduction will present the nature, basic insight, and linguistic difficulties of process philosophy; Chapter 1 will give an overview of Whitehead's initial, non-technical formulation of the philosophy of organism in SMW. The remainder of the work will follow the structural divisions of PR so that both can be read concurrently, each throwing light on what might be obscure in the other.

A final note is in order. Whitehead would be utterly inconsistent if he had intended PR as the formulation of an ultimate metaphysics to be at worst slavishly parroted and at best explicated and commented on by a narrow coterie of adoring followers. To be a genuine Whiteheadian is to see his thought as seminal, as tentative, as demanding the kind of development, rethinking, and revision which results from the confrontation of a theory with its application to broad-spectrum practice. In such a confrontation, practical issues receive new dimensions and new interpretations, and theory displays its strengths and its weaknesses. Some of these are already evident with respect to Whitehead's speculative scheme: on the credit side, the extraordinary relevance and utility of process philosophy to the physical, biological, psychological, social, and theological sciences; on the debit side, the almost inaccessible abstruseness of the scheme, its technical neologisms, its metaphysical complexity begging for simplification. Only in the dialectic between theory and application can the weaknesses be overcome. Such is the vocation of the Whiteheadian scholar, and to such a task the author has set herself.

In this context, the following examination of PR can be seen as complete in itself and yet the prelude to a larger enterprise. Chapter 6 begins that enterprise, being the barest sketch of a volume (currently straining for birth) developing the classic issues in theology in Whiteheadian categories. If present intentions can become future facts, this will be followed by similar works centering in other areas of interest to the author: ethics, aesthetics, mathematics, etc. It is my firm belief that the Whiteheadian categoreal scheme, if treated as an organism capable of adaptive growth, can provide the kind of metaphysical infrastructure sorely needed to ground and unify contemporary thought.

THE METAPHYSICS
OF EXPERIENCE

INTRODUCTION

PROCESS PHILOSOPHY is an answer to the being *vs.* becoming, permanence *vs.* change problematic which has been central to metaphysical speculation since the time of the Greeks. Most attempted solutions resolve the antitheses either by denying the reality of one or the other of the paired alternatives or by making it in some sense less real than, dependent upon, or derivative from the other. Despite the implications of its name, the process philosophy of Alfred North Whitehead does not opt for the Heraclitean alternative; nor does it attempt to make permanence in any way the subservient member of the pair. Rather, it asserts that being and becoming, permanence and change must claim coequal footing in any metaphysical interpretation of the real, because both are equally insistent aspects of experience.

> In the inescapable flux, there is something that abides; in the overwhelming permanence, there is an element that escapes into flux. Permanence can be snatched only out of flux; and the passing moment can find its adequate intensity only by its submission to permanence. Those who would disjoin the two elements can find no interpretation of patent facts [PR 513].

This is not to say that the permanence affirmed by Whitehead can be identified with substance in any of its classic forms (Aristotle, Aquinas, Descartes, Spinoza, etc.). These conceptualizations of the unchanging element in experience fall, in one way or another, into the Fallacy of Misplaced Concreteness: the error of reifying what in fact is a high-order abstraction. Nor can Whitehead be interpreted as rejecting the classical notions of substance in an unqualified manner. On the contrary, he acknowledges his debt to Aristotle, Descartes, Locke, et al. for various cogent aspects of their theories. His rejection of substance focuses on an error which was introduced into European philosophy by the medievals and found its most eloquent spokesman in Descartes: namely, that a substance is "an existent thing which requires nothing other than itself to exist" (*Principles of Philosophy*, I.51). It is this notion of substance as independent, as "just its individual self with no necessary relevance to any other particular" (PR 79), which Whitehead sees as fatal to a metaphysics which would purport to remain faithful to the modern experience of the world as an eco-system. Although the error originated with the Schoolmen, it has its roots in the Aristotelian dictum that substance is always a subject and can never become a predicate in the sense of inhering in another subject (*Categories*, 2A).

A twofold difficulty is hidden in the classic view of substance. First, it exalts the categories of quality and quantity over the category of relation, failing to realize that the former themselves are relational in that they express the ways in which substances *are for* other substances, and are not attributes of isolated substances. In other words, the subject–attribute mode of predication has been mistaken for a metaphysical paradigm. Secondly, and more fundamentally, the classic view makes an unwarranted dichotomy between a substance and its predicates, attributing permanence to the former and changeability to the latter, and in the same act renders substance *qua* substance transexperiential and unknowable (incapable of being present in another substance—in this case, in a knowing subject), graspable only in and through its accidental modifications. To put this in other language: the problematic conception is substance not as "that which is"—substance in the truly metaphysical sense—but substance in its categoreal distinction from accidents, substance as a logical and/or linguistic category. Whitehead himself retains the former sense in his notion of actual entities as the "final real things of which the world is made up" (PR 27); yet he denies the sort of radical aseity which accrues to substance when, in addition, it is considered as suppositum for accidents and hence as supporting qualities which it possesses in its own right, independent of its relation to the world. He sees this rejection of the essential relatedness of things as leading inexorably either to a Leibnizian rationalism of windowless monads or to a billiard ball universe of blindly interacting, qualityless particles. Both alternatives spell death to the metaphysics of experience, which for Whitehead must be a metaphysic of the patterned intertwining of all things: a philosophy of organism.

What is permanent in the Whiteheadian scheme is not, therefore, some underlying stage upon which accidental change is played, but rather the value achieved, the world-unification effected by and in an entity whose self-creative process is the growing together of the public world in the privacy of a perspective. It is important to note that this permanence is not to be construed as the endurance of the "is" of "that-which-is." To exist in the Whiteheadian sense is to self-actuate, to create a moment of "for-one's-self–ness," to be *now*. The product of the self-creative act, *being*, is immortal and permanent; the activity, *becoming*, is not. The activity perishes as it achieves the goal of determinateness aimed at in the process. An actual entity " 'never really is' " (PR 130). It is a drop of process, a pulse, a throb of existence, an event, a happening of value which sacrifices its immediacy in the instant it is gained, in the same manner as any "now" loses its nowness to a subsequent "now." Just as permanence cannot be attributed to the nowness of "now," so also the actual entity cannot endure in its subjective immediacy. By the same token, just as the content of any "now" becomes an historical "then" to be taken into account by all future "nows," so the structure of the subjectivity achieved by an actual entity in its process is transformed into objectively functioning, stubborn, past fact. The final causality operative in self-creative process becomes efficient causality transcending the process. "For-one's-self-ness" becomes "for-the-others-and-for-the-totality." "Everything that in any sense exists has two sides, namely, its individual self and its signification in the universe" (MT 151). These two poles cannot be torn apart. Each finds its fulfillment in the other via their dialectical relation. Thus, becoming is for the purpose of being (signification in the universe) and being is for the purpose of novel becoming (the emergent individual self).

Objectivity, facticity, is the permanent aspect of reality—immortal achievement immortally realized; subjectivity, immediacy, process, is its changeable aspect—its advance toward novelty. But subjectivity is not the result of an underlying subject's activity of relating objects to itself, of a one weaving a many into the pre-existent unity of its oneness. It is, rather, the "growing together" (con-crescence) of objects to create a novel subject which enriches the many from which it springs. "The many become one, and are increased by one" (PR 32). The entire world finds its place in the internal constitution of the new creature, and the new creature lays an obligation upon the future: that it take into account the value achieved by the new creature. Thus every creature both houses and pervades the world.

Two inseparable notions therefore constitute the foundational insight of Whitehead's process philosophy: the permanence of value achieved and the ongoingness of value achievement. To construct a metaphysical scheme capable of elucidating the implications of these notions was his purpose in writing PR.

II · THE FIRST FORMULATION

Whitehead's initial grasp of the primacy of relations came in that period of his life when he had not yet made the move from the philosophy of science to pure speculative metaphysics, a time during which the focus of his concern was the construction of a theory of knowledge adequate to the scientific endeavor post-Einstein. Early works such as CN and PNK reveal him abandoning the traditional interpretation of perception as a grasp of the properties of "things" and moving toward a view of its being an apprehension of relations: of things *in* their relations and *as* related. He came to see that the qualia as perceived are not properties of an underlying supposit or of the act of experience itself, but are the relations between events in nature. The perceiver *infers* "things" from perceived relations, not vice versa. Nor is the perceiver external to the perceived, as a privileged observer uninvolved in the system observed. Nature for the perceiver is a total relational event of which the perceiver is a part. A perceptive event is situated "here" and "now" within nature and is bound to the relativity of a perspective. An adequate theory of perception must therefore take into account the event perceived (no longer conceived as an object but as a happening), the event of perceiving (no longer construed as a perceiving subject), and the complete event which is nature as simultaneous with the perceiving event, which total event is the togetherness of a manifold of other particular events.

In this context, to perceive an event is to grasp or to become aware of the natural relations of the perceiving event to the rest of nature. The qualia are, therefore, neither purely subjective nor purely objective. In a relational context, the opposition between these terms evaporates. Both are equally valid descriptions of perception, for it is a grasp "here and now" of the relation between events: one perceiving and the other perceived, a relation which makes each to be what it is. Considered from the standpoint of the spatio-temporal position of the perceiving event, perception is subjective—which is to say, not that the qualia are qualities of mind and not of things, but that perception by its very essence is an event within nature: "here" within and "now" within. Perception is objective in that the qualia perceived *are* the natural relations of the perceived event to the perceiving event.

Furthermore, the relations are perceived in the making and because of the making, not as having been made. Linguistic structures force us to speak of the perception *of* relations, as though the perceiving event, the relations perceived, and the events related were separable in the concrete. It is more accurate to say that perception *is* the relationship between two events: from one point of view, the self-manifestation of the objective event; from another, the self-relating activity of the subject. Just as a line is not drawn between two separate, pre-existing points thereby joining them but rather contains and constitutes its endpoints as limits, so the relation of perception constitutes both perceiver and perceived and is not an accidental linkage between already constituted entities. The co-presence in the forest of falling tree and ear constitutes the tree as noisy and the ear as a sensing organ. Without the ear, the tree is silent; without the tree, the ear is a vestigial structure of flesh and cartilage. With both as interrelated events within the totum of the forest, the sound is the tree-event in its relation to the ear and the ear-event in its relation to the tree.

Only in the abstract can one talk about ears and trees as though they were things involved in relations with other things. All that perception yields to awareness is reality as a complex of interrelationships, within which complex are foci of relations inextricably intertwined with each other and with the totality. "Things" are never perceived; yet non-substantial and interdependent foci of relations cannot be thought. To think is to predicate: to analyze a totum into subject and attributes which can be conjoined or disjoined in a judgment. The activity of predication, therefore, necessitates a double abstraction from the organic complex of relations grasped in perception. The logical subject must be isolated from the natural eco-system, and the predicate separated from the quasi-infinity of relations whose focus has thus been isolated. Predication is therefore the exclusion of irrelevance (and, correlatively, the *abs*-traction of relevance) which makes finite expression possible. The entity or "thing"—the bare "it" which serves as subject of a proposition—has no metaphysical status in the universe. It is an abstraction which perforce must be used to make thought about the universe possible. All that has metaphysical status is the fact of nature and the many factors which can be vaguely discriminated within it. "Things" in their barren individuality are these factors abstracted and functioning as termini of thought. This is to say that thought creates its own objects out of the welter of sense experience, separating the entity as bare "it" from the factor and making it the substrate of which the factor is predicated. The conclusion to be drawn from this interpretation is not a postulate of anti-intellectualism such as that ascribed to Bergson when he reached a similar insight into the functioning of thought. On the contrary, it must be realized that if thought is to be possible, such abstractions are *de rigueur*; but they cannot be projected back into reality as the foundations of a realistic metaphysics. "Thing," "entity," property" are tool concepts essential to reasoning about the world: *entia rationis*, and not ontological realities. The metaphysically real is the relational complex of events grasped in perception.

The epistemological model of perception as laid out thus far is still abstract, since it fails to take into account the processual character of the relational complex. "Nature is ever originating its own development . . ." (PNK 14). It is not a static whole given once for all, but an ongoing, creative process. Our sense of action is "the direct knowledge of the percipient event as having its very being in the formation of its natural relations," "a self-knowledge enjoyed by an element of nature respecting its active relations with the whole of nature in its various aspects" (PNK 14). Perception therefore stands at the utmost point of creation, and is the other side of action. In a Bergsonian sense, it traces the lines of our interaction with the world, of our contribution to ongoing process. The broadening of these epistemological considerations to metaphysical dimensions is the *Ur-sprung* of the philosophy of organism.

III · THE LANGUAGE PROBLEM

A difficulty of monumental proportions stands in the way of any philosopher attempting to express his insights: i.e., the language into which they must be cast. As Bergson pointed out in *Creative Evolution*, language was the first human artifact and, as a tool, was forged for utilitarian purposes: to give the individual a "handle" with which to manipulate more effectively the important aspects of his world. As an essentially pragmatic instrument, language functions superlatively. In a very real sense, the process of "naming the gods," as Heidegger would put it, renders the "gods" mundane, discrete, and controllable. However, the "gods" named are those elements in experience which have survival import for the individual—those vividly apprehended because they contribute to or detract from the being and/or well-being of the organism. The act of naming "cuts" these elements out of the tissue of experience in which they come and go and stabilizes them, so that they may be anticipated in their absence, controlled in their presence, and communicated to others. However, these elements with respect to which language is so rich in its denotative and connotative power are those which are trivial to the metaphysician in his attempt to give linguistic expression to the massive core of experience, that which is all-pervasive and not transitory in its influence. "Words, in general, indicate useful particularities. How can they be employed to evoke a sense of that general character on which all importance depends?" (MT 7). Any philosopher, therefore, finds the lingua franca inadequate to the philosophical enterprise, and begins his work with the creation of special terminology in which his ideas can take flesh.

While Whitehead is no exception to the rule, he goes further than most philosophers in his construction of a novel philosophical language—further not in the direction of precision but in the direction of what might be called deliberate imprecision. For him, philosophy is "the endeavour to find a conventional phraseology for the vivid suggestiveness of the poet" (MT 68–69), "the endeavour to reduce Milton's 'Lycidas' to prose" (MT 69), while retaining that vivid suggestiveness in the resultant reduction. The Whiteheadian vocabulary is not at all like the precisely defined terms of the Rationalists. It retains the evocative character and deliberate ambiguity of poetic usage.[1] Whitehead begs the reader to recognize the elliptical character of his words and to allow their meanings continually to be stretched beyond the boundaries of ordinary usage, to be sought for in an imaginative leap similar to that demanded by the language of the poet. On no account is the reader to fall into the Fallacy of the Perfect Dictionary by identifying a symbol and its obvious meaning in a "nothing but"

---

[1] Take for an example the term "feeling" central to PR. In ordinary language it can mean an emotional response, an aesthetic sensitivity, or a physical contact with an object. Whitehead intends his technical use of the term to connote all three meanings. Even his artificially created words like "prehension" or "concrescence" are richly suggestive to anyone familiar with Latin or with the Romance languages. For further examples, see AI 235–37.

fashion. Nor are words and phrases to be taken as complete explications of objective states of affairs. At all times, they are bare signposts mutely appealing for a transcending leap.

The same must be said for the philosophical concepts themselves. The clarity and distinctness of an idea is to be taken as more of a sign of its triviality than as an index of its truth. Clarity marks merely the familiarity of a concept; distinctness, its degree of remotion from the reality which it supposedly expresses. Too often, philosophy mistakes an analysis of abstract ideas for an interpretation of reality and unwittingly reduces metaphysics to logic and/or linguistics.

For a process philosopher, the problem of terminology is particularly acute, in view of the intertwined character of the aspects of experience symbolized in concepts and language. A clear and distinct idea would be a falsification of experiential realities. Just as nature and all aspects of it have a ragged edge, so their philosophical expression cannot have the sharply defined contours and precise internal structure for which a Cartesian would strive. This is not in any way to imply that process philosophy is de jure fuzzy, but rather that it must contain an element of vagueness in its language—its concepts themselves must have a ragged edge. Any philosophical system must be self-referential. If "you cannot abstract the universe from any entity . . . so as to consider that entity in complete isolation" (PR 42), likewise you cannot precisely define any Whiteheadian term in isolation from his system of terms: "an apparent redundancy of terms is required. The words correct each other" (AI 236).

The difficulties with process terminology are minor when compared with the central linguistic problematic a process philosopher must confront. Technical terminology constitutes only a small portion of the linguistic tool kit. Words and phrases must be strung together in the linguistic structures—grammar and syntax—of ordinary speech if philosophy is not to be reduced to lexicography. But language in this broader sense is one of the facts of the metaphysical situation to be interpreted in the philosophical scheme—a fact whose factors are as intertwined and mutually dependent as are the factors in the larger fact of nature. The process philosopher is forced to concede that the structure of the universe of discourse does not necessarily reflect the structure of the universe as he conceives it. The philosopher, and particularly the process philosopher, consciously works in the continual shadow of his own Uncertainty Principle. Just as, in particle physics, the technique of observation modifies what is observed, philosophic expression runs the serious risk of altering what is expressed because of the distortion which the medium introduces into the message.

To put this in more concrete terms: for a linguistic proposition to be meaningful, it must be set within a systematic universe of propositions, involving that universe for its own definiteness.[2] Any proposition about the world is therefore a *flatus vocis* unless it simultaneously implies the general character and connectedness of the world and its own place within that larger picture. There can be no self-contained, isolated propositions. This is to say, therefore, that every proposition implies a metaphysics, that syntax, grammatical structure, and the like are disguised metaphysical assertions. Granted: the metaphysics is naïve, unexplicated, and uncriticized; but it is nevertheless a metaphysics. Until that metaphysics is explicated, no proposition can be fully determinate. But the explication can only be done propositionally—and the vicious circle closes, leaving language by its very nature indeterminate, and a precise metaphysical language impossible. The philosopher must therefore maintain a thoroughgoing distrust of any linguistic formulation. It is only a simplistic metaphysics which believes it can start with precisely formulated axioms and proceed to unfold itself deductively. Dogmatism is the classic example of the Fallacy of the Perfect Dictionary.

The linguistic Uncertainty Principle compounds the problems of the process philosopher, for the metaphysic implicit in the language used, the metaphysic veiled in the "S is P" structure of the verbal proposition, is diametrically opposed to the metaphysic explicated through the language. Nouns imply static, independent entities as their referents; adjectives and verbs connote qualifiers of and activities performed by these entities. Propositions constructed out of these elements subliminally broadcast the pincushion notion of substance and accident in its crudest form. If the problem is critical for the process philosopher, it is hypercritical for the student of process philosophy. How *can* one learn process metaphysics in a "thing" language? The answer is, one cannot, if what one anticipates is finding the ideas freeze-dried in the linguistic expression. But if the distrust of language which Whitehead urges is taken seriously— in this case a distrust of his own language—if his demand that expression be viewed as metaphorical and elliptical, and his continual plea for the imaginative leap from language to meaning, are complied with, the task becomes possible. But a continual effort must be made by the student, for the linguistic metaphysics of "things" slips back into thought insidiously like the evicted demon of the New Testament.[3] The distrust of

---

[2] For example, "the wind is blowing the ashes" is utterly meaningless outside of a context of other propositions indicating whether "ash" refers to a species of tree or the results of combustion. Its meaning also depends on more abstract sets of propositions defining and distinguishing nouns and verbs, and elaborating grammatical and syntactical structures, etc., as well as on propositions detailing the implied metaphysical context. The full meaning (definiteness, structure) of the original proposition involves all these elements if it is to be grasped.

[3] Note how even a technical expression like "an actual entity physically prehends its actual world" is a self-falsifying statement, for an actual entity is not a fully constituted thing performing a transitive activity (prehending) upon an already

language called for is therefore a constant leap toward insight coupled with a negation of what is actually said—a never-ending "yes" and "no" dialectic in the mind of the reader, an ongoing attempt to see Milton's *Lycidas* through and in spite of its prose rendition.

IV · THE LANGUAGE OF FEELING

An additional clarification must be appended with respect to Whitehead's technical vocabulary: namely, his use of the language of consciousness in interpretations of non-conscious processes. It is bewildering at first glance to encounter terms such as "feeling," "emotion," "enjoyment," "decision," "freedom," "purpose," "satisfaction," "subjectivity," and the like in discussions of the self-creative activity of an actual entity; and the bewilderment leads the novice to accuse Whitehead of psychologizing the real, of constructing an animism or spiritualism of the crudest, most mythological sort. If Whitehead does not intend these terms to be taken in their literal, i.e., conscious, meaning, how are they to be understood? The answer to the question is difficult to formulate, but must be attempted in the very beginning in order to forestall grave misinterpretations. One way out of the box would be to call the language of feeling metaphorical, as indeed it is; but metaphor can too readily be taken as expressing nothing real about the reality it represents. None of the classic modalities of analogy works either, because they do not express the peculiar similarity between "feeling," "decision," "emotion," etc. as used by Whitehead and their human, conscious counterparts. What Whitehead intends to express in the language of feeling is the fact that conscious phenomena are further specifications of the more primordial, less abstract activities symbolized in the language of feeling, related to them as species to genus. To discover the intended meaning of one of Whitehead's feeling-terms, one has therefore to negate those aspects of the activity signified which are peculiar to consciousness, and to grasp those more general characteristics which are not properly conscious via a leap or stretch of the imagination. This is an admirable instance of the "take-off" of the airplane which initiates the abstract, metaphysical flight. It also instantiates the difficulties latent in that take-off, for if all one has ever encountered is *this* species (i.e., conscious feelings), how is it possible to isolate the more general, non-conscious activities and relations which they specify? The answer, quite simply, is that at the outset the move to generality is impossible if that move is construed as the positive grasp and delineation of the general aspects sought. The initial phase of the dialectical movement is one of negation—the "yes" and "no" attitude already described. If the student

constituted set of objects (its actual world) as the language implies, but rather the prehensive activity constituting a perspective on that world.

approaches the language of feeling with "yes, he means 'emotion,' but no, he does not imply consciousness," its import will eventually become meaningful; and emotion, for instance, will be seen as a personal, subjective, private appropriation of a datum, as its "value" from the standpoint of the self-creative perspective as opposed to its public factuality. "Enjoyment," "satisfaction," etc., are not conscious phenomena for Whitehead, they are *subjective*; and for him the goal of creative process is the achievement of a drop of subjectivity: an event whose structure is internally self-conditioned as well as externally other-determined.

"To experience" for Whitehead is to synthesize a given public multiplicity into a private unity; to be a subject is to be the focus of that experience; "to decide" is to select those aspects of the manifold unifiable from that focus. "To enjoy" is to exist as a unity self-created out of the manifold; "to be satisfied" is to have eliminated all indeterminations as to what that existence might be and thus to have become an "object"—a superject—added to the manifold and given for the future.

SCIENCE AND THE MODERN WORLD AS A ROMANTIC VERSION OF PROCESS AND REALITY

LEARNING, be it a philosopher's growth in insight or a student's grasp of that insight, proceeds via a natural rhythm if it is to be genuine and not the mechanical acquisition of inert ideas and dead facts—a rhythm which moves from ferment to exactness of formulation to fruition. In the language of AE, the educative process completes itself in three stages: Romance, Precision, and Generalization. No one of these can be singled out as the most important, for all are interfertilizing; however, the rhythmic process, if it is to begin at all, must begin with a moment of romance.

No better description of this period of intellectual ferment can be given than that which Whitehead sets out in AE:

> The stage of romance is the stage of first apprehension. The subject-matter has the vividness of novelty; it holds within itself unexplored connexions with possibilities half-disclosed by glimpses and half-concealed by the wealth of material. In this stage knowledge is not dominated by systematic procedure. Such system as there must be is created piecemeal *ad hoc*. We are in the presence of immediate cognisance of fact, only intermittently subjecting fact to systematic dissection. Romantic emotion is essentially the excitement consequent on the transition from the bare facts to the first realisations of the import of their unexplored relationships [AE 28–29].

SMW represents Whitehead in his moment of romancing the metaphysical implications of his earlier epistemological theories, the full schematization of PR having yet to be constructed. The work has the "vividness of novelty," the "unexplored connexions," the "possibilities half-disclosed . . . and half-concealed," and hence the vital immediacy which makes it an admirable introduction to the complexities of PR. Furthermore, it provides an experiential grounding for the later, more abstract superstructure, showing as it does that the metaphysics springs not from a vacuum, but from a solid basis of human experience[1] given form, universality, and stability in science, mathematics, philosophy, literature, religion, language, and social structures. There is, therefore, no more admirable entry into the intricacies of PR than the route which Whitehead himself took: through SMW.[2]

A detailed analysis of the work would be superfluous; however, a careful limning of the key ideas as they evolve from the pivotal warehouses of human experience will both prepare the student for the metaphysical difficulties of PR and provide an experiential referent when the abstractness of PR's speculative analyses become dizzying.[3]

II · SCIENTIFIC MATERIALISM AND THE FALLACY OF SIMPLE LOCATION

A scientific paradigm holds sway as long as it fulfills its purpose of giving a rational account of physical phenomena. Whitehead's pre-Romantic works were written at a time when the classic paradigm, derived explicitly from Newton but ultimately from the cosmological speculations of the ancient Greeks, had become inadequate to handle modern discoveries. At issue was the very rationality of nature, the basic postulate of all prior science, ancient or modern. That nature was regular and lawful had been an explicit assumption of Greek and medieval cosmology, an assumption not overthrown by the Scientific Revolution but merely thrust into the background as the undemonstrable condition for the possibility of induc-

---

[1] ". . . experience drunk and experience sober, experience sleeping and experience waking, experience drowsy and experience wide-awake, experience self-conscious and experience self-forgetful, experience intellectual and experience physical, experience religious and experience sceptical, experience anxious and experience care-free, experience anticipatory and experience retrospective, experience happy and experience grieving, experience dominated by emotion and experience under self-restraint, experience in the light and experience in the dark, experience normal and experience abnormal" (AI 226).

[2] In presenting the philosophy of organism through SMW first, in no way do I intend to imply that PR is merely a further explication of the doctrines already contained in SMW. It may even be the case that Whitehead subsequently perceived difficulties and inadequacies in the earlier formulation and reworked many notions (see the discussion between Lewis S. Ford and Victor Lowe in *International Philosophical Quarterly* ["Whitehead's First Metaphysical Synthesis," 17 (1977), 251–64, and "Ford's Discovery About Whitehead," 18 (1978), 223–26, respectively]). My choice of SMW as a prolegomenon to PR is motivated by reasons more pedagogical than philosophical. These same reasons have prompted me to develop the fundamental notions in SMW further than Whitehead does in that seminal work, and to introduce material from later works wherever it can clarify the issue being explored. I therefore ask the reader to remember that this chapter is *not* to be construed as a companion to SMW, systematically explicating the doctrines it contains; it should be read, rather, as an introduction to PR.

[3] Those wishing a more complete understanding of the "wealth of material" contained within SMW are urged to read it in its entirety.

tive methodology. The New Science, despite its claims to the contrary, was a thinly disguised rationalism, one which may have rejected the specifics of the Aristotelian and medieval cosmologies in the professed anti-rationalism of its demand for the "patience of minute observation" (SMW 7) and of its return to " 'irreducible and stubborn facts' " (SMW 3) as the sole justification of a theory, but one which at the same time uncritically accepted the explicit first premiss of the old science: that nature is both rational (regular) and accessible to human reason.

From the seventeenth to the late-nineteenth centuries, this naïve rationalism sustained itself by a gradual expansion of the only path open to it: (a) the rejection or relegation to a phenomenal, illusory, or merely subjective realm of those elements of nature not readily forced into rational (i.e., quantitative) categories, elements such as quality, chance spontaneity, freedom, final causality, and internal relations; and (b) the correlative exaltation and absolutization of those aspects of nature amenable to thought: i.e., its spatio-temporal, mathematical, quantitative properties. The seeds of this attitude had been planted by Descartes, with his assertion in *Meditation VI* that with respect to corporeal things "we must at least admit that all things which I perceive in them clearly and distinctly, that is to say, *all things which*, speaking generally, *are comprehended in the object of pure mathematics*, are truly to be recognized as external objects."[4] He could attach no such certainty to qualitative, non-extensive phenomena. From these beginnings to the hypothesis of universal mechanism which dominated all departments of nineteenth-century science was but a small and logical step.

The attitude culminated in the climate of scientific materialism, whose post-Einsteinian scientific and philosophic inadequacies provoked Whitehead to say:

> Time, space, matter, material, ether, electricity, mechanism, organism, configuration, structure, pattern, function, all require reinterpretation. *What is the sense of talking about a mechanical explanation when you do not know what you mean by mechanics?* [SMW 16; emphasis added].

It was not the case that science, in its pursuit of "stubborn facts," had been too empirical; rather, it had not been empirical enough! It had fallen into the most dangerous version of Misplaced Concreteness in its reduction of matter to its quantitative properties, and by so doing had sundered the world in two: one part, a world of mechanically interacting, externally related particles, real but not experienced—the world of conjecture; the other, a "booming, buzzing confusion" of qualities, purposes, freedom, and spontaneity, experienced but not real—the world of the dream. White-

---

[4] *The Philosophical Works of Descartes*, trans. Elizabeth S. Haldane and G. R. T. Ross, 2 vols. (New York: Dover, 1955), I 191; emphasis added.

head set about to construct, therefore, a new empiricism, radical in the Jamesian sense, to overcome this strange offspring of Cartesian dualism.

The focus of his critique in SMW is what he termed the Fallacy of Simple Location, an error which he had previously attacked from an epistemological standpoint in CN and PNK, and which he now approached metaphysically. In a nutshell, it is the attitude that the basic element of the real is the simply located particle,

> the ultimate fact of an irreducible brute matter, or material, spread throughout space in a flux of configurations. In itself such a material is senseless, valueless, purposeless. It just does what it does do, following a fixed routine imposed by external relations which do not spring from the nature of its being [SMW 17].

It is the "entity" previously described as the thought-created terminus of thought, now "bared of all characteristics except those of space and time" and having "acquired a physical status as the ultimate texture of nature" (CN 20). Nature as described by the scientist then becomes the "distribution of material throughout all space at a durationless instant of time" (PNK 2); and her development, "merely the fortunes of matter in its adventure through space" (CN 20). In itself, the particle has no intelligibility, no internal structural content, having been reduced to a bare "it" which can be designated but not thought. All value accruing to it is superadded in virtue of its external relations and hence is purely utilitarian. Barren of any interiority, it is likewise incapable of self-initiated, purposeful action, and is merely "moved around" by the mechanical causality of its environment. Since the totality of its behavior is induced by external, observable, and quantifiable forces, its future is totally explainable and absolutely predictable.

The Rationalists, in their initial formulation of this view of matter, had exempted mind and possibly life from the dominance of mechanical causality, as a result throwing a sop to human experience at the expense of the internal coherence of their cosmologies. This dispensation was voided by the scientists of the nineteenth century in the interest of a unified theory, and so the embryonic notions of psychology, biology, and evolution themselves fell victim to mechanistic interpretations.

Whitehead's fundamental objection to the quasi-metaphysics of Simple Location Theory was basically the same as Bergson's: that such a conception of the particle renders time irrelevant both for the particle and for the universe of particles, and thereby any interpretation of change, process, or motion an easy prey to Zeno's critique. To take an illustration of the simplest sort: the spatial displacement of a body in uniform rectilinear motion is given in the formula $s = vt$, which is to say that at the end of "t" units of time, a body moving with the constant velocity of "v" has traversed "s" units of space. Note, however, the latent inconsistency. "T" represents a discrete quantum of time stretched between t_1, its beginning point, and t_2, its terminal point. These are cuts arbitrarily introduced into the continuum of time—abstract, non-temporal instants at which the spatial position and change of position are being noted. As Bergson expressed it in *Time and Free Will*, the observer is counting simultaneities: between the positions of the clock hand and the spatial positions of the moving body. When the equation is solved for "v" and the appropriate variables plugged in, the result is the velocity of the body at t_2, which by definition is a durationless instant of time. The velocity is therefore an instantaneous velocity, a paradoxical motionless moving. What is going on *between* t_1 and t_2—time in its *passing* and motion in its *moving*—is irrelevant to the equation.

But when it is the motion itself which is under consideration—when, for instance, a problem concerns itself with changes in velocity (i.e., acceleration) and not merely with changes in position—theoretical problems arise which crippled the mathematics of motion (the calculus) for the centuries between Newton/Leibniz and Whitehead/Russell. Newton and Leibniz, in their attempt to apply the instantaneous velocity notion to changes of velocity, had to postulate a smallest increment of change (the fluxion, for Newton)—the quantum of increase or decrease in velocity in an infinitesimal unit of time, one greater than zero but less than any assignable number.[5] Both time and motion were thus construed as the summation or serial addition of these now existential units. They were, in a sense, the mathematical equivalent of the simply located particle of the physicist, and posed similar philosophical dilemmas; for just as an un-

---

[5] The result for Newton was the paradox of calculus' becoming an inexact science —a scandal to mathematics as a whole. This becomes obvious in an examination of his derivation of the relation of rates of continuous change. Take $y = x^2$ as a function varying continuously. If o is an infinitesimal time interval, and $\dot{x}$ and $\dot{y}$ are increments of x and y respectively, then $\dot{y}$o and $\dot{x}$o are infinitely small increments in the variation of x and y. If $y = x^2$, then $y + \dot{y}$o $= (x + \dot{x}$o$)^2$ or, as expanded by the binomial theorem, $x^2 + 2x(\dot{x}$o$) + (\dot{x}$o$)^2$. Since it is the relation of the increments which is the point of concern, all terms in which o does not appear are dropped, yielding $\dot{y}$o $= 2x(\dot{x}$o$) + (\dot{x}$o$)^2$. This expression can be simplified to yield $\dot{y} = 2x(\dot{x}) + \dot{x}^2$o. Thus far, the procedure is in accord with classical mathematics. The next step, however, is problematic. Following the procedure of Newton, all terms remaining with an o are dropped, for o is considered as infinitely small, giving the value of $\dot{y}$ as $2x(\dot{x})$ and the relation of the increments as $\dot{y}/\dot{x} = 2x$, the same result as would have been obtained by applying the modern formula for a first derivative: $dy/dx = nx^{n-1}$. The inconsistency in Newton's method lies in his dropping of the o terms, since o by definition is greater than zero, though less than any assignable number. Newton's result, by modern standards, is the correct answer; by his own theoretical assumptions, an inexact approximation. The infinitesimal had to be banished and replaced by a conceptualization of continuous variation in terms of a serially ordered set of values between any two of which there were additional values (a dense set), which set is bordered by limits. Within this framework, the exactitude of the answer can be theoretically justified. Simply located values can have no place in the mathematics of continuity.

broken line cannot be constituted out of discrete unextended units no matter how small, so continuous motion cannot be made up of discrete immobile segments. In both instances, the philosophical problem centers in the way in which the units are connected. If the mode of connection is in any way external to the units connected, then true continuity cannot be achieved. Simply located particles, be they "bits" of space or "bits" of time, remain eternally outside each other, incapable of being joined into anything with a unity greater than that of a mere assemblage. Only if the relations are internal—that is to say, if t_2 is somehow an outgrowth of t_1— can motion be analyzed without the specter of a frustrated Achilles haunting the theoretical background of the calculations.[6]

When the phenomenon at issue is the causal relationship rather than motion, Zeno is replaced by Hume as the principal antagonist if simple location is the paradigm. In the case that event B follows event A, if there is nothing intrinsic to B which relates it to A, all that can be said with any certainty about their relation is that which was the content of the original observation, i.e., that B follows A. If enough B's are observed as following A's, it can be generalized that their sequence is probably invariable, with the probability a function of the number of observations; but that probability can never become certainty. For the natural scientist, this amounts to a denial of the possibility of inferring the general laws of nature from particular observations and, more fundamentally, to a destruction of the theoretical assumption of induction: i.e., that B's relation to A is invariant because it is of the nature of A's to produce B's and of B's to be produced by A's.[7] Although science "has remained blandly indifferent to its refutation by Hume" (SMW 16) and has proceeded to great heights despite its naïveté, the philosophers of science could not take the same path—hence Whitehead's work in CN and PNK as a response to Hume on the epistemological plane.

On the metaphysical level, however, a reinterpretation of perception is not sufficient to ground the edifice of science and its methodology. Hence Whitehead saw as a primal necessity in SMW the construction of a theory of internal relations to justify causality as a relation implying more than mere sequence of events. In the language of time, this involved a conception of the "now" which does not divorce the present from the past and the future but sees it as constituted from them.

[6] Note Charles Sanders Peirce's attempt to resolve the difficulties latent in the notion of the infinitesimal, while maintaining a postulate of its reality by describing infinitesimals as "overlapping" in a continuum, as "neighborhoods," and hence as mediately connected. See *Collected Papers of Charles Sanders Peirce*, edd. Charles Hartshorne and Paul Weiss, 6 vols. (Cambridge: Harvard University Press, 1931–1935), 4.125–27.

[7] ". . . science is impossible, except in the sense of establishing *entirely arbitrary* connections which are not warranted by anything intrinsic to the natures either of causes or effects" (SMW 4).

III • PREHENSION AS THE BASIS OF INDUCTION

In SMW, the theory of internal relations takes the form of the doctrine of prehensions, a doctrine given a variety of expression in images drawn from significant modes of human experience. Since it was the scientific experience which was pre-eminently in need of clarification, Whitehead devotes considerable attention to the problematic of induction in order to expunge the hidden irrationality in the naïve faith of the physical scientist. He states the issue quite baldly: "Either there is something about the immediate occasion which affords knowledge of the past and the future, or we are reduced to utter scepticism as to memory and induction" (SMW 43–44): as to memory, for unless the past is retained in some real way in the present, memory is reduced to a species of fantasy; as to induction, for unless the future is in some sense prefigured in the past and present, predictive statements are entirely arbitrary. Unless an occasion embodies in its present both its past history and its future possibilities, all that can be said of it is where it is—its instantaneous configuration.

It is to be noted that Whitehead takes induction in its most limited sense, as the derivation of a particular future from a particular past, rather than as the extrapolation of the universal laws of nature from particular observations. More metaphysical groundwork must be laid before such generalizations as the latter have any significance. What is ultimately needed is (a) a general doctrine of the organic character of nature; and (b) a more specialized doctrine of the hierarchy of social relations within nature to give "depth" to the organic paradigm, lest the stress on organism give rise to a reductionist "block universe" conception wherein all law is univocal. Before these notions can be worked out, however, the simplest case of organic structure must be interpreted: the intrinsic relation of a particular occasion to its own past and future and to the past and future of the environment. The interpretation must carefully sidestep any modality of the retention of the past in the present which would bind a future occasion to its past in a woodenly deterministic fashion, and at the same time must avoid disjoining the future from the past so radically that the future becomes purely arbitrary. Both these pitfalls would render an adequate account of life, organism, function, instantaneous reality, interaction, and natural order impossible.

Whitehead takes his imaginative leap toward an initial interpretation of the organic character of an individual occasion from the basis of Bacon's insight as recorded in Section II of the *Silva silvarum*:

"It is certain that all bodies whatsoever, though they have no sense, yet they have perception; for when one body is applied to another, there is a kind of election to embrace that which is agreeable, and to exclude or expel that which is ingrate . . ." [SMW 41].

This extract contains, for Whitehead, the nucleus of the foundational assumption of the philosophy of organism: the doctrine of prehensions. Instead of taking the path which would be followed by eighteenth- and nineteeenth-century science (the path in which the unconscious, the inert, the inorganic are the paradigm in terms of which consciousness and organic life are interpreted), Bacon takes the alternative course in his use of terms from the vocabulary of conscious organisms—"perception," "embrace," "exclude," "agreeable," "ingrate"—to describe inert matter. This is precisely the direction Whitehead sees must be taken if the Simple Location Fallacy is to be overcome. Following Bacon, he carefully distinguishes between "sense" (conscious perception) and "perception," making the former merely a more advanced, more abstract process than the latter, in much the same way as that in which Leibniz discriminated apperception from perception in the *Monadology*.[8] That Whitehead selects the term "prehension" to designate the internal relatedness of one entity to its world is significant in itself. "Apprehension" linguistically indicates a subject *to* (*ad*) which the object is united as a result of the activity of seizing (*prehendere*), a notion foreign to Whitehead's insight. "Prehension," on the other hand, denotes the bare process of seizing, excluding the extraneous notions of subject and of consciousness.

To present a complete explication of the doctrine of prehension and the correlative doctrine of the organicity of the world is virtually impossible in a subject–predicate language;[9] however, an analysis of various types of experience can reveal elements whose synthesis in the imaginative leap yields a model at least adequate for Whitehead's purposes. The experience of volume is a case in point. When abstractly considered, from the standpoint of the geometer, a volume presents itself as a bland multiplicity of endlessly divisible subvolumes, a continuum in which there are no topically singular points—which is to say that all possible subvolumes share the same mode of connection. None has any individuality, any unique characteristics unshared by the others. However, when a volume is an object of conscious experience, it possesses a unity of structure of a different sort—not the sort of structure which would be grasped by a privileged observer in his view from no viewpoint, but a structure unique to each possible perspective within the volume.[10]

[8] *Gottfried Wilhelm Leibniz: Philosophical Papers and Letters*, trans. Leroy E. Leomker, 2 vols. (Chicago: The University of Chicago Press, 1956), II 1045–46.
[9] See below, at note 16.
[10] A concrete example may serve to make this point clearer. If you view a doughnut from an angle, it appears to be an ellipse whose degree of flattening is a function of the obliqueness of the viewing angle. If you view it on edge, it appears to be a solid object, the hole having been obscured. If you view it "head on," it assumes the characteristic torus shape, but the reverse side is invisible. No one of these perspectives on the doughnut can be absolutized as "*the* way a doughnut *is*." Each is the way a doughnut looks *from* a particular position in the environing space.

Furthermore, each position *is* the perspective which it takes on the other included subvolumes. In other words, the structure of the volume from the perspective constitutes the perspective.[11] It is important to note, in addition, that it is not the full determinateness of each subvolume perspectivally grasped which is appropriated in the grasp, but only an aspect of it. The aspect *from* the perspective enters into the constitution *of* the perspective.[12] Therefore, it is equally true that the togetherness of the perspectival aspects constitutes the perspective and that the perspective "decides" the aspects. Each is what the other makes it to be.

Finally, not all perspectives on the volume produce the same intensity of subjective experience. Some are more aesthetically pleasing than others because of the more "artistic" character of the aspects and the unification of aspects decided by the perspective. In concrete human conscious experience, there is no "bare" perception of space; space is experienced as beautiful or ugly, sacred or profane, important or trivial. The togetherness of the elements in a perceived volume has a subjective, emotional character over and above but not separable from the aspects contributed objectively by the data. In PR this will be interpreted by the doctrine of subjective forms, a doctrine ascribing an emotional–purposive side to any form of prehension, even the most primitive. The theme is hinted at in the poetic analysis of SMW V (75–94), but not fully elaborated. It is a necessary component of a theory of prehensive unification if a perspective is to be more than the merely public togetherness of its geometric relations to its world.

The model from experiential geometry, although bringing out certain notes in the concept of a prehension, must be further supplemented if the full meaning is to emerge. The Castle, Planet, and Cloud model which Whitehead borrows from Berkeley's *Alciphron* further clarifies the meaning of a perspectival aspect. From the realization that " 'neither the castle, the planet, nor the cloud, *which you see here* [i.e., the small round tower, the bright disk, or the fluffy white mass], are those real ones which you suppose exist at a distance' " (SMW 68), Berkeley moves into the idealism of *esse est percipi*. Whitehead, on the contrary, makes an alternative move,

---

[11] To take a two-dimensional example: given A, B, and C as three coplanar

points, A is the unity of its perspectival relations to B, C, and BC. The same can be said of B and C, as themselves perspectives.

[12] In the doughnut example, from no single position can the entire doughnut be seen, only that aspect of it visible from whatever position in the environing space the observer takes. The doughnut "in itself" is the unity of all possible doughnut-views, each of which is *sui generis*.

arguing that perception constitutes its subject, not its object: "realisation [i.e., the process of becoming actual] is a gathering of things into the unity of a prehension; . . . what is thereby realised is the prehension [i.e., the prehending subject], and not the things" (SMW 69). Prehension is therefore a gathering of aspects located "there" into the immediacy of a "here." In that immediacy, the things do not lose their objective "there-ness" as they do for Hume.[13] The aspect of an object prehended into a perspectival "here" is irrevocably tainted with its origins; it has, as part of its very being, an essential relatedness to its proper "there." Prehension, in the language of physics, is vector feeling. In the language of consciousness, subjectivity and objectivity are inseparably interdependent in the concrete and cannot be torn apart without mutual destruction. An actual occasion *experiences* its world—enjoys it, suffers it in a manner not necessarily conscious—and *is* its experience.

What has been said about "here" and "there" must likewise be asserted of "now" and "then." Just as conscious perception is a grasp and display of a past object in present experience with a view to future action, so the more fundamental process of prehension synthesizes the agency of the past factual world into the unity and immediacy of a new present. The past is lifted into, made operative in, the emergent "now" without losing its vector origin in the past. The unification thus realized through the prehensive activity is the actual entity or actual occasion, a concrete, fully determinate, spatio-temporal perspective which contributes its aspects objectively to the future as causal agencies to be taken into account by future occasions. The vision of this "pragmatic afterlife" guides the process of self-realization. An entity thus "decides" both what it is in itself and what it will be for the future; each mode of functioning (subjective and objective) is a function of the other. In a very real sense, then, matter remembers and anticipates, and is the togetherness of its memory and anticipation. There *is* "something about the immediate occasion which affords knowledge of the past and the future" (SMW 43–44), that something being the very essence of the immediate occasion as a perspectival unification of past and future. With one bold stroke, the problem of induction in its limited form is solved, for previous events in the life history of a contemporary occasion[14] are part of the past out of which that occasion creates itself; and its future course must likewise bear the impress of that past.[15]

---

[13] "Here" has no meaning if divorced from "there"; and, conversely, "there" requires a "here" to give it meaning.

[14] A history conceived as a succession of interlocked occasions, each prehending its predecessors.

[15] How this interpretation of the life history of an occasion does not lead to rigid determinism must be explicated in future pages.

IV • THE ACTUAL OCCASION AS A SPACE–TIME QUANTUM

The classical space–time model which led inexorably to the Fallacy of Simple Location presented time under the same abstraction as space—as a container in which events were inserted, as an unbroken, undifferentiated continuum which both separated and externally connected those events, enabling them in the case of time to be placed in an absolute system of "before," "after," or "contemporaneous" relations to each other. Correlatively, enduring objects were conceived as just that—i.e., enduring in an unbroken, linear continuum of existence, be it that of either a bit of matter or of a mountain. The emergence of relativity physics and quantum mechanics in the early-twentieth century was a death blow to these naïve conceptions. In Whitehead's words, "scientific theory [was] outrunning common sense" (SMW 114), especially the commonsense understanding of time, temporal sequence, space, spatial relations, and matter. Though these ordinary conceptions functioned well enough in the pragmatic world of everyday experience, they failed totally to give an adequate framework in which to interpret events observed on the micro- and macro-levels of the cosmos. Here, both space and time had to be considered as relative to the system in which the measurement was being made. The notions of enduring matter and of continuous change had to be replaced with quixotic ideas of vibratory entities and quantum jumps in the attempt to create a paradigm adequate to the new experience of matter. These aspects of modern scientific theory provided an additional inspiration for Whitehead in his development of the notion of the actual occasion. In fact, they are so intimately related to his theory that they seem deductions from it rather than provokers of it.

The prehensive unity of an actual entity, the fact that it sums up its life history in its present, demands that that life history be composed of discrete, spatio-temporal drops, episodes, or occasions of experience. To realize why this is so, the doctrine of prehensions must be explored further. Thus far, the notion of unity in the theoretical interpretation of an actual entity as a prehensive unification of the world from a perspective has not been explicated. It must be if the epochal theory of time is to be seen as a logical result of the doctrine of prehensions.

If any manifold is to be brought together into a genuine unity, and if that unity is to avoid the extremes of fusion on the one hand and mere additive aggregation on the other, the unifying process is possible only if the elements of the manifold are *patterned* together, thereby participating in the oneness of the pattern without losing their individual identities. In the doctrine of prehension, this is precisely what occurs. The multiplicity of aspects which is the world from a possible perspective is woven together in the determinate structure which constitutes the perspective as real. "The definite finite entity is the selected mode which is the *shaping* of attainment; apart from such shaping into individual matter of fact there is no attainment" (SMW 94; emphasis added). An actual entity is a realized perspectival harmonization of the world. The realization is ephemeral—it perishes when the determinate pattern is attained; but the harmonization—the pattern unifying the manifold aspects—is "obstructive, intolerant, infecting its environment with its own aspects" (SMW 94). In a word, it endures, which is to say, it is reiterated in processes of realization beyond itself.

An enduring object is therefore to be conceived as a succession of occasions each structuring its definiteness via the same pattern. In each occasion of that thread, the achieved pattern is displayed, the serial order and sheer succession of these displays being what constitutes time in its most concrete and relativistic form. An enduring object reveals itself as a temporal whole embodying as a whole the same pattern exhibited in its sequential parts. Its importance in its environment is proportionate, in part to this temporal dimension,[16] and in part to the aesthetic complexity of the pattern.[17]

What is significant for our purposes at this point is the awareness of two factors: (*a*) that the process of realization culminates in a structured quantum of space–time; and (*b*) that the process itself is neither temporal nor spatial: i.e., it does not occur *in* space or *in* time.[18]

Whitehead is driven by his sensitivity to Zeno's criticisms of continuity to regard the actual entity as the achievement of a drop of space–time. If it is the case that a real temporal span has no smallest unit, it is impossible for an entity to endure through a time, inasmuch as any contained duration is divisible into likewise divisible subdurations ad infinitum, each one of which has to be run through, from the smallest to the largest. Unless there *is* a smallest unit, an indivisible quantum, a temporal sequence can never begin.[19] The same arguments can be leveled against conceptualizations of real space in terms of either endless divisibility or ultimate, unextended units. Whitehead clearly sees that if Zeno is to be over-

---

[16] A flash of existence having no life history is trivial in its impact on its environment; but an electron exhibiting the same pattern in the discontinuous throbs of its life history so that it remains *this* electron is a force to be reckoned with by the environment.

[17] This aspect will be discussed later in the treatment of eternal objects.

[18] Both dimensions are aspects *of* the determinateness of the concrete entity and hence are relative to its perspective. Space–time systems are abstract schematizations of the mutual interrelatedness of entities. That these schematizations have a foundation in the concrete will be demonstrated in later discussions.

[19] In much the same way as that in which an enumeration of the rational fractions between 1 and 2 can never begin. But if this smallest unit is an instant with no temporal extensity, no collection of units however great could ever produce a temporal span.

come, the space–time of experience must have extended and undivided spatio-temporal units as its ultimate constituents: atomic blocks of experience. He maintains therefore that a spatio-temporal quantum—a duration—results from the prehensive process, an undivided pulse of space–time in which the achieved pattern is displayed. This quantum has limits —a beginning and an end, so to speak—but it appears all at once. It is not run through sequentially from beginning to end. "There is a becoming of continuity, but no continuity of becoming" (PR 53). The continuity which is becoming—the spatio-temporal drop—is considered as "the field of the pattern realised in the actualisation of one of its contained events, . . . an epoch, *i.e.*, an arrest" (SMW 125).

Unless this notion of a duration is grasped with perfect clarity at this juncture, the subsequent analyses of an actual entity in PR will be falsified. Unfortunately the model of duration and time which most readily comes to mind in a first reading of SMW is the "beads on a string" model which Bergson attacks in *Time and Free Will* as being a spatialization of temporality. Interpreted according to this model, each duration or epochal drop would be distinct, self-contained, and external to all others. Actual entities would be represented by the beads; and time, by their linear succession. It is to be regretted that Whitehead himself occasionally uses images such as "historic thread" which reinforce this misinterpretation. The model is most unfortunate, for it totally distorts the point Whitehead tries to make. The difficulty lies in the incapacity of any linear time-model to explicate the relations between spatio-temporal drops in such a way that their connection can be seen as internal. The point to be illustrated is that each drop contains as elements in its constitution, as its proper "parts," all previous drops, each of which contains its own parts in the same manner. Thus every duration is endlessly divisible (though undivided) into parts ordered in dependency relations. A duration is a continuum, in the modern sense of the term—a dense set—given in its totality rather than run through.

A better explanatory model can be borrowed from Whitehead's descriptions of abstractive sets in his philosophy of science works, a description which he elaborates in Part IV of PR. Since the latter analysis will be explored in detail in later pages, it would be more appropriate to stay within the context of the earlier descriptions. The pivotal notion is that of "covering," which Whitehead defines in the following manner: "An abstractive set p covers an abstractive set q when every member of p contains as its parts some members of q" (CN 83), those members further down the converging tail of q (i.e., those members closer to the ideal limit toward which the set converges). Without a visual model, this notion is extremely difficult for a non-mathematician to grasp; yet a visual model which will convey Whitehead's insight while remaining in the realm of empirical feasibility is impossible to create. Therefore I would ask the reader to suspend critical judgment for a moment and to imagine the following: We have all seen ripples spreading out in a calm pool when a stone is dropped in the center. If one were to make the unlikely assumption that each ripple could freeze as soon as it is formed, the resultant configuration would resemble the schematization in Figure 1—a nest of concentric waves radiating from the point of disturbance. If each wave (and the area it circumscribes) is considered as a set, it "covers" the smaller waves, including them as parts of itself. Each wave, together with its contained waves, can be taken to represent a duration in Whitehead's

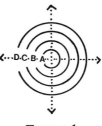

FIGURE 1

sense of the term. Their ordered succession can serve as a model of time. If the system is allowed to propagate in the direction of the arrows, each wave being circumscribed by a larger wave, the spreading process can be taken as a model of the process of temporalization; the spreading totality, as an enduring object. Note what the model, inept and physically impossible as it may be, illustrates with respect to the successive durations it represents. Duration B "contains" A, C "contains" B. . . . The durations are not isolated, self-contained, simply located beads of time. They are, rather, increasing in "content," in extensity, overlapping each other in the sense that the later durations in the enduring object embrace earlier ones. Each duration as a whole exhibits the wave pattern, as do its included parts. It is in this sense that a duration is a "field of the pattern realised in the actualisation of one of its contained events" (SMW 125).

It is also in this sense that a duration is extended and divisible. It is given with its parts and "not realised *via* its *successive* divisible parts" (SMW 125): i.e., it is not run through sequentially. Every duration has parts, those parts have parts, and all parts are contiguous—a duration is a continuum. But note the difference between this notion of continuity and that usually symbolized by an endlessly divisible line. The parts in a linear continuum are external to each other; those of a duration are internal to each other like the parts and subparts of an organism. Note also that continuity, though an attribute of a duration, is not at all a property of time. Time is sheer sequence, not divisible extension, "the succession of elements in themselves divisible and contiguous. . . . Temporalisation is not another continuous process. It is an atomic succession" (SMW 126).

The model illustrates this "epochal" character of time in the individual waves of the system. Each is an "arrest" of the temporalizing process, a further display of the pattern, retaining its identity even when superseded by another encircling wave. Furthermore, a certain extended quantum is necessary for the display of the pattern. A geometric circle—a locus of *points* equidistant from a center point—cannot display a wave pattern; it can only mark the limit or boundary of a wave. The wave pattern stretches from trough to trough, and *is not* unless it does. The quantum therefore possesses a spatial dimension, an extensity concretely inseparable from its durational aspect—it is a drop of space–time with its own "here" and "now" which synthesizes other "here's" and "now's." Temporalization is "the realisation of a complete organism," "an event holding in its essence its spatio-temporal relationships (both within itself and beyond itself) throughout the spatio-temporal continuum" (SMW 127). The organism (in the model, the spreading-wave system) endures (*a*) because it has been able to discriminate space-as-divisible-extension from time-as-sequence; and (*b*) because its environment is a matrix possessing a degree of order capable of sustaining such a differentiation. Endurance is possible only in an ordered context, as the analysis of societies in PR will reveal.

Whitehead's understanding of time and duration provides the basis for an interpretation of motion and change which is invulnerable to Zeno. In the classic beads-on-a-string time concept, one cannot talk in terms of a genuine continuity of change without postulating some unchanging substrate (the string) to unify the stages in the change. Without this substrate, the stages are at best externally related (in invariant sequence); at worst, they represent the mere substitution of one state by another. In Whitehead's conception, it can be clearly seen that although the *sequence* of changes may be atomic, the transition is continuous and internal to the intensity of the organism-in-transition. The "organic deformation . . . is within the duration which is already given" (SMW 135) in the same way as that in which the discrete changes in the spreading-wave system are given with the outermost wave.

If the illustrative model which has been detailed in the past few paragraphs is pushed too far, it breaks down. In the model, each wave is not created "all-at-once," as an atomic block in the manner of Whitehead's conception of the creation of an actual entity. The second factor noted before must be continually borne in mind: i.e., that the self-creative process, the spatialization or arrest of a duration, does not take place *in* space or *in* time. A realized duration appears in a quantum jump. The process of realization has stages which may be distinguished in it—stages which Whitehead details in PR—but these stages do not follow one another in a linear fashion. The whole of the process is not constituted by the summation of its parts; rather, it *evokes* and *pervades* its parts: the actual entity is an organism both directing and emerging from the synthesis of its various prehensions.

The doctrine of the organic character of the world is simply the doctrine of prehensions without the foregoing limitation to an interpretation of the emergence of one actual entity. It must not be taken as a separate doctrine holding the unity of the world to be a unity over and above that of the entities intertwined in it; "nature is conceived as a complex of prehensive unifications" (SMW 72), the unity of which results from the immanence of the whole in each part and of each part in every other part. Every actual entity is the totality of nature in microcosmic perspective; every perspective is therefore essentially linked with every other perspective. The four-dimensional space–time of the physicist is the abstract schematization of these linkages within and relative to an internally self-constituted, quasi-independent system or cosmic epoch. It is not a framework *in which* the system is set.

V · THE LITERARY EXPERIENCE

For a more vivid rendering of the organic universe, as well as for further clarification of the doctrine of prehensions, Whitehead turns to literature, particularly to the works of the Romantic poets. Why literature? Because it corrects the excess of objectivity and consequent remotion from the concrete latent in the experience of the scientist. Poetic insight is, paradoxically enough, one of the most concrete renderings of human experience, for it does not de jure exclude emotion from its formulations. If one were to structure the doctrine of prehensions solely on the basis of scientific experience, the subject emergent from the growing together of the world could be interpreted as a completely public reiteration of that world from the subject's perspective. Through the promptings of the poets, particularly Wordsworth and Shelley, Whitehead sees that prehension is an emotional grasp *even when it is not conscious*, that there is a subjective reaction to what is objectively appropriated.[20] In this emotional reaction, the subject, whether animate or inanimate, conscious or unconscious, achieves a privacy and intensity of experience proportionate to the importance of the emotional reaction to the unity achieved.[21]

In Wordsworth, Whitehead finds an expression of the organic char-

---

[20] "And 'tis my faith that every flower, / Enjoys the air it breathes" (William Wordsworth, "Lines Written in Early Spring," lines 11–12).

[21] Whitehead does not fully work out this notion in SMW; however, it becomes the doctrine of subjective forms in PR.

acter of nature which plunges beneath the abstract schematizations of the scientist to reveal "the dark, inscrutable workmanship that reconciles / Discordant elements, making them cling together in one society" (*The Prelude*, I.341–42). The brooding presences of nature were to the poet "like workings of one mind, the features / Of the same face, blossoms upon one tree" ("The Simplon Pass," lines 16–17), causing him to admonish:

> Then, dearest Maiden, move along these shades
> In gentleness of heart; with gentle hand
> Touch—for there is a spirit in the woods
> ["Nutting," lines 54–56].

Wordsworth does more than merely personify nature as a poetic device; he feels her to be like an organism *in solido*;[22] in Whitehead's language, a complex of "entwined prehensive unities, each suffused with [the] modal presences of others" (SMW 84). The whole looms over every part, pressing in inexorably, demanding to be taken into account, be it the whole which is the life history of an electron, a man, or a universe. Each organic creature is a cosmos, an ordered environment for its parts, ordering those parts according to the organic plan. There is an expansiveness about nature. Each whole is environed in a larger whole; each plan, a species of a wider plan. The totality pours into each individual perspective, giving nature the inescapable permanence, the eternality, the "Unknown modes of being" (*The Prelude*, I.393) which pursued Wordsworth in his boat upon the night-shrouded lake.

Shelley, on the other hand, glimpsed the transitoriness of nature, the "endless, eternal, elusive change of things" (SMW 86), a change not so much in their external trappings as in their inner character. "Naught shall endure but Mutability" ("Mutability," line 16). Time in its never-ending passage leaps forward from prehensive occasion to prehensive occasion, from past to present, from value achieved to value achieving. No duration is final, no attainment ultimate. All perish to be reborn in a new synthesis. "I change, but I cannot die" ("The Cloud," line 76).

In the contrast of the two poets, Whitehead sees the togetherness of permanence and change in experience which marks the character of his resolution of the being–becoming problematic. What endures is fact, value immortal *in* its achievement, stubbornly infecting all future environments *with* its achievement. What is transitory is the micro-process of realization, the activity of achieving value. The dialectic between the two is the macro-process of temporalization, the transition of any reality from exist-

---

[22] Whitehead borrows the *in solido* notion from Roman law, in which each individual obligation is immersed in, and hence derives its obligatory force from, the totality of obligation.

ence for itself to existence for the others and for the totality, from immediate to modal existence.

To the poets in general, Whitehead is indebted for their vision of the aesthetic element in nature. It is obvious that they discover a value infinitely transcending such trivialities as "prettiness" or "utility" (value in the crass aesthetic and moral senses), a value which is permanent in the flux and yet fluent in the permanence of nature. But how is this value to be characterized? To put the question more metaphysically: What does it mean to say that an occasion within nature, or nature herself for that matter, achieves value? What meaning is to be ascribed to the term if the ordinary aesthetic and/or moral meanings are not far-reaching enough?

What emerges from Whitehead's exploration and imaginative generalization of the nature of value is a trivalent relationship underlying the surface meaning of the term. In the first place, value refers to the in-itselfness and for-itselfness of the process of self-realization and of the fully determinate existent.

> At the base of our existence is the sense of "worth." . . . It is the sense of existence *for its* own sake, of existence which is its own justification, of existence with its own character [MT 147; emphasis added].

> Each actual entity is an arrangement of the whole universe, actual and ideal, whereby there is constituted that self-value which is the entity itself [RM 98].

Value is "the intrinsic reality of an event" (SMW 93), "the selected mode which is the shaping of attainment" (SMW 94). Each of these extracts repeats a common theme: the identification of value with "character," "shape"—in a word: with the pattern being realized and made fully determinate in the existent.

However, this "in-itselfness" of achieved value does not leave the existent confined in a solipsism. Value achievement immediately and by its very nature becomes a datum for the other individuals in the environment and for the environment itself.

> There is the feeling of the ego, the others, the totality. . . . Everything has some value for itself, for others, and for the whole. . . . no unit can separate itself from the others, and from the whole. And yet each unit exists in its own right. It upholds value-intensity for itself, and this involves sharing value-intensity with the universe. Everything that in any sense exists has two sides, namely, its individual self and its signification in the universe. Also either of these aspects is a factor in the other [MT 151].

It is value, therefore, which binds together being (objectivity) and becoming (subjectification), the many (the facts given for prehension) and the one arising out of that many (the actual occasion). Value is to be understood both as the pattern of achievement aimed at in the achieving (abstract value) and as the achieved pattern (concrete value) transitional beyond the achievement to the environing world.

It must be carefully noted that the mode of being of abstract value, or form, is totally unlike that of concrete value or enformed fact. Fact coerces recognition; form lures realization. Fact is fully determinate in all respects—is a "this"; form is partially indeterminate—is a "what" always capable of being determined further. Fact is essentially temporal, involved in a time sequence; form is essentially atemporal, a visitor in time but unaffected by its sojourn. Form gains efficiency and full determinateness from its factualization; fact gains immortality beyond its drop of self-existence—and hence significance in the universe—from its enformation. In a certain sense, however, abstract value has priority over concrete value. Fact is unthinkable without form, for its very intelligibility stems from its patterned structure. Form, on the other hand, retains its intelligibility and its character when not exemplified in facts. It has the mode of being of a possible. Form is therefore an ingredient in events, is exemplified in facts, but is not an event or fact itself, lacking as it does the insistent particularity of an event. It is the condition or set of conditions determining "how" a manifold could be structured together into an event, yet transcends any given manifold. The essential poetic insight, i.e., that nature has an aesthetic character, translates as "Nature immortally embodies eternal values in its aspects, and hence is valu*able* for future manifestations of herself."

VI · ETERNAL OBJECTS

The question which arises at this point is: Given form or abstract value or pattern as a set of relations or conditions exemplifiable in some concrete universe, what can be said of the nature and interrelatedness of these relations? Because of his extensive background in pure mathematics, it was quite logical for Whitehead to turn to that field for the necessary tools with which to explicate his doctrine of form. Mathematics is, in a very real sense, the science of form, since its objects themselves are purely abstract conditions and relations considered without reference to any concrete exemplifications. What it reveals to the philosopher is an image of the organic character of possibility in the systematic relations of those objects.

Abstract mathematical conditions condition each other, in the sense that given condition A, conditions B and C must necessarily follow. The only external condition laid upon such sets of conditions is that they be rational: i.e., internally non-contradictory, or possible. This is not to say, however, that alternative, mutually contradictory systems cannot be compossible. What is affirmed is that the acceptance of one set of conditions (the axioms of Euclidean geometry, for instance) entails the acceptance of all equivalent and derivative sets and subsets of conditions. Taken as a unit, this complex defines the mathematical universe in question. Within such a system, it is possible to move from elementary postulates to remote conclusions with no gaps, no surds, no inexplicables encountered beyond the original assumptions. Thus, a mathematical system is an intelligible, organic whole—a realm.

It should not be assumed, however, that every mathematical system is exemplifiable in the idiosyncratic dimensionality of this cosmic epoch. Mathematics continually transcends the power of the human imagination, tied as it is to four-dimensional space–time, but by definition it remains within the domain of human reason. Non-Euclidean geometries, n-dimensional geometries, bichronal systems, and the like are as rational as Euclidean systems despite their unimaginability. They are equally intelligible, alternative realms of relations and conditions.

When this view of the connexity of mathematical objects is translated into a metaphysics of forms, it yields valuable insights into the nature and relation of the abstract values or patterns in terms of which entities are structured. Like mathematical objects, patterns retain their possibility even when unexemplified in a given cosmic epoch. They are both eternal (unaffected by time) and objective (being what they are irrespective of what anyone thinks of them).[23] The forms structuring the togetherness of data into a datum of experience—eternal objects in Whitehead's language —are given for all times in ordered, intelligible, interrelated sets like mathematical systems.[24] If it is the case that eternal objects stand to each other in intelligible relations of this sort, and, further, that they form the patterns structuring concrete fact, it follows that the world disclosed in and for experience is itself intelligible, that it reveals no surds, no gaps, no inexplicables beyond the initial ordering of the system of eternal objects. Whitehead expresses this essential knowability of the real as the principle of relativity. Its epistemological formulation is:

> No statement, except one, can be made respecting any remote occasion which enters into no relationship with the immediate occasion so as to form a constitutive element of the essence of that immediate occasion. . . . The one excepted statement is: —If anything out of relationship, then complete ignorance as to it. . . . Either we know something of the remote occasion by the cognition which is itself an element of the immediate occasion, or we know nothing [SMW 25].

---

[23] In a very real sense, mathematics is a science of discovery, in that it uncovers interrelated sets of conditions already *given* eternally.

[24] Is it surprising, therefore, that Plato, whose paradigmatic footnote Whitehead writes, should have so disappointed Aristotle by delivering a lecture on the Good which was largely a mathematical dissertation?

As a metaphysical doctrine this becomes:

> the full universe, disclosed for every variety of experience, is a universe in which every detail enters into its proper relationship with the immediate occasion [SMW 25].

The relationship is necessarily intelligible, for an unintelligible relationship is a contradiction in terms.

Reason can thus indefinitely explore the richness of relations synthesized into an individual occasion. Note the difference between this notion of the intelligibility of the world and that proposed by the mechanists. The latter assumed intelligibility to entail a rigid determinism of the sort which affirms: given complete knowledge of the present position and velocity of particles, all futures are absolutely predictable.[25] In contradistinction to this view, Whitehead attributes an open-ended character to the intelligibility of an individual occasion. Since it houses the world in a patterned unity, in a "reasonable harmony of being" (SMW 26), that pattern can be unfolded indefinitely.[26]

With this preliminary notion of an eternal object in mind, it is possible to clarify further the relation between eternal objects and the events incarnating them. It has already been seen that any actual entity as an event is a patterned interfusion of all other events and that eternal objects are the abstract patterns making that interfusion possible. Eternal objects, therefore, "ingress" into (enter into the constitution of, become ingredient in) the process of realization which culminates in the synthesis of possibility and actuality into a concrete, fully determinate value.[27] This ingression can take various forms. In one mode, an eternal object can serve as the "how" of the subject's relation to the object prehended—it is an adverb, not an adjective.[28] Eternal objects relational between subjects and objects in this fashion are termed qualia: the simplest kinds of eternal objects, having no structural complexity of their own, but structuring the relationship between an emerging subject and each event which it prehends into itself. The full complexity of the subject is the perspectival togetherness of its manifold of adverbially qualified prehensions of the

---

[25] In this sense, the "last" physics book could be written; the only thing hindering its completion is lack of data.

[26] No one will ever write the "last" mathematical treatise, for each newly discovered condition opens up others to be explored.

[27] It is all too easy at this point to slip back into subject–predicate modes of thought and their consequent but implicit substance–accident metaphysics by considering the relation of an eternal object to the event which it structures—be that event a prehending subject or a prehended object—in terms of the classical relation of a quality to a fully constituted substance. It cannot be said too often that the subject *emerges* from the prehensive activity, that it is not the pre-existent substrate of that activity.

[28] Just as the eye does not see a red object but appropriates a certain environmental event "redly," so the hand might appropriate the same event "hotly."

events in its environment. This togetherness achieves its unity through the ingression of another, more complex eternal object which serves as lure for the process of realization and structures the achievement. It is the "shape" or pattern of the fully determinate, concrete value precipitated by and in the process.

Aspects of this eternal object, qualia subsumed in the overarching unity of the complete pattern, serve to objectify a completed actual occasion to future occasions. Thus subjects do not prehend objects in their full determinateness; they prehend objectifications of completed occasions, which objectifications are selected, adverbially qualified prehensions integral to the constitution of the completed occasions. In another language, prehension is feeling the *feeling* of another, not feeling the other. In the simplest case, this is a description of energy transfer from occasion to occasion in a route; in the most complex case, it describes the personal identity reiterated in a life history. In all cases, it gives the metaphysical groundwork for the inheritance of the past by the present and for the endurance of the objects of experience. Both what is inherited in a causal chain and what "endures" in a life history are eternal objects,[29] either qualia (or subjective forms in the language of PR) or overarching value-structures (i.e., defining characteristics).

Both these types of eternal objects transcend any occasion in which they are realized. Positively conceived, this transcendence means that the possibilities for realization of an eternal object are not exhausted by any occasion or set of occasions in which it may be realized. Part of the very nature of any eternal object is an indeterminate relation to occasions-in-general; for what else does possibility mean, save possibility-for-an-actuality? From a negative point of view, certain eternal objects are *not* embodied in the event and hence are impossible *for* it. These eternal objects are the predicates of all false propositions which could be constructed about the event—what it could have been but is not. Realization therefore implies decision—the selection of relevant eternal objects to be embodied and the rejection of the others. Every actual occasion takes a determinate stance toward all possibles.

Notice, however, that all inclusions and/or exclusions are not on the same footing with each other, are not equally relevant aspects of the value

---

[29] I do not mean to infer that in a causal sequence *all* that is inherited is the eternal object, for to me such a statement would reduce causal chains to mere sequences of identical patterns, removing the "force" from efficient causality. I interpret causality as a transfer of *energy* from past to present. But energy is always a *kind* of energy, always structured, always displaying a form. An emergent occasion feels into itself the "pressure" of the past, displays the im-pression (structure) of that pressure in its present and ex-presses (transmits) the pressure received to the future. The eternal object may represent the energy structure received from the past, but the necessity of the reception constitutes the energy *qua* energy.

achieved by means of them.[30] From the standpoint of any given perspective, the eternal objects are arranged in degrees of importance to that perspective, to be included or excluded in gradations of relevance. Without this graded ingression of eternal objects, an actual occasion would be the mere logical conjunction and disjunction of what it includes and excludes, resembling by analogy a painting with neither focal point nor perspective. Thus the understanding of any actuality entails a necessary reference to the forms it includes *and* the form of the inclusion, and to the forms it excludes *and* the form of the exclusion.

The previous analysis of the concrete value achieved by an actual occasion revealed it to have an intrinsically trivalent character: being something in itself, for the others, and for the totality. The world of possibility is no exception to the protean relativity evidenced by actuality, and manifests the same trivalent character. Each eternal object is uniquely individual yet is inextricably intertwined with all other eternal objects and has a definite status in the realm of eternal objects in addition to its patience for exemplification in the world of fact. To understand an eternal object is therefore to grasp its particular individuality (or individual essence) as well as the way that individuality is enmeshed in the system of possibles and bears a general relevance to actuality (its relational essence).

But to speak of an eternal object as having a unique character of its own would seem at first glance to be introducing a crack into the organic character of possibility by setting the eternal object up as a "simply located" form, which is what it is independent of its relation to other forms. This is not the case, however. What an eternal object is in itself is precisely the togetherness of its relations to all other eternal objects. An individual eternal object is therefore to be conceived as the togetherness[31] of the world of eternal objects from its perspective and its individuality as the structure of that togetherness.[32] Each eternal object is what the others make it to be. Possibility emerges from this view as inseparably organic as is actuality.

Just as the affirmation of the uniqueness of each eternal object does not destroy its organic relations with the others, so the affirmation of the internal, organic relatedness of eternal objects does not vitiate the uniqueness of each. In this sense, an eternal object is "in itself" in a manner not shared by actualities. An actual occasion has *no* meaning apart from its world, whereas an eternal object has its personal, private nature in quasi independence of the other eternal objects to which it is related. The in-

---

[30] To take an analogue from the moral sphere: in the embodiment of justice in an interpersonal situation, the pattern of justice is more significant to the interchange than the fact that one of the persons involved is wearing a green dress.

[31] The character of this togetherness will be explored later.

[32] This is simply another way of expressing the fact that description is always in terms of universals, even when it is universals which are being described.

dividual essence of an eternal object—the unitary quality of the quality—is something perfectly definite and is self-identical in all its modes of ingression into actuality.

The relational essence of an eternal object must be described in a somewhat different manner. It includes (a) the indefinite plurality of relations which constitute the status of the eternal object in the realm of possibility, for every possible relationship of an eternal object is itself an eternal object entering into relationship with all other eternal objects . . . ad infinitum; (b) the generalized relation of an eternal object to actuality; and (c) the limitation placed on (a) by the spatio-temporal conditions exemplified in the actual course of events, which conditions themselves are eternal objects. In combination, (a) and (b) would seem to preclude the possibility of finite truth, since their conjunction might appear to exclude the possibility of limited relations between eternal objects—r(AB), for example. Whitehead eludes the Bradleyan alternative, however, by carefully clarifying the nature of this manifold of internal relations constituting an eternal object. On the assumption that eternal object A, taken in the infinitude of its relations to the other eternal objects, were related to them in the fullness of their internal relations, Bradley would win. To say anything about an eternal object would entail saying everything. For Whitehead, the other eternal objects to which A is related (an infinite number) enter into relationship with A as mere relata, as termini of the relationship, not as themselves infinitely related to all other eternal objects. They are, in Whitehead's language, "isolated" from A, bearing explicitly within themselves only that aspect of their own relational complex necessary to support the relationship with A. Possibility, though an organic realm, does not evidence the radical togetherness which characterizes actuality. The relational essence of an eternal object is not unique to it, as is its individual essence. Insofar as eternal objects are related as foci of their internal relations, these relational patterns are uniform schemes—matrices of relations demanding of their relata only that they have the characteristics pertinent to their particular position in the scheme.[33] They are variables in the sense in which logicians use the term. Therefore, the infinity of organic relationships which constitutes the realm of eternal objects is divisible from the perspective of any eternal object into an infinite plurality of limited relations.

When an eternal object ingresses into an actual occasion, it brings with it the totality of these relations as further limited by the conditions im-

---

[33] For example, the relation "sine" requires of its relata only (a) that they be sides of a right triangle, (b) that one be opposite the angle in question, and (c) that the other be the hypotenuse of the triangle. All other characteristics of the lines are irrelevant to the schematic relationship. The lines are the "x's" in the relationship; they are "any" lines with the requisite character.

posed by the space–time continuum. The relational essence is self-identical in content in whatever event embodies the eternal object in question. However, the way in which that content is "valued" varies from event to event as a function of the occasion's perspective—which is to say that certain of the limited relations within the eternal object are more relevant to the perspective, more important to its self-creative, aesthetic synthesis, than others. Some may positively inhibit the synthesis insofar as they are contraries, and these enter into the event by the positive act which excludes them from the event. Thus, though a general relation to actuality is internal to any eternal object, the specific modes of ingression, which are constitutive of and hence internal to an actual occasion structuring itself via that eternal object, are external to the eternal object.

From the standpoint of actuality, the most concrete eternal object embodied in an occasion is the one which in its complexity is the pattern of value achieved in the event. It represents a grading in degrees of positive and negative relevance of all eternal objects vis-à-vis that event. It is the fully determinate character of the event, that infinity of detail which would have to be run through in order to describe the event exhaustively: in Whitehead's terminology, its associative hierarchy. To speak of hierarchies in the realm of possibility is to describe the logical relation between complex eternal objects and those more simple.[34] To explicate the notion of hierarchies of possibility in schematic form, take for example the simple (non-structured) eternal objects A and B. Each contains within itself the full infinity of its relational essence—its status in the realm of eternal objects. When A and B are considered as involved in a limited relation, however—r(AB)—they are more abstract than A or B *simpliciter*, since only those aspects of their relational essences warranting their status in the relation are retained in the relation. The relation itself—r(AB)—is an eternal object bearing its full relatedness to all other eternal objects. When r(AB) itself becomes one pole of a more complex relation— r[r(AB)][r(CD)]—it likewise retains only those of its manifold of relations which are relevant to its status vis-à-vis the other pole. In such a manner, hierarchies of abstraction can be constructed from a base of simple eternal objects. Some of these have a vertex—an eternal object of maximum complexity—and hence are finite. Others are infinite, lacking a grade of maximum complexity.

The associative hierarchy of an actual occasion is an abstractive hier-

---

[34] It must be noted to avoid confusion that the movement of abstraction from possibility takes a direction diametrically opposed to that of abstraction from actuality. In the latter case, the simple is more abstract than the complex; in the case of possibility, the complex is more abstract than the simple. For example, to say that an object is green is to say less about its concrete reality than to say that it is a tree; whereas to say that a color is green is to say more about it than to say that it is a sensum.

archy of the latter type, differing from other infinite hierarchies in the fact that the simple eternal objects from which it springs are "together" in the most concrete way—as *realized* together in the physical constitution of an event rather than as together in the abstraction of a limited relation. In their joint embodiment in the occasion, they relate the entire realm of eternal objects in ascending degrees of complexity to this base, thus providing the inexhaustible intelligibility of the event, its conceptual structure.

Eternal objects are not limited to such concrete ingression in events, however. When seized in imagination, memory, anticipation, or thought, they are grasped as just a "this" and nothing more, as abstracted from the multiplicity of their internal relations and considered only as the focus of those relations. If the eternal object in question is complex, it is grasped as the vertex of a finite hierarchy including its component eternal objects but isolated from the rest of the realm.[35] In Whitehead's language, it is seized "abruptly." The individual essence of the eternal object seized in this abstract manner remains self-identical with that in the more concrete modes of ingression, thus providing the condition for the possibility of a correspondence theory of truth. There can be, therefore, an adequation between an eternal object grasped conceptually by a knower (appearance) and those integrated into the physical constitution of the knower as structuring the received causality of the object (reality). This distinction, as fully worked out in PR and AI, grounds Whitehead's epistemology.

VII · CREATIVITY

Thus far, two elements of the speculative scheme which SMW proffers for the interpretation of reality have been limned out: the notions (a) of the actual occasion as the unity emergent from a concrescence of prehensions, and (b) of eternal objects as the qualia and patterns making that unity possible. As a metaphysics, the scheme remains incomplete, for both elements represent the static aspects of reality: completed fact and eternal form. What is needed is an additional element capable of grounding the dynamic character of the real by answering the question: *Why* does a settled past grow together through the mediation of eternal objects to form a newly patterned present? Without such an element, the scheme is as incoherent as Descartes' arbitrary disconnection of mind and extended matter, and can offer no cogent interpretation of experienced reality.

Whitehead's response is in terms of an element which in SMW he variously calls "underlying activity" or "substantial activity."[36] The lat-

[35] The situation resembles that exemplified in a limited relation between possibles, but in this case only one relatum is a possible—the eternal object abstractly grasped. The other is the event which is the knower.

[36] In PR, the term "creativity" replaces these earlier formulations.

ter term is perhaps the more revealing, insofar as it underlines the fact that, like a primary substance, the primordial activity cannot be characterized because it is the source of all characters and, as such, the ultimate subject of predication. All realizations, all individualizations, all characterizations are its modal manifestations; hence its attributes are the multiplicity of realized individuals and the eternal objects which make realized individuality possible. It is not to be considered an *Urstoff* analogous to that sought by the Milesian philosophers, however; for in no way can it be likened to an entity. It is "the synthetic activity which prehends valueless possibility into superjicient informed value" (SMW 165). But that is precisely the activity exercised by an actual occasion in its self-creative process, which is to say therefore that the self-creative activity of an actual occasion is a modal individualization of the substantial activity. It is "the one underlying activity of realisation individualising itself in an interlocked plurality of modes" (SMW 70). The plurality is "interlocked" because each prehensive activity, as a modal manifestation of the one underlying activity, is hence primordially related to all other prehensive activities. Likewise, the mutual and dynamic relevance of possibility and actuality is to be accounted for in terms of their both being "creatures" of the same protean activity.

The underlying activity does not "exist," for to exist means to be determinate; yet it is the ground for all determinacy. Neither is it possible, for it likewise grounds possibility. It is as far beyond the reach of language as is the One of Plotinus, yet is foundational to the metaphysical system, in that everything described in the system is one of its modal differentiations.

Perhaps metaphor can serve better than precise philosophical formulation at this point. The underlying activity is the eternal urge "that all shall be one," that realized multiplicity be fused into the unity of concrete value. Out of its unity, it engenders manifold creatures which it weaves together into new epiphanies of its unity. It is the activity at the heart of all activities, the becoming latent in all becomings; uncreated, because it is no-thing, creating all things out of its dynamic formlessness; refracting itself endlessly into individual creative activities, formal possibilities, and determinate creatures. It is the "something far more deeply interfused" of Wordsworth's "Tintern Abbey,"

> Whose dwelling is the light of setting suns,
> And the round ocean and the living air,
> And the blue sky, and in the mind of man:
> A motion and a spirit, that impels
> All thinking things, all objects of all thought,
> And rolls through all things . . .

["Lines Composed a Few Miles Above Tintern Abbey," lines 97–102].

VIII · GOD

With the addition of the dynamic element, the speculative scheme is still incomplete, lacking an account of the prior limitation of eternal objects necessary for them to become relevant to actuality. To review briefly the complex account of eternal objects: it has been noted that every eternal object is something in itself (its individual essence), for the others and for the totality of possibility and actuality (its relational essence). From the perspective of an individual eternal object, its relational essence proved to be its net of relations to all other eternal objects, each considered not in the totality of its own internal relations, but merely as terminus of its relations to the eternal object in question. From the standpoint of the totality, each of these relations between pairs of eternal objects is itself an eternal object, albeit of a higher grade of complexity. The component eternal objects are component only insofar as they stand *in* that relation to each other—they lend their relevant aspects to that relationship, and could be replaced with any other eternal objects having as part of their internal relations the same aspects. A complex eternal object is the schema of a limited relationship and not a real togetherness of the full internal relatedness of the relata. Carry this complexification further and it becomes evident that the realm of eternal objects is indeed organic, but that its organicity and connexity involve the *status* of included eternal objects and not their relational content. The world of eternal objects emerges as a realm bearing a *generalized* relation to actuality, but at the same time indifferent to any particular actualization.[37] Eternal objects are thus isolated from each other, since no one contributes its totality to another, and in a sense are likewise isolated from actuality because of their indifference to particular individualization. Such a realm of eternal objects, taken in combination with the substantial activity of individualization, is not sufficient to account for the full determinacy of achieved actuality displayed in the associated hierarchy of an actual occasion—the gradation of eternal objects in degrees of relevance to *that* perspective. This incoherence of the metaphysical scheme can be overcome only by postulating a prior limitation of the eternal objects, a limitation through which they are ideally realized, i.e., *thought together* in a manner overcoming their isolation, a limitation which itself is a modal manifestation of the creativity.[38]

The necessity for an aboriginal limitation of eternal objects becomes

---

[37] For example, if any eternal object of the sort A (color) ingresses into an event, eternal object B (shape) will be necessarily connected with it. But there is nothing in the nature of possibility to demand that red and the customary shape of an apple are necessarily connected.

[38] It should be noted that for Whitehead, "to limit" always means "to structure," and lacks the negative connotation attached to limitation in medieval thought.

more critical when it is remembered that there can be no such thing as an isolated actual occasion. Each occasion is essentially social, creating itself out of the data contributed by other realized occasions, each of which is itself (has its own unique associative hierarchy), but creates that self out of the contributions of still others. Each occasion, therefore, is set in the midst of a course of interlocked events which it appropriates and orders from its vantage point through the ingression of relevant eternal objects. The substantial activity is particularized in its organically related, modal manifestations, each of which is itself and not other because of the uniqueness of its perspective on the totality as displayed via its associative hierarchy. But the course of events itself displays limitations which cannot be accounted for from within it: logical and causal relations of a general sort which do not have to be what they are, and more particular, idiosyncratic relations which could be other than what they are. Since these are not decided *by* the course of events, they must be decided *for* it, in an antecedent limitation of the general conditions for courses of events to be the *particular* conditions for *this* course of events.

Furthermore, (*a*) if the outcome of process is a unit of realized value, (*b*) if value is the structuring of fact into aesthetic achievement, and (*c*) if aesthetic achievement is aesthetic precisely because it is displayed against a background of relevant alternatives, it follows that decision among these alternatives entails the application of standards of value given *for* the achieving process and not created *by* it.[39] An antecedent valuation of isolated, abstract value systems is necessary, delimiting them into "contraries, grades, and oppositions" (SMW 178) in order for aesthetic decision to be possible.

Whether one looks, therefore, at the actual course of events or at the achievement of fully determinate occasions within that process, one sees the necessity for a principle of concretion, an activity limiting the generality of the conditions for process and for realization in order to bridge the gap between the abstract and the concrete. Eternal objects may be the conditions for the possibility of actuality-in-general, but they cannot be the conditions for actualities without additional limitation. They must be ideally realized (conditioned) before they can become real conditions.

This limiting, this ordering of the eternal objects so that they are relevant to finite process in both its macro- and its micro-forms, is what Whitehead calls God in SMW and the primordial nature of God in PR. The primordial limiting, though the source of rationality, is itself transrational, in that no reason can be given why the limitation takes the form it does, inasmuch as the primordial limitation is the source of all reasons.

---

[39] Multiple standards would isolate the value achieved by one occasion from those achieved by other occasions, rendering them all "windowless" values, without sufficient communality to achieve interfusion in newly emergent values.

"There is a metaphysical need for a principle of determination, but there can be no metaphysical reason for what is determined" (SMW 178). This is not to ground rationality on irrationality, however. It is simply to ground it on an ultimate connexity which is the necessary source of all rationality.

It must be carefully noted that God does not usurp the metaphysically ultimate position heretofore accorded to the substantial activity. God too is to be construed as "a creature of the creativity" in that he shares with actual occasions and eternal objects the property of being a modal individualization of the substantial activity. It should be noted that for Whitehead "creature" does not carry the connotations of existential dependence with which the medievals clothed the term. In a Scholastic context, since the act of creation is a production *ex nihilo sui et subjecti*, the *esse* of the creature is contingent—i.e., non-necessary—and the creature is assigned a lower grade of reality than the creator who as a necessary being *has to be*. Whitehead does not hold to a doctrine of *creatio ex nihilo*; hence, to call God a creature is not to place him below the substantial activity (but above temporal occasions) in some hierarchy of being. To be actual has but one meaning for Whitehead: to be an actual entity, a fully determinate drop of realized value existing in and for itself and for the others. The substantial activity, lacking such individuality, *is not actual*, and since only actualities can function as causes, *does not cause* God, i.e., is not his "creator" and hence a "superior" order of being.

Likewise, the valuation of eternal objects in such wise as to make them relevant to process is not to be conceived as the full extent of the metaphysical character of God. This aspect merely denotes God's primordial nature—God in his activity of making self-creative process possible, God as the principle of concretion. Although SMW does not explore the other aspects of the divine nature, these are sketched out later in PR.

The metaphysics of SMW centers, therefore, in four organically interrelated, interdependent notions: the actual occasion (and the derivative notion of prehensive activity), eternal objects, the underlying or substantial activity, and God. This conceptual system, romantically glimpsed in SMW, becomes the backbone of the fully elaborated metaphysics of PR, there to be elucidated, explicated, ramified, and raised to the level of Precision.

2

THE SPECULATIVE SCHEME

(PR, Part I)

In *Modes of Thought* Whitehead describes the task of philosophy as "the understanding of the interfusion of modes of existence" (MT 97). But what does it mean to understand? If the word is taken in its classical sense, any grasp of what Whitehead purports to do in PR and of the way in which he views his speculative scheme as an interpretation of reality is vitiated from the outset. In its Aristotelian meaning, to understand anything is to know it in its causes: to grasp principally its form and purpose. Knowledge, thus interpreted, is a moving away from the thing in its concrete singularity, which *qua* individual is unintelligible, toward a grasp of the universals which it embodies. To know an object is to be able to place it in its appropriate category, having delimited its genus and differentiae. When based on this notion of understanding, philosophy is viewed as a purely abstract, *a priori*, apodictic, and deductive science, whose certainty and purity are a function of its remotion from the concrete.

Whitehead totally repudiates this conception of the philosophical enterprise and the notion of understanding from which it springs. He is a Platonist with respect to knowledge, realizing that it is not theoretical understanding but rather the ability to rule well. If it entails a departure from the concrete, that departure is justified only in virtue of a subsequent return. Even the departure itself takes a different form from that evidenced in the traditional notion of abstraction, in which the individuating notes of an object are left aside in the endeavor to seize its universal essentiality. For Whitehead, the movement of abstraction is indeed toward higher generalities, but in the move the individuality of the starting point is not analyzed away. In his view, a fact is understood when it can be placed in a wider systematic context which gives an account of its interconnections with other facts. The technique of analysis presumes that facts are isolated, self-contained units whose character can be revealed by systematic dissection, and it thereby loses itself in barren abstractions. The true activity of understanding consists in a voyage to abstraction which is in fact a voyage to the more fully concrete: to the system in which the fact is enmeshed. That system *as conceptualized* may be more abstract than the fact itself in that it is more general, but the real systematic context is more concrete, and its elaboration yields more about the existential relations of the fact.

When a given systematic context itself is taken as a fact, it demands a voyage to a still wider context for its comprehension. Thus there is a dialectical movement in understanding, a movement encompassing the exploration and explication of wider and wider contexts, each step of which further enriches the knowledge of the original fact.[1] The task of philosophical understanding is to criticize these contexts in the sense of constructing a conceptual macro-system capable of elucidating their interrelationships.

However, no philosophical system can completely formulate the ultimate context, for any conceptual scheme, as an eternal object, is still abstract, lacking the full particularity of the fact which it purposes to interpret. It is asymptotic to reality rather than a dogmatic statement. Therefore, the philosophical voyage, the attempt to formulate the most general relationships exemplified in every fact, can never reach its destination; the perfect system is unattainable. "The object of this discipline [speculative reason] is not stability but progress" (FR 82).

Nor is the philosophical enterprise an end in itself. If the goal of knowing is to rule well, then the function of philosophic reasoning is "to promote the art of life" (FR 4; emphasis deleted) by rendering human life and the experienced world meaningful. A philosophy is successful when it expresses "the general nature of the world as disclosed in human interests" (FR 85),[2] and its success transforms life from absurdity to aesthetic achievement.

In the phraseology of PR, "Speculative Philosophy is the endeavour to frame a coherent, logical, necessary system of general ideas in terms of which every element of our experience can be interpreted" (PR 4). Just as knowing is neither analysis nor classification, so "interpreting" is not explaining. To explain is to take apart the puzzle, discover how the separate elements are put together, reassemble it, and put it away in a box labeled "done." Though a pleasant diversion, such an exercise leads no-

---

[1] It must be carefully noted that this movement in no way resembles an ascent of the Porphyrean tree, each limb of which is more abstract *qua* further from reality. It more closely resembles the progress from cell to organ to system to organism in the evolution of life.

[2] "Philosophy is the attempt to make manifest the fundamental evidence as to the nature of things. . . . It makes the content of the human mind manageable; it adds meaning to fragmentary details; it discloses disjunctions and conjunctions, consistencies and inconsistencies. Philosophy is the criticism of abstractions which govern special modes of thought" (MT 67).

where, for it reveals nothing about other puzzles save the fiction that they too have discrete parts and can be disassembled and reassembled at will. To interpret, on the other hand, is to search out the more general law of which the fact is an instance, and to see that law as predictive of still other instances. Thus interpretation moves from the particular to the universal and back to the particular, in a passage Whitehead likens to the flight of an airplane. A philosophical scheme takes off from experience, is formulated in the stratosphere of abstraction, and returns to experience for the verification of its predictions. It is "a matrix from which true propositions applicable to particular circumstances can be derived" (PR 13). The landing not only verifies the abstract formulation, but also reveals otherwise unnoticed elements in the initially observed facts, since observation tends to be selective and to overlook what is irrelevant to practice. Philosophy is thus a voyage toward abstraction in order to render experience more concrete. It is "an adventure in the clarification of thought" (PR 14), which adventure begins with concrete experience and comes to fruition in a generalized theory concretely applicable to experience. The philosopher must take care, therefore, (*a*) that the experience provoking philosophical reflection *be* concrete, and (*b*) that it represent the common experience of mankind.

To satisfy the first norm, experience must transcend the narrow limits of rational experience—it must be the "experience drunk and experience sober, experience sleeping and experience waking . . ." of AI, ranging through the full gamut of human experience in its most concrete form. This is not to say, however, that experience *can* be fully concrete. The mere fact that it is conscious makes it selective and hence abstract. Consciousness lights up merely a portion of the data affecting the organism— that portion relevant to the organism's being and well-being.

Nor is experience to be taken as a bare, uninterpreted datum which subsequently acquires interpretation. By the principle of relativity, that which is uninterpreted—i.e., not related to its world via some sort of scheme— is unknown, unexperienced. Therefore, the philosopher must take off from experience recognized as already abstract and interpreted, seeking by his scheme to rectify the inadequacies of the starting point: criticizing and justifying its interpretation, correcting its initial abstract character.

In order to guarantee some universality to the interpretations from which the speculative philosopher begins, Whitehead demands that they be selected from the great warehouses of human experience: the physical, social, and life sciences, the arts, ethics, religion, social institutions, language, etc. With such interpretations as its starting point, the resultant scheme can avoid to some extent the provincialism which might otherwise taint it, and be assured of a focus of practical application as well. For a scheme to be genuinely metaphysical, it must be applicable beyond the limited confines of its starting point, having achieved some relatively universal perspective.

The manner in which a scheme transcends its starting point is critical, however. It cannot be the case, for example, that laws generalized from mechanics be taken as univocally applicable to psychology or sociology. In this instance, no real generalization, no genuine philosophical movement, has taken place. The locus of application of the law has been generalized, not the law itself. In the philosophic generalization of a law, those characteristics idiosyncratic to its original locus must be recognized and abstracted from. However, those characteristics can be discovered only in the context of a more general formulation. It is obvious, therefore, that philosophy—the attempt to formulate the most general notions in terms of which any experience can be elucidated—is an eminently fallible endeavor. "The aim at generalization is sound, but the estimate of success is exaggerated" (PR 11). Hence the tie to practice cannot be broken, for therein lies the only possibility for verification. In the dialectic between the scheme and confirmatory experience, the scheme undergoes continued modification. "The proper test is not that of finality, but of progress" (PR 21).

From an epistemic point of view, how is it even possible to move from the provincialism which must accrue to any sort of experience, however "common," to a metaphysical generalization? Granted: every limited context is a subset of a larger context and hence displays the more general characteristics of the larger context; but how can these be distinguished from the more idiosyncratic characters? The problem is particularly acute when it is the ultimate generalizations which are sought, for, exemplified in every experience, they are for that very reason ordinarily unexperienced. They cannot be recognized in the contrast of their presence and absence because of the "no vacations" clause binding them. Therefore, the ultimate generalizations cannot be derived either by deduction from other generalizations or by induction from experience. Both methods leave the metaphysician taxiing around his home airport, unable to discern the nature of airports in general.

The only way to leave the ground is through an imaginative leap.

> The reason for the success of this method of imaginative rationalization is that, when the method of difference fails, factors which are constantly present may yet be observed under the influence of imaginative thought. Such thought supplies the differences which the direct observation lacks. It can even play with inconsistency; and can thus throw light on the consistent, and persistent, elements in experience by comparison with what in imagination is inconsistent with them [PR 7].

Thus, a philosophical scheme begins not with a set of clear and distinct ideas, but with a vague, artistic sort of imaginative grasp of the nature of things: too vague to be judged valid, invalid, true or false, lacking explicit logical structure and concrete implications. Adequate formulation is the goal of philosophic endeavor, not its starting point.

This goal is reached by the gradual elaboration of the categoreal scheme, an elaboration which moves from the initial inchoate vision of the whole to progressive levels of detail, thus making the scheme more and more determinate. The best example of this sort of movement can be found in PR itself. From the romantic insight of SMW, in which he vaguely grasped the organic ongoingness of the world and the necessity for a four-element scheme to interpret it, Whitehead derives in PR first a basic categoreal list in terms of which the most general relations between the elements as vaguely conceived are rendered explicit. In Part II, these notions are shown to be genuine responses to the philosophical and scientific problems of the modern world and at the same time to be grounded in the work of previous philosophers and scientists. The explication of the tie to experience serves to concretize the abstract formulations of the categoreal lists. Parts III and IV continue the elaboration, now in abstraction from experience and in terms of the scheme itself. Part V marks the landing of the airplane, a return to the romantic, lyrical language of SMW, only now with the clarity attained in the flight.

The elaboration of a speculative scheme does not proceed in an ad hoc manner, but is controlled each step of the way by the norms which govern the ideal product. The most fundamental criterion of any metaphysics is that it be self-referential, interpreting not only the world of experience but itself, its process of formulation, and its relation to other theories as well. Any philosophical theory should be the prime exemplification of itself if it is not to be useless speculation. For Whitehead's scheme, this entails that the theory manifest the same organic interconnections as it ascribes to the world. The various elements involved in it cannot be "simply located" or self-sufficient, but must each be what the others make it to be: "what is indefinable in one such notion cannot be abstracted from its relevance to the other notions" (PR 5). In a word, any scheme must exhibit coherence as its prime requisite. It must likewise be internally consistent or logical, though a defect in this area is not prima facie justification for abandoning a scheme; it is merely an indication that more work must be done. Furthermore, inasmuch as the theory asserts the indissoluble relation of form and facts, its abstract character must be capable of exemplification in the concrete. It must have experiential ties. Insofar as it springs from concrete experience, a speculative theory will always be applicable—at least in the locus of its starting point. Its adequacy to interpret data from other areas is the empirical norm which is critical, for as a metaphysical generalization purporting to interpret all possible modalities of experience, it implicitly asserts its own necessity, which necessity must be borne out in fact.

The test for adequacy is the landing of the airplane, where the confrontation of theory with fact weeds out the bizarre, the impractical, and the irrelevant, and ensures the avoidance of pure fancy in the imaginative flight. This is not to say, however, that any theory can exhaust experience —explain it by explaining it away. Such expectations are the worst form of Misplaced Concreteness: the Dogmatic Fallacy. There will always be a gap between theory and fact, a mutual dialectic which progressively purifies the former while it elucidates the latter.

II • THE CATEGOREAL SCHEME AND DERIVATIVE NOTIONS

Anyone who has attempted to read the Preface to Hegel's *Phenomenology of Spirit* has found it to be unintelligible before the remainder of the work has been read. The same may be said of the categoreal scheme which begins PR. It represents the entire work raised to the utmost power of generalization and hence cannot be genuinely grasped until it can be seen in its details. To attempt an explication of it at this point would therefore be folly. However, it will be of value to indicate those areas in which the romantic vision of SMW has reached further precision in terminology, in the elaboration of the basic conceptual elements, and in the introduction of principles only foreshadowed in the earlier work. As set forward in SMW, the doctrine of prehensions concerned itself with concrete facts of relatedness among entities: their bond with all other entities. Implied but not explicit until PR is the fact that prehensions sort themselves into two varieties, depending on what kind of entity is being absorbed into the self-creating creature: another actual entity, an eternal object, or an earlier prehension in the concrescence. In the instance that an emerging occasion is "feeling" the causal agency of other occasions in its environment, the prehension is termed "physical." It is this manner of prehension which displays the vector character described in SMW, being a feeling "here," in the immediacy of the subject, of an influence causally "there" in a completed or "satisfied" occasion. The latter is not a merely passive given, to be appropriated by subsequent occasions. It is the "provoker" of its absorption into the future. Its perishing—the completion of its self-creative process—has spelled the death of its immediacy, of its self-functioning, but has initiated its "pragmatic afterlife" as an insistent, obstructive fact forever operative in the future. The efficiency of the past in the immediacy of a present occasion is what constitutes a physical prehension. No concrescent occasion may ignore the facts in its relevant environment, in its actual world. It becomes what they, in their insistence, make it to be. In the language of PR, an entity positively prehends or feels every item in its actual world.

The same cannot be said with respect to an occasion's prehensions of eternal objects, that is, with respect to its conceptual feelings.[3] Insofar as some eternal objects are contraries of others, all cannot ingress into the same entity, cannot become structural elements in its definiteness, without vitiating its internal unity. Therefore, relevant eternal objects are appropriated by the occasion; irrelevant or contrary ones, excluded from the emergent unity—they are negatively prehended.

The notion of negative prehension must be carefully qualified. It is not to be conceived of as an "ignoring" of irrelevant forms, for this would constitute a violation of the principle of relativity as it pertains to the relatedness of the realm of eternal objects and an emergent occasion (see Category of Explanation iv, PR 33). Every occasion takes a positive stand toward every eternal object, positively incorporating it into its definiteness or positively excluding it—holding "its datum as inoperative in the progressive concrescence of prehensions constituting the unity of the subject" (Category of Explanation xii, PR 35). In the simpler language of SMW, an occasion acquires the determinate character it has because of the forms it excludes as well as because of the forms it includes.

Furthermore, just as satisfied entities are not passively given for prehension, so eternal objects are not inert forms waiting to be appropriated. They have about them all the unrest of the Platonic Eros. They are lures for feeling finding a response in the "appetition"[4] of conceptual prehension, whether that prehension is conscious (as it can become in higher phases of the concrescence of certain actual entities) or unconscious (as is more normally the case). The relevance of eternal objects to process is an active relevance: not the brutal activity of efficient causation, but the seductive activity of final causality.

Any entity is, therefore, essentially dipolar, creating itself out of an interweaving of physical and conceptual feelings which are respectively the expression and ingression in its constitution of the actual and the non-actual worlds, of fact and of form. This interweaving is not accomplished all at once, however. It comes about in successive, atemporal stages in which prehensions other than those initiating the concrescence can arise. These may be additional conceptual prehensions: the feeling of eternal objects not factually exemplified in the data but related to those so exemplified—reverted feelings (see Categoreal Obligation v, PR 40), which feelings can be a source of novelty for the occasion. These subsequent prehensions can likewise be integrations of previous physical and conceptual prehensions. In this case, Whitehead calls the prehensions "impure," since

---

[3] A pure conceptual prehension is the grasp of an eternal object as a possibility *for* exemplification, not *as* exemplified in another occasion. It is "a direct vision of some possibility of good or evil—of some possibility as to how actualities *may* be *definite*" (PR 50).

[4] "Appetition is immediate matter of fact including in itself a principle of unrest, involving realization of what is not and may be" (PR 47–48).

they involve a synthesis of fact and form. They may be "transmuted feelings," "physical purposes," "propositional feelings" (see Categoreal Obligation vi, PR 40), or other more complex prehensions such as PR III will describe. Yet they all display one characteristic in common: their datum is a modality of the togetherness of an actual entity or set of actual entities and an eternal object.

The actual entity arising from the final synthesis of its many prehensions represents the transformation of the original incoherence of its manifold data into the coherence of its drop of unitary experience, of its one synthetic feeling. By Category of Explanation ii, "the *potential* unity of many entities—actual and non-actual— acquires the *real* unity of the one actual entity . . ." (PR 33). This real unity is immediate and subjective, which is to say that the public character of fact and of form is privatized in the unity of the subject. Any prehension has, therefore, a subjective form which is "how" the occasion in which the prehension is an element feels the datum of the prehension. This "how" is the adverbial quality of experience referred to in SMW's discussion of prehension; it involves the "emotions, valuations, purposes, adversions, aversions, consciousness, etc." (Category of Explanation xiii, PR 35) which transform objectivity into the perspectival realization of private fact.

Since any actual entity is the result of a synthesis of a manifold of prehensions, the subjective forms of the prehensions must be such as to render synthesis possible. They must be "sympathetic" rather than mutually inhibiting (see Categoreal Obligation i, PR 39). Furthermore, if genuine unity, and not mere addition, is to be achieved, no element can play inconsistent roles in it; nor can diverse elements play the same role (see Categoreal Obligations ii–iii, PR 39). All this points to the necessity of an overall purpose guiding the concrescence from its inception, a vision of the goal to be achieved in the process, immanent in and normative of each step no matter how complex the process is. Therefore, any process must originate with a conceptual prehension of its subjective aim, which then becomes its "living aim at its own self-constitution" (PR 373), controlling the becoming by its final causality. As initially grasped, the subjective aim is a proposition, a hybrid entity whose subject in this case is the actual world given for the concrescence and whose predicate is a complex eternal object indicating the general scheme in terms of which that actual world could be integrated.[5] The proposition lures the subsequent integration. The reason for the predicate's displaying the pattern it does must, by the ontological principle,[6] be sought in another actual entity, for to seek

[5] As will be seen in later discussions, Whitehead uses the term "proposition" to designate a hybrid form of entity not restricted to the logical sphere. It is a mode of togetherness between a fact (its subject) and a form (its predicate).

[6] ". . . every condition to which the process of becoming conforms in any particular instance, has its reason *either* in the character of some actual entity in the

a reason is to seek for an actual entity. But the actual entity in question cannot be bound to the limitations of a finite perspective; if it were, the organic character of the world would be destroyed. It must be a view from a transcendent viewpoint, a view which can therefore provide a system of sympathetic and hence integrable patterns for all viewpoints. The subjective aim of any entity must be ultimately grounded in that protean ordering of eternal objects which constitutes the primordial nature of God. God's primordial envisagement of the eternal objects orders them in degrees of relevance to finite perspectives, limits fathomless possibility to possibility *for* actualities, thereby providing finite perspectives with systems of value concretizable in process and relevant to future processes. The subject's prehension of its subjective aim enables it to synthesize its actual world via the ingression of relevant eternal objects, to coordinate the subjective forms of its feelings, and to achieve thereby a fully determinate unity.

It would seem, at first glance, that the doctrine of the subjective aim destroys creaturely initiative in the self-creative process, that God in a sense "hands out tickets" to destinations which concrescences meekly attain. Such an interpretation is far from the truth. What Whitehead is saying is (*a*) that a creature is limited by the real potentiality given in the environment, and (*b*) that within that context an emergent entity can function autonomously.[7] This autonomy is evidenced in the modifications an occasion introduces in its subjective aim, whereby the initially general pattern becomes progressively more determinate and "personal," through the self-creative process of the subject.[8] By analogy, the associative hierarchy fully realized in the satisfaction of an occasion is to its initial aim as received from God through the actual world as an individual is to the species in which it participates. In each pair, the latter member, though imposing a definite limitation on the former, is in many respects indeterminate or general; whereas the former has resolved in a perfectly definite way the indetermination latent in the latter—it is particular and anti-general.

The subjective aim, therefore, governs the becoming of an actual entity and is fully personalized and concretized in that creature's satisfaction: "*how* an actual entity *becomes* constitutes *what* that actual entity *is* . . ." (Category of Explanation ix, PR 34). The subject becoming under the lure of its subjective aim becomes, in Whitehead's terminology, the

---

actual world of that concrescence, *or* in the character of the subject which is in process of concresence" (PR 36).

[7] To take a homely example: the rules of chess limit the ways a knight *can* be moved, but do not determine the ways a knight *is* moved within those limitations. These are determined in part by position of the other pieces on the board and in part by the ingenuity of the player.

[8] How much autonomy is possible to a creature is, however, a function of its environment. See subsequent discussions of order as the condition for creativity.

superject of its own experiences: a fully determinate matter of fact which is efficient cause of futures. The two—subject and superject, becoming and being—cannot be torn apart. To be a subject is to be a subject of experience emerging out of the weaving together of experiences into a concrete unity. It is quite literally to be "thrown under" experience as the possibility progressively realized through the processive synthesis of experience. To be a superject is to have reached that fully determinate synthesis (subjectivity) aimed at in the process of subjectification (of synthesis) and to "throw over" or "throw beyond" experience the unity achieved in experience as a fact forever operative in the future under aspects or "objectifications" of that unity. It is obvious, therefore, that subject and superject are inseparable terms with respect to the actual entity: the former underlining the private internal process whereby subjectivity is realized, the latter stressing the public pragmatic afterlife of that realization in future processes. Each is what the other makes it to be. The actual entity's vision of itself as operative in the future (as superject) guides its process of subjectification; the process (as subject) determines the future efficient causality emerging from it. The subject is a self-creating creature functioning in regard to its own individuality, having significance and value in itself through its concrescence of prehensions. The superject is the definiteness achieved in the satisfied subject, fully determinate with respect to the process of its becoming, its future agency and its relation to every item in the universe of facts and the realm of form (see Category of Explanation xxi, PR 38). In achieving this definiteness, its immediacy —its self-functioning, its self-value—perishes; but the occasion then becomes a value for the others and for the totality, pervading the future world in objective immortality.

This transcendent functioning of an actual entity is termed its objectification, and is inseparable from the entity's self-functioning. An entity is not to be viewed as "selfishly" directing its decisions *only* toward its own achievement. Its superjective functioning is as much a part of its initial aim as is its subjective activity. In this sense, the superject cannot be torn from the subject without destroying the temporal organicity of the world. Just as in human conscious behavior consequences are as important as immediate gratification and hence influence the deliberative process, so in the becoming of an actual entity its pragmatic afterlife in the relevant future partially conditions its subjectification. The relevant future "consists of those elements in the anticipated future which are felt with effective intensity by the present subject by reason of the real potentiality for them to be derived from itself" (see Categoreal Obligation viii, PR 41). Thus every occasion "anticipates" in addition to "remembering" and "enjoying."

This inclusion of memory and anticipation in an actual entity grounds the togetherness of actual entities in an actual world. In virtue of their mutual immanence in each other, they form a nexus, a public matter of fact (Category of Existence iii, PR 32) as real, individual, and particular as the actual entities comprising it. Togetherness in a nexus is, therefore, the most general form of togetherness among actual entities; all other modes are specifications of it. When there is an additional real togetherness between a nexus and an eternal object considered in its character as a potential for realization, a proposition results: a hybrid entity considered true if the predicative pattern is exemplified in the satisfactions of the members of the nexus, false if it is not. As grasped in an impure prehension, a proposition is a lure proposed for feeling and is the doorway through which novelty enters the world. Without propositions (particularly false propositions) and propositional feelings, the universe would be condemned to an endless reiteration of the forms it already exemplifies.

The false proposition reveals the fact that possibilities not actualized in an actual world are nevertheless relevant to it. The ground for this relevance is again the primordial nature of God: that ordering of eternal objects which limits their general relevance to actuality to be a graded relevance, a specific togetherness. Thus the primordial nature is a primordial datum for any finite process, immanent in it—prehended into its constitution—as the condition for the possibility of its advance toward novelty, yet transcending it as the condition for the possibility of *all* creative advance.

When God is considered in this manner, however, he is considered in abstraction from the universe of concrete particulars—"alone with himself" (PR 50) as the self-sufficient togetherness of otherwise isolated eternal objects. In the language of feelings, his conceptual prehensions alone are being taken into account—his atemporal envisagement or valuation of the eternal objects. As "alone," he is an exception to the principle of relativity, an exception intolerable to the organic vision of reality, in which all reality is inseparably intertwined. God must have physical feelings if he is to be an *actual* entity (i.e., real *qua* capable of *acting*), and in virtue of the fact that he is the *reason* for the graded relevance of eternal objects, he *must* be an actual entity, albeit not one bound to the spatiotemporal limitations of a finite perspective.[9] The data for his physical feelings are the manifold of creaturely achievements in the universe. There is, therefore, an appropriation of God (in his primordial nature) by the world and an appropriation of the world by God. Whitehead terms this latter appropriation—the result of God's physical feelings—his consequent nature and sees it as the divine synthesis of creaturely fact, the

---

[9] By the ontological principle, to search for a reason is to search for an actual entity.

final togetherness of actuality, which overcomes the limited togetherness achievable from a perspective.[10]

The exigencies of the scheme, however, demand a still further synthesis, for though divine conceptual feelings provide the forms for finite togetherness and divine physical feelings redeem achieved togetherness from its necessary partiality, the two poles of divine feelings remain unsynthesized: God is incoherent. Therefore, an additional aspect must be predicated of God: his superject nature, in which this ultimate synthesis takes place and becomes a datum for the world.[11] As will be more fully discussed later, it is through God's activity of feeling together (*a*) his physical feelings of the actual world of a concrescent occasion and (*b*) his primordial envisagement of the eternal objects that that additional limitation of the eternal objects by means of which a subjective aim relevant to a determinate actual world—the real potential for a novel creaturely synthesis—comes to be and to stand in propositional togetherness with that actual world as a datum proposed for creaturely feeling.

An actual world is the *real* potentiality of the universe *for* the perspective as physically felt *into* that perspective: the mutual implication of occasions relative to a concrescence and defined by its perspective. It represents the unique character of space–time from the perspective, bringing out the fact that "here" and "there," "past," "present," and "future" have no meaning in abstraction from a concrescent occasion. This is not to say, however, that actual worlds are, in consequence, as isolated as the universes inscribed within Leibniz's monads. Actual worlds are "connected" in the ways to be described in Chapter 5. Most fundamentally, they "overlap," in that some occasions causally efficacious and hence "past" from the standpoint of one occasion may be not physically felt (and hence "present" or "future") from the standpoint of another; still others may be in the past for both. The actual world of one actual entity is a subordinate nexus in the actual world of others.

Using the concentric wave model of Chapter 1 will clarify this notion. In Figure 2, from the standpoint of B, A is in its actual world, and A's

FIGURE 2

[10] This doctrine will be explicated in detail in later pages, particularly in Chapter 4.
[11] For a full discussion of Whitehead's trinitarian interpretation of God, see Chapter 6 and PR V.

actual world is a subordinate nexus in B's actual world. From the vantage point of C, both B and A and their actual worlds are past elements, and D is future. If C is considered as a multiplicity of occasions, c_1, c_2, . . . c_n, these will be contemporaneous: i.e., not causally influencing each other, yet providing part of the real potentiality for d_1, d_2, . . . d_n in the nexus D by their pragmatic afterlife. Despite their contemporaneity, c_1, c_2, . . . c_n do not share identical actual worlds, for the causal elements in B and A (b_1, b_2, . . . b_n; a_1, a_2, . . . a_n) influence each occasion in C in a manner unique to its perspectival "location." This is to say that the prehended occasions are objectified for concrescences in C under different aspects of themselves.[12]

The doctrine of selective objectification concerns itself with the pragmatic afterlife of an occasion—what it is as a given fact for the others after its moment of for-itselfness has perished. Any concrescent occasion decides the different modalities under which it can "live on" in the future, but which if any of these aspects are relevant to an emerging occasion is a function of the latter's perspective. For example, a fire is relevant to a hand under the aspect "hot," to an eye as "red," to an ear as "crackling," etc.[13] Our habitual subject–predicate mode of thought and its underlying substance–accident metaphysic makes this extremely difficult to grasp, for in verbally separating the heat, color, sound, etc. from the fire, we tend to think of the fire as something in itself, as though its "fireness" were a fact for the others in the environment in independence of its modifications. It must be continually borne in mind that "hot" *is* the fire as appropriated by a hand—*is* the modal existence of the fire for the hand—and not an accident *through* which an underlying reality is grasped. Objectifications *are* past entities functioning in the present under the limitations of the present perspective. The "fireness" of the fire, the unity of all its aspects—the fire considered in its self-functioning as creating its own drop of unified, immediate experience—has perished.[14] " 'It never really is' " (PR 130). What *is* is its various modal activities in the actual worlds of occasions beyond itself, in its future. The difference between self-functioning and objective functioning is the difference between subject and superject. They are inseparable[15] yet distinct modes of existence, marking the difference between process and reality, between perishing and objective immortality.

---

[12] Since the model is spatial and hence homogeneous, it cannot illustrate differences in objectification and must be dropped at this point.

[13] But it is not an important item in the actual world of a taste bud. It is not a fact *for it*: its relevance is negligible.

[14] Although the fire example serves admirably to bring out the point at issue, the reader is cautioned to take it *only* as an illustration and not to infer that in actual fact a fire is an actual entity. Under Whitehead's interpretation, it would be a type of society (see Chapter 3, Section 3).

[15] Because each determines the other.

3

DISCUSSIONS AND APPLICATIONS

(PR, Part II)

TO BE AN ACTUAL ENTITY for Whitehead is to be fully formed, fully definite, with no indeterminations left unresolved. From the welter of what it could be, an actual entity decides what it will be: realizing certain potentials and positively excluding others; taking a definite stance with respect to everything in the ideal and actual worlds. Its real essence, structured by its associative hierarchy, comprises the full particularity of its status in the universe and of the universe in it: its unique way of housing and pervading *this* world populated by *these* actual entities. The result of the status decision is a new fact in the world, inexplicable in terms of anything outside its own self-creative process—ultimately its own reason for being what it is and what it is not. It presents itself to all subsequent occasions, therefore, as a new "given," irrational in the sense that its decisions are effected from within itself and are not mediated by any outside agency. It is "externally free" (PR 41). But its freedom is not to create itself *ex nihilo*. It still is what the others make it to be as a result of their own free decisions. The manifestation of its creativity is its own internal synthesis of what is given for it. Because of this self-functioning every actual entity has an element of exclusiveness. Its satisfaction cannot be tampered with, by either the addition or the subtraction of elements, without the destruction of the unique character of the entity. In its process the actual entity has established a fully determinate bond with each element in the universe, positively including that element in a determinate way in its nature or positively excluding (negatively prehending) it in a manner which makes the excluded item impossible for it. The freedom of an actual occasion is therefore both limited and limiting, conditioned by past achievements and conditioning future process, a decision arising out of previous decisions and provoking future decisions. Decision "constitutes the very meaning of actuality" (PR 68).

The decision which superjects givenness is a "decision amid 'potentiality' " (PR 68): the real potentiality latent in the actual world stubbornly given for that occasion as a brute fact. This world is particular (unique to the occasion) and particulate (a disjoined multiplicity of individual facts apt for synthesis). In virtue of its individuality and that of its included members, it is actual; in virtue of its real potentiality for synthesis, it is a world. This real potentiality is ultimately tied to the primordial decision limiting the disjoined welter of possibilities to be conjoined possibilities. God's primordial nature is therefore the ideal realization of possibility, the ultimate activity conditioning possibility by its decision and grounding all subsequent decisions. As internal to God, it is a free and hence reasonless synthesis of eternal objects, limiting their indeterminate relevance to actuality and overcoming their mutual disjunction. As given for the world, it is the irrational conjugation and gradation of possibility which mediates objective givenness and subjective decision, making possible the synthetic unity of the emergent creature.

This mediation is first apparent in the objectification of actual entities. Each, though achieving a fully determinate, peculiar, and exclusive satisfaction shaped by a complex form, superjects[1] that achievement to emergent perspectives as a plurality of potential objectifications, each of which is an element in the complex pattern structuring the entity. As has been seen before, every actual entity is a concrescence of prehensions, each seizing its datum with its own subjective form. A satisfaction is therefore a unitary feeling which represents the togetherness of a manifold of prior feelings. As will be seen in the analysis of Part IV of PR, these feelings are inseparate but separable. From the point of view of the physical pole of a concrescent entity, the objectification of a past occasion felt into the subject is one of these separable feelings as structured by the subjective form it possessed in the satisfied occasion. The subjectively formed feeling felt by the concrescent occasion is the aspect or modal limitation under which the past occasion enters the present—an aspect or modal limitation of the fully determinate unitary satisfaction achieved in the past. As separable from that unity while at the same time inseparate from it, the objectification conveys the value achieved from

---

[1] It will be noted that I occasionally employ "superject" as a verb—a usage not explicitly found in PR. My reasons for so doing are central to my reading of Whitehead, for I see that unless the superject be interpreted dynamically, as not merely "given for" but more importantly "acting in" a subsequent subject, then that subject is not the "cumulation of the past" but a *mere* "stage-play" (PR 363) about it. I interpret the past as "looming over" the present, as "pressing in," as "insistent," as "a flying dart hurled at the future," not as a passive, inert "given." I believe a case can be made for the fact that Whitehead himself leans toward this view, although this is not the place to develop my argument. I must admit, however, that many Whiteheadian scholars would disagree with my reading.

past to present under an abstraction from itself which is not disconnected from the satisfied occasion. The metaphysical basis for this separable–inseparate character of a satisfaction lies in the primordial nature of God. These pattern elements, like the total pattern concretized in a satisfaction, are eternal objects, which, although selected from the other eternal objects comprising the total pattern, maintain a real relatedness to them. If this were not the case, actual occasions would be a synthesis of isolated fragments of their past and hence radically subjective and alone.

This doctrine can be clarified by reference to the fire example in the last chapter. If "red," the objectification of the fire, its modal existence *for* the eye, were not as an eternal object *intrinsically* bound up with the eternal objects "hot" and "crackling" in the complex eternal object "fire," then to appropriate "red" would be to appropriate it as an isolated possibility—redness-in-itself—and not as "red-fire-which-must-also-be-hot-and-crackling." If appropriated in the former way, the "red" in the actual world of the eye would have no connection whatever with the "hot" and "crackling" in the actual worlds of the hand and ear. Not only the fire would have perished, but also the real togetherness of the forms which structured its definiteness. If formal togetherness is reduced to mere existential juxtaposition, the universe is fragmented into as many realities as there are perspectives, making any objectivity impossible. But if prior to any instantiation "red," "hot," and "crackling" are inextricably related in the eternal object "fireness," then the givenness of fire-as-red for an eye includes the potential relevance of the other eternal objects involved but not exemplified in this particular objectification. In other words, because the togetherness of eternal objects not merely is a product of finite process but represents a synthesis antecedent to all created fact, the "selection" in Whitehead's conception of "selective objectification" is not an annihilation of the relevance of alternatives. The way lies open for reverted conceptual feelings—a "secondary origination of conceptual feelings with data which are partially identical with, and partially diverse from, the eternal objects forming the data in the first phase of the mental pole" (PR 40). Every actual entity therefore actualizes a nexus of eternal objects whose togetherness is already ideally realized in the primordial nature of God.

The mediation of ordered and mutually relevant eternal objects is likewise responsible for the fact that the appropriation of various items in a public world can be synthesized into a drop of private experience. Eternal objects not only serve to objectify data; they also clothe the feelings whereby data are grasped, functioning as the subjective forms of feelings and in their togetherness constituting the private emotional complex. That they are sympathetic is a function of the subjective aim; that they are capable of being sympathetic is a function of their primordial togetherness in God. As a result of the ingression of eternal objects as subjective forms, feelings acquire a private character such that an actual entity can be said to "enjoy" its experience rather than merely to undergo it. There is thus no bare feeling, no absolute objectivity, no mere inheritance of influence from a causal past. Both physical and conceptual prehensions add not only their data to the satisfaction but their emotional character as well. Even in the case of negative prehensions which eliminate their data from feeling, the subjective forms add to the definiteness of the occasion.

The subjective forms arise under the influence of the subjective aim of the concrescence—the hypothesis prepared for the concrescence in God's synthesis of his primordial envisagement and his consequent physical assimilation of the entities in the actual world of the concrescence. From this synthesis arises the abstract value realizable from the perspective; this, from the standpoint of the perspective, forms a proposition with the nexus of the actual world, a lure proposed for feeling, to be concretized—i.e., its indeterminations solved by the concrescence. When the lure is finally realized, the fully determinate value achieved becomes a condition limiting subsequent creativity because of the real potentiality embodied in it. The initial valuation of eternal objects in the primordial nature provides a background of graded eternal objects against which the subjective aim is set. Without the background, actual entities would be Leibnizian monads, achieving autonomy but incapable of contributing that achievement to future process. The primordial nature undergirds the solidarity of the world, supplying the communal conditions which make individuality possible. It "constitutes the metaphysical stability whereby the actual process exemplifies general principles of metaphysics, and attains the ends proper to specific types of emergent order" (PR 64). Thus, despite the exclusive character of the satisfaction of an actual entity, despite its privacy, it can arise out of the equally exclusive and private achievements of the others in its actual world and bequeath itself as a new condition laid upon the future.

II · THE EXTENSIVE CONTINUUM[2]

A further limitation must be introduced into the realm of possibility in order to guarantee the solidarity of an actual world. In previous discus-

[2] Whitehead introduces the notion of the extensive continuum by means of a preliminary discussion of conscious perception. But to discuss perception at this point in the analysis requires that certain thus far unexplicated notions such as "society," "social order," "personal order," "causal objectification," and "presentational objectification" be grasped in preliminary form. Rather than anticipate what will be fully elaborated in subsequent sections, I shall use a more general derivation of the necessity for and nature of the extensive continuum, which will be further amplified in the discussions of perception which follow.

sions of actual occasions, it has been mentioned that, as a result of the self-creative process, each occasion actualizes the drop of space–time which is its fully determinate perspective. In its satisfaction, it synthesizes the "there's" and "then's" in its actual world from the vantage point of its "here" and "now," thus producing the unique, perspectival "here–there," "now–then" relationships into which its concreteness can be analyzed. In the same manner as that in which the ideal realization of eternal objects in God's primordial nature had to be invoked to guarantee the metaphysical communality of occasions, an additional limitation of potentiality must be postulated as the condition for their physical togetherness. Without some more general uniformity, diverse, perspectival, spatio-temporal drops could never be coordinated to form a new occasion.

In grappling with the correlative problem in mechanics, Newton was forced to postulate absolute space–time as a container composed of an infinity of immovable, spatio-temporal positions with respect to which relative motion could be measured. Whitehead cannot opt for this explanation, for to him actual entities do not undergo "adventures" in space–time. They literally do not move. Each finite satisfaction is fixed and unchanging: objectively immortal and resembling more the absolute spatio-temporal places of Newton than it does his bodies in relative motion. What is to be accounted for is not the relativity of motion but the solidarity of an actual world populated by entities "at rest" in their perspectival places. In other words, the spatio-temporal unity of an actual world needs grounding. Nor can Whitehead choose an explanation of a Kantian sort by postulating a synthetic activity of mind as the source of the spatio-temporal coordination of actual occasions; mind can unify only what is already given as unifiable, being in Whitehead's view merely a later, more complex phase in the concrescence of an occasion—a concrescence which, like all others, originates in the physical prehensions of the entities in an actual world. What Whitehead seeks is, therefore, neither something actual (such as an absolute space–time system in which events are situated) nor something purely subjective (such as an *a priori* form) but rather something which itself is an aspect of the real potentiality given for any concrescence.

He finds this in the notion of the extensive continuum as an overarching scheme of relational possibility of which the relativistic space–times of actual occasions are further specifications. This coordination of spatio-temporal possibility is not to be construed as a geometric schema—for it is more general than geometries, which themselves, as metric, are perspectival. It is "one relational complex in which all potential objectifications find their niche" (PR 103). As a locus for *potential* objectifications, it is a continuum with indefinite divisibility and unbounded extension, containing no singularities, no privileged "places," no asymmetrical relations, and no metric characteristics, for these are properties of actuality in its stubborn atomicity. In other words, it is not exemplified in actual occasions in its generality. Occasions particularize it, rupture it, specify its generality from their perspective. Yet the general coordination remains as the first limitation of the real potentiality for subsequent occasions—as a schema of possible spatio-temporal relations in terms of which the achieved drops of space–time in the actual world are coordinatable from the perspective of the concrescent occasion.

It must be carefully noted that this schema does not specify the idiosyncratic characteristics of the space–times peculiar to various cosmic epochs (e.g., that they be four-dimensional, five-dimensional, bichronal, etc.). These are further determinations introduced by the course of events in a cosmic epoch and are relative to the cosmic epoch in question. The determinations introduced by the extensive continuum are the more general conditions which must be shared by all dimensional systems if they are to be systematic and dimensional.[3] These are the properties of extensity as such, irrespective of its dimensionality, and concern relations such as inclusion, connection, overlap, etc., without which any modality of spatio-temporal relatedness is impossible. The extensive continuum is therefore the "spread" of space–time conceived as the potential public relatedness of private relations in an actual world. When this spread is atomized and specified in a concrescence, it allows the multiplicity of the past to achieve the solidarity of one world for the concrescence and for the future. It provides a spatio-temporal mutuality which transcends the limitations of each perspective so that each actual occasion can pervade and house all spaces and all times.

III · ORDER, SOCIETY, ORGANISMS, AND ENVIRONMENT

The descriptions of actual entities thus far built up from SMW and PR are still far removed from a description of the concrete world given for human experience—the world of concete, enduring yet changing objects. Actual entities have been described only in terms of their general character and relations to each other, not in terms of the more particular relations which join them together into atoms or stones or trees. An actual world has been spoken of only as a nexus of mutually implicated occasions. What has been left out of the previous discussions are the more specialized kinds of order which can be manifest in an actual world, those in virtue of which the concrescence relative to that actual world

---

[3] For this reason, in Part IV of PR Whitehead is compelled to redefine the basic spatial notions such as "point," "line," and "plane" in purely formal terms not peculiar to our cosmic epoch.

can achieve greater intensity in its satisfaction, greater importance and value for itself and for the future.

In general terms, order is that factor in an actual world which limits a concrescence, deciding for it what it can and cannot become. No actual occasion can outgrow its actual world, since it is an outgrowth of that world. This is the root meaning of givenness. The real potentiality, the real options offered a concrescence are settled for it by its antecedent world, by the limited potentialities for synthesis in the data.[4]

What differentiates order from mere givenness is the fact that an ordered world does not merely *provoke* a satisfaction, it *promotes* intensity in resultant satisfactions in view of the coordination already present in the data. This is not to say that every element in an actual world manifesting order is therefore bound up in the dominant order. Disorder is a necessary part of the given as well—the disorder introduced by mutually inhibiting or incompatible elements, which will have to be negatively prehended or synthesized as contrasts if an aesthetic unity is to be achieved. It is the proportion of order to disorder in an actual world which conditions the intensity of a resultant satisfaction, which intensity is the private aim of the concrescence, that which the entity seeks for itself—the subjective form or emotional tone of the satisfaction. Why this is so remains to be seen.

The intensity of a satisfaction is a function of the aesthetic structure of the concrete value or pattern exemplified in it. If, for example, the actual world of a concrescence is excessively diverse and uncoordinated, the resultant synthesis will have a trivial value, in that the various feelings do not strengthen each other. In Whitehead's terminology, it will manifest an excess of width without reinforcing narrowness. (Cacophony as opposed to harmony, randomly repeated sound as opposed to rhythm serve as illustrative analogues.) On the other hand, an excess of identity among the original data produces an unaesthetic vagueness in the satisfaction: the many are integrated into a formless one. In this instance, the defect is an excess of narrowness. An intense satisfaction arises from the proper balance of width and narrowness, a balance achieved through the progressive unification of the incompatibilities in the manifold in terms of contrasts and rhythms through which the necessity for negative prehension is overcome. An intense satisfaction will therefore manifest width in its earlier stages and progressively simplify that width in the later stages. It resembles a painting with a carefully detailed foreground set against yet growing out of a vaguely discriminated background. The right

---

[4] One cannot make a silk purse out of a sow's ear; but one could make a leather wallet, or a pouch. "Imperious Caesar, dead and turn'd to clay, / Might stop a hole to keep the wind away" (*Hamlet*, V.i.235–36) because he embodied that potentiality (among others) for the future.

kind of narrowness is essential if the painting is not to become a cartoon; the right kind of width and vagueness if it is not to degenerate into chaotic busy-ness.

Thus the aesthetic value of a satisfaction finds its inspiration or lack of inspiration in the order–disorder given for it in the environment. That each actual world is unique to the occasion arising out of it entails that there be no absolute or ideal order in a universal sense; there are only the limited orders relative to perspectives and their actual worlds. Nor can an actual entity achieve an absolute ordering of its own given. All attainment is partial, involving the elimination or trivialization of elements unsynthesizable (*qua* disorderly) from the perspective. However, the partiality of any finite attainment is the ground for subsequent creative endeavor in which the disorderly elements may be positively unified in the order of a new perspective.

Although no absolute order is possible, actual worlds will exhibit dominant orders relative to them: the "moral order" proper to a given culture, or the "physical order" dominant in a cosmic epoch. These, though not absolute in either their universality or dominion, provide an emerging entity with an environment whose incompatibilities have been partially overcome through their shared order, an environment whose further synthesis can evoke a more intense satisfaction than that growing out of an environment not already structured. The right order and the right disorder are therefore the conditions for the possibility of intensity. Both too little and too much order evoke low-grade satisfactions: the former, because it necessitates wholesale rejection of incompatible data, thus impoverishing the content of the satisfaction; the latter because it compels uncreative reiteration of the overdominant pattern, thus robbing the perspective of its originality. The doctrine of social order is Whitehead's interpretation of the ways in which this fine balance is maintained in the world.

Social order is not an addition to the doctrine of actual entities, tacked on to make aesthetic achievement possible; it is a special case of the organic interfusion of actual entities, reinforcing the mutual connectedness of members of a nexus by the exemplification of a common element of form in each—the defining characteristic of the social nexus. This is not to imply that the satisfactions of members of a society are identical. In their full particularity, they are still diverse. They share in common, however, certain general characteristics which mediate and canalize their diversity, making it a relevant diversity, one unified through the contrast-in-identity of the various members. Thus, the presence of a defining characteristic lends an order to a social environment which is not found in a nexus. For a member arising within a social context, the shared form in the data allows the diversity (disorder) to be *aufgehoben* rather than negatively prehended; hence more complex integrations and more intense satisfactions are possible. "The dominance of societies . . . is the essential condition for depth of satisfaction" (PR 142).

A nexus becomes social when the already present similarities among its members become important for them as a group.[5] That set of similarities —a complex eternal object—gains significant relevance in the objectifications of the members, and is inherited by new members arising in the social environment, who reproduce the defining characteristic in their own definiteness and further propagate it, thereby ensuring analogous similarities in the future. "Thus a society is, for each of its members, an environment with some element of order in it, persisting by reason of the genetic relations between its own members" (PR 138).

The endurance of a society is temporally limited, however. There are no self-contained, "simply located" societies, needing nothing but themselves in order to survive. Every society exists within a wider framework, needing a background of social order to ensure its continuance by supplying the more general characteristics necessary for the maintenance of its specialized characters. Members of the included society are members of the larger society as well, and depend on the more general characters in the larger environment as the base for their specialization.[6] The same must be said for the larger environment as well. The most general society of which we are aware is that manifesting the order of protonic and electronic occasions peculiar to our cosmic epoch.[7]

Actuality therefore presents itself as a nest of social environments providing more and more complex orders for included members. This nest must not be conceived after the model of nested boxes, however. In such a spatial construct, the environment would be construed as external to the environed society. The organic model is the only apt one, for, in this, all nested environments pervade each other, so that an actual entity receives objectifications from the members of all environing and environed societies in the nest.

An unfavorable change in the proximate environment can lead to the

[5] This importance would arise because of conditions in which the embryonic society finds itself.

[6] For example, a cell in an organ has specialized characteristics in virtue of its inclusion in the organ, characteristics not shared by cells in other organs. But in addition to being a liver cell, for instance, it is likewise a bodily cell and shares certain general characteristics with all other bodily cells. Without these more general characteristics, it could not support its specialized ones. Its social environment is the liver *and* the body.

[7] Leaving metaphysics aside for the moment and concerning himself solely with the spatio-temporal characteristics of occasions, Whitehead hypothesizes that the extensiveness manifested in this cosmic epoch may itself be a specialization within a broader framework of order: a society of alternative geometries each determined by the congruence-definitions which hold within it. This geometric society forms a subset of the society of pure extension whose defining characteristics are the relations manifest in the extensive continuum. The mind cannot push the boundaries further back than this.

collapse of an included society, rendering its members incapable of prop- agating the defining characteristic. This collapse is not to be interpreted as the annihilation of the members. The society vanishes when the defin- ing characteristic is no longer a relevant, important item in the satisfac- tions of its members. The endurance of societies is therefore epochal: they arise, flourish, and decay as a function of the background order in the environment, with societies requiring more specialized environments having a higher mortality rate than more primitive ones. Even the widest society—the cosmic epoch—is itself mortal, being set against a back- ground of disorder which will eventually overcome it. This does not spell its annihilation any more than its arising entailed creation. Both birth and death are marked by the incoming of a new order, not by the initiating and cessation of existence. God creates by providing forms relevant to self-creative factualization, not by calling fact forth from nothingness.

This fundamental description of social order as the genetic inheritance, display, and propagation of a defining characteristic in a nexus of actual entities is strictly applicable only to entities arising in a physical field in empty space—those intermittent flashes of existence which manifest no temporal continuity of inheritance relations and hence are not particles in the sense in which physics uses the term. (They are not enduring ob- jects.) The notion of temporal endurance demands a further specification of "society," transforming merely social order into "personal order." What differentiates the latter is the fact that the members of the nexus are arranged in a one-directional series via a linear propagation of the defining characteristic. Each occasion of the thread arises out of and sums up its own history in a peculiarly intimate way, and is provoked to reiterate its past character in the present, thereby allowing us to speak of particles, wave trains, and the like as enduring entities. What endures through a lapse of time is not a factual actual entity, but a defining char- acteristic, an eternal object reiterated in a thread of occasions, enabling each to sum up its "personal" past in a peculiarly intimate way.

The macro-objects of experience are social organizations of strands of such personal order woven together by an additional defining character- istic. In Whitehead's language, they are corpuscular societies. These may vary in complexity from the simple coordination of personal threads man- ifested in an atom to the more and more complex groupings of simple corpuscular societies as subsocieties in higher societies, represented by molecules and crystals, cells and organisms.[8]

A corpuscular society provides a highly favorable environment for members arising within the included personal threads. Their data exhibit a massiveness of shared order, which promotes both intensity in the result-

---

[8] That the latter pair cannot be interpreted solely in terms of social inheritance will be dealt with shortly.

ant satisfactions and stability for the social organization. Each included occasion in its grasp at intensity inherits and ratifies its position in the whole, and the whole thereby tends to endure. This same massiveness of order inhibits the originativeness of the members, however, since it "binds any one of its occasions to the line of its ancestry" (PR 159), thereby oversimplifying diversity in the environment, blocking out detail not relevant to the dominant order. As a result, included entities are not sensitive to environmental change—it is either negatively prehended or reduced to trivial relevance—and cannot react adaptively to it. Inorganic structured societies are capable of long endurance only if the environment is relatively stable.

If the society is specialized with respect to the presence of certain characteristics in the environment, its endurance is more a function of environmental stability than that of an unspecialized society. The former may offer higher-intensity satisfactions than the latter because of the increased complexity of the defining characteristic, but it nevertheless breeds reactionary, maladaptive members which are ultimately at the mercy of the environment, to be either dominated by its order or rendered "stateless" by its disorder. The appropriate response to the problematic of a shifting environment cannot be made from within an inorganic society, since in such a society the new can only be cast in the mold of the old.

Life is the alternative response to change. It manifests itself in an escape from inheritance, as "a bid for freedom" (PR 159): freedom *from* the pressure of the past and *for* reaction dictated by the present— for the capture of intensity and the grasp at vivid immediacy. By definition, therefore, life is antisocial. Living occasions form non-social nexuses, not societies or personal orders. They are mutually implicated but not mutually determining, representing the triumph of final over efficient causality. Since they are unbound by conceptual inheritance, living occasions can grasp novelty as novel and can initiate novel, adaptive responses through the increased operations of their unfettered conceptual pole. Life manifests a degree of autonomy not found in the inorganic world of corpuscular and structured societies. Yet its very autonomy makes it paradoxically the most destructive as well as the most fragile of forces. Without a highly structured environment to pattern its data and assimilate its reactions, it is merely a moment of valueless, anarchic disorder, resembling a revolutionary so radical as to eschew any contact or communication with the society he revolts against, thereby forfeiting both the platform and the fruits of his revolt.

If a living occasion is to achieve any value in its satisfactions—i.e., in itself, for the others, and for the totality—it must originate from within a highly structured social context which orders its data in such a way that environmental disorder (novelty) is included as relevant contrast rather than dismissed in negative prehensions, and must superject its novelty to an environment complex enough to withstand and appropriate it.[9] Life is impossible outside the shelter of a structured society with a certain amount of complexity. Within that context, a living occasion can be sensitive to the social past, since that past forms part of its actual world, yet not be bound by it; and at the same time can bequeath relevant novelty to the sheltering society, thus ensuring and enhancing the organism's survival in the welter of change.

A structured society harboring living occasions is termed living when the living nexus is regnant. However, the notions of "harboring" and "regnancy" must be carefully explored to avoid their being interpreted in classical soul–body terms. Inasmuch as living occasions are not social either in the generic sense (as unified by a defining characteristic) or in the more special sense (as possessing personal order), they are not elements in the enduring structural pattern of the host organism; nonetheless the data patterned by occasions arising within that structure are available to them, constitute their actual world, and are the source for their intense physical experience. The entirely living nexus is therefore situated within the bodily society but not as a structural and hence social element. For this reason, a living occasion is not bound to reiterate the defining characteristic dominant in its bodily region and can react spontaneously to the data.

The reason for the living occasion's ability to superject novel responses to the data is not attributable to some inner characteristic of the living occasion. All actual occasions are exactly the same in that they are what the real potentiality of their environment allows them to be. Life arises, therefore, as a function of environmental data, requiring complex data "on the edge of a compatibility beyond that to be achieved by mere inorganic treatment" (PR 161), if it is to arise at all. In the realm of the inorganic, environmental disorder is either negatively prehended or integrated in faint contrasts. The eternal objects embodied in the disorderly elements are not directly prehended by a social occasion: they become an element in its definiteness either through the integration of the subjective forms of the negative prehensions (in which case they are not operative constituents in the occasion or for the future) or as variables, "x's," in the contrast pattern (in which case though not operative in the present save as bare relata in the contrast, they are potentially operative in the future, having achieved a minimum of ingression in the present). A future occasion, in grasping the exemplified contrast in its feelings, can initiate reverted feelings[10] of the eternal objects, seizing them in pure

[9] Too much novelty may destroy the "animal body," the way a runaway auto-immune response can "kill" its host.

[10] A reverted feeling occurs when the feeling of one eternal object results in a

conceptual feelings which "recognize" the disorder–novelty and appropriate it via novel subjective forms. Since these reverted feelings must be integrated with the feelings of the orderly data, the subjective forms of the latter feelings are modified (according to the Category of Subjective Unity) so as to be sympathetic to those of the former feelings; out of the totality of feelings a drop of relevant novelty emerges, to be superjected to the "animal body"—the structured society harboring the living occasions. It is assimilable by the animal body since it does not mark a total break with the social, bodily past.[11] In other words, it is the organization of the data which is responsible for the origination of non-social occasions: for the intensity of their experience and for their ability to escape the necessity of inherited modes of response and to respond originatively. It is this novel yet historically relevant datum superjected by a living occasion which gives its host the adaptive flexibility which is the hallmark of a living body.

Living occasions arise, therefore, wherever such environmental conditions prevail within the body—"in the interstices of each living cell, and in the interstices of the brain" (PR 161), surrounded by the inorganic lattice and enabling it to function organically. Thus living occasions populate the body without any historical or social continuity among themselves, appearing wherever the complexity of the data can evoke them. Therefore, it is totally inappropriate to speak of an enduring vital principle animating a body. A living occasion can have no history, no inherited mode of response, to shackle it (save the history of the animal body and the ambient environment) if it is to be free to introduce relevant, novel solutions to novel problems.

An entirely living nexus becomes regnant in a stuctured society and enables that society to be termed living when the contributions of that nexus become important for the society. By the same token, an occasion is living when novel forms assume importance in its satisfaction. Therefore, no sharp line of demarcation between the organic and the inorganic, between the living and the non-living, can be drawn. One can speak of thresholds of life, however—but not with any exactitude.

The operations of a regnant, living nexus disturb the ordinary functionings of the inorganic host. In a sense, the physical laws which form part of the defining characteristic of the subservient inorganic societies are modified by the actions of the living members. As Whitehead said in SMW, "The electron blindly runs either within or without the body; but it runs within the body in accordance with its character within the body;

derivative feeling of other eternal objects relevant to it. Thus, a feeling of a contrast may elicit a feeling of the contrasted eternal objects.

[11] Of course, the case described above is an oversimplification of vital processes, but it serves to illustrate in ideal outline the mechanism at work.

that is to say, in accordance with the general plan of the body, and this plan includes the mental state" (SMW 79). A breakdown in inherited social bonding—in the statistical, physical laws keeping the society "together"—comes about in the transmission of energy across the interstitial empty space[12] when it harbors living occasions, thus producing an instability and disruption in the ordinary "blind-running" of the body's inorganic societies. Chemical dissociations occur which would not take place outside a living body and which require repair if the bodily society is not to lose the structure it needs to support the living occasions. Therefore, a living organism continually requires food: inorganic societies "robbed" from the ambient environment to repair the inorganic damage life causes, returning the disturbed region to chemical stability. This larcenous character of living organisms orders them in systematic social relations of food-chains and eco-systems, making nature herself social in the ordinary meaning of the term.[13]

In living organisms of sufficient complexity, strands of personal order may appear among the living members, arranging them into "living persons" with personal histories. It would seem at first glance that such an ordering would vitiate the originativeness of occasions within such threads, and a thread itself would resemble a particle. If what were inherited in the strand were a defining characteristic of the inorganic type, i.e., a determinate mode of response, this would certainly be the case. However, the defining characteristic of a living occasion is not the structure unifying the content of its satisfaction but the structure of that structure: a life style or personality. In the same sense as an artist's style unifies his life's work without inhibiting his genius, the defining characteristic of a living person canalizes the novelty achieved in the many occasions of its existence—making it more intense because of the continuity attained with past novelty. Through the origination within it of a personality with historical continuity, a living organism is further protected from the possibly rampant and destructive originality of the included living occasions. The living occasions themselves achieve greater intensity in their satisfactions. Thus creativity is mated with historic continuity, originality with inheritance, in overcoming the essentially anarchic character of life.

With these various notions, the model of a high-grade organism emerges as a complex of subordinated, inorganic societies and subsocieties protecting and protected by a regnant personality.[14] "Thus in an animal body

---

[12] "Empty" means containing no permanent structures, not sheer nothingness.

[13] Nature is social in Whitehead's technical sense, in that the basal society is the society of electromagnetic occasions which characterizes this cosmic epoch. An organism is not *in* this macro-society as in a container; it is a regional budding of this society in more complex forms.

[14] In the case of lower life forms, the personal strands are more loosely structured in a "democracy."

the presiding occasion, if there be one, is the final node, or intersection, of a complex structure of many enduring objects" (PR 166–67). If the organism is envisioned as a nest of concentric circles, the presiding occasion is the center point, receiving as its data the patterned and repatterned data superjected by the various levels of the bodily society. "The harmonized relations of the parts of the body constitute this wealth of inheritance into a harmony of contrasts, issuing into intensity of experience. The inhibitions of opposites have been adjusted into contrasts of opposites" (PR 167). In the case of man, the human mind at any occasion of its existence is "conscious of its bodily inheritance. There is also an enduring object formed by the inheritance from presiding occasion to presiding occasion. . . . This route of presiding occasions probably wanders from part to part of the brain, dissociated from the physical material atoms" (PR 167),[15] arising in the region receiving the most input from the bodily system. When cortical activity is at a lower ebb, its dominance may fade for a time and be replaced by more democratic relations among living strands.

IV · THE MODAL THEORY OF PERCEPTION

When conscious perception is discussed, it must be borne in mind that for Whitehead consciousness is a subjective form qualifying the experience of the living occasion or thread of occasions regnant in a highly complex society which provides the data for the percipient occasion's feelings. Perception is not therefore an exception to the doctrine of actual entities and of society already laid down; rather it represents a further refinement in feeling possible to a concrescence because of the real potentiality of its data: a mode of experience which is a further synthesis of the data out of which the percipient occasion arises. The immediate environment for the percipient occasion is the animal body, with its manifold of interrelated and hierarchically structured subsocieties, which likewise harbor living occasions. The data from these societies (or from some of them) as further correlated by the society of neurons in the brain form the actual world from which the percipient occasion arises, the actual world whose final synthesis the percipient is, and to which it partially conforms in its self-creative process. Therefore the classic image of perception as the soul's immediate and concrete grasp of the outside world via the senses must be carefully qualified if it is not to distort the model Whitehead creates. The outside world is indeed an element in the actual world of the percipient occasion, but its data have been structured and restructured by the occasions in the bodily society, particularly in the sensory

[15] This "consciousness of bodily inheritance" is critical to Whitehead's epistemology. What the "soul" primarily knows is the antecedent physical states of the body, which themselves are modal appropriations of the ambient environment.

organs and central nervous system, so that in no way can it be said that perception is a concrete grasp of an external object. It is abstract: in a temporal sense, many operations removed from the physical appropriation of environmental causality by the basal societies in the animal body; in the genetic sense, many phases removed from the physical experience of the percipient occasion in the brain. The simplistic view of perception which takes it to be the direct experience of the qualitative aspects of environmental objects is the metaphysical naïveté which rightly provoked the Humean and Kantian critiques—a prime example of the Fallacy of Misplaced Concreteness.

In PR, Whitehead gives two accounts of perception: (a) the more general analysis of the three modes it takes (presented in PR II, Chapters IV–IX, and again in S); and (b) a situation of perception in the genetic and coordinate analyses of a concrescence presented in PR III and IV. The two accounts are not contradictory, though their mutual consistency is not explicitly demonstrated in PR. It may be the case that Whitehead realized that detailing the specifics of the various modes in the genetic and coordinate accounts would make the complexity of those accounts so massive as to be impenetrable, and left the task to the reader.

The ontological basis of perception is the interpretation of an actual entity as a drop of experience, which interpretation has been detailed in previous chapters. Since experience is the self-realizing process of any actual entity, conscious experience is merely a further refinement of the more fundamental modes of experience (physical and conceptual functioning) and not a radically new activity introduced by a percipient. It is a more sophisticated form of "the 'self-enjoyment of being one among many, and of being one arising out of the composition of many' " (PR 220). To keep a discussion of conscious perception from falling into Misplaced Concreteness, it is necessary therefore to insert it into the wider framework of the becoming of experience, so that its genetic relatedness and continuity with basal physical and conceptual experience can be maintained.

Whitehead sees an actual entity as moving from the givenness of its data, which provide its objective content and real potentiality as decided by occasions in the past, to the superjection of its own decision to the future, via a non-temporal concrescence of phases culminating in the satisfaction or closing up of the entity.[16] In this process, the data, under

---

[16] See the schema of these phases given in Figure 3. Unfortunately, any spatial representation of a concrescence must perforce give the impression that the phases succeed one another in linear order from initial data to terminal satisfaction. Therefore, the reader must bear in mind that no phase is ever completed and passed beyond. Each reaches completeness *only* in the satisfaction, the fully determinate drop of space–time which closes up an entity's process of self-actualization. "There is a becoming of continuity, but no continuity of becoming" (PR 53).

limitations determined by their own decisions, are met with "the rush of feelings whereby secondhandedness attains subjective immediacy" (PR 235). The indeterminations in the data—how the many are to be felt as one, how they are to be objectified and subjectively felt—are solved in the concrescence.

> Every individual objectification in the datum has its perspective defined by its own eternal objects with their own relevance compatible with the relevance of other objectifications. Each such objectification, and each such complex of objectifications, in the datum is met with a correspondent feeling, with its determinate subjective form, until the many become one experience, the satisfaction [PR 234].

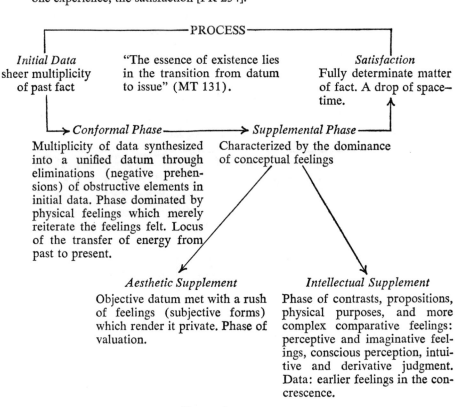

FIGURE 3

Eternal objects have a twofold functioning with respect to this subjective appropriation of objectivity: (a) they structure the objectifications of the data; and (b) they qualify the subjective feelings of those data, ingressing as their personalizing subjective form. In the initial phase of a concrescence—the phase of objective conformation—the eternal object qualifying the subjective form reproduces the eternal object in the objective datum: thus a concrescence originates as a feeling of the feeling of another, as a subjective re-enactment or reiteration of what is objectively given for it. In the supplemental phase, so called because additional eternal objects ingress to "supplement" those given in the data, the diversity in the data is overcome through the mediacy of sympathetic subjective forms, eternal objects conceptually felt as compatible with each other and hence promoting the realization of subjective unity. In the initial phase of the supplement, called aesthetic because it has to do with the personalizing harmonization of the given, these subjective forms are predominantly emotional and purposive in character, determining the relative importance of items in the data with respect to the guiding ideal of the concrescence—its subjective aim. In the intellectual supplement, the emphasis shifts to further integrations of already grasped material—in contrasts, rhythms, comparisons, and the like through which feelings previously arising in the concrescence are adjusted and wedded into more complex unities. It is in this stage that consciousness arises as the subjective form of certain feelings. As the subjective form of a supplementary feeling, what it illumines are the feelings in the stage in which it arises, and not primarily the physical experience from which the concrescence originates. If the latter is rendered conscious at all, it is illumined vaguely and derivatively, in proportion to the relevance it still retains to the concrescence. Despite its remotion from the basal, physical experience of the percipient, conscious perception is nevertheless an outgrowth of it, and hence is rooted in "stubborn fact" as "the cumulation of the universe and not a stage-play about it" (PR 363).

a. *Perception in the Mode of Causal Efficacy*
The most primitive form of awareness for Whitehead is not the vivid display of the ambient environment normally termed sense perception, but the vague feeling of causal presences which he terms "perception in the mode of causal efficacy," or "sense reception." In an organism which achieves a significant consciousness of its present environment (sense perception in its ordinary meaning—to be discussed later), the causal perception is rendered conscious as well, as the vague awareness of causative agencies underlying and provoking the vivid display. For organisms without such consciousness, causal efficacy remains unconscious—as the basic receptivity of the percipient occasion manifest in its conformal and aesthetic phases.

In the ideally simple case of one concrescent actual entity feeling one objectified actual entity, the datively functioning eternal object whereby the past actual entity is objectified ingresses into the relationship as its subjective form, making the concrescent feeling conform to the feeling felt. A transition of feeling from entity to entity, from past to present, comes about as a result of the two-way functioning of this sort of eternal object, called by Whitehead a sensum. It is important to note that the term is used here in a sense more primitive than that normally employed in epistemology. It refers to an emotional feeling-tone which is inherited by the concrescent subject from the object, not the vivid colors, sounds, etc., displayed in ordinary conscious perception. A sensum is simply the primordial form of the subject–object relationship, a simple eternal object of zero width, not involving any lower-grade eternal objects to make possible its ingression. It is the form of the efficiency of the object, superjected by the object and grasped into itself by the subject, the "kind" of energy decided for and felt by the concrescent occasion.

The conformal phase of any actual entity is a reception and coordination of sensa through the mutual sensitivity of their forms,[17] so that the multiple re-enactive feelings can become the unified experience of one subject and hence relevant to future concrescences. These feelings are blind, vague, and heavily emotional, concerned with "a beyond which is determinate and pointing to a beyond which is to be determined" (PR 247). Hence there can be a transmission of feeling from past to present to future through the mediation of sensa which allow past efficiency to enter the constitution of present subjective immediacy. In the event that a manifold of causal influences is objectified (and hence appropriated) by the same sensum, the multiplicity is only vaguely felt, the eternal object being transmuted as derivative from a more generalized, regional source. In accordance with the Category of Transmutation,[18] such a feeling has a vector character and a quantitative intensity proportionate to the number of reinforcing point sources of energy in the region. These regional feelings attain importance in higher modes of perception, for the present counterparts of those regions are what are vividly illustrated via the geometry and sense qualia of sight, hearing, etc.

When this oversimplified account of causal perception is amplified as a description of the receptive phase in human experience, it must be borne in mind that the experience described is that of the final percipient: the living occasion in the brain assuming temporary dominance because of the richness and complexity of its data. Its proximate actual world is the neuronic society in the brain, which itself receives data from the nervous

---

[17] This sensitivity has its ground in the gradation of eternal objects in degrees of relevance to any possible perspective accomplished in the primordial nature of God.

[18] By the Category of Transmutation, "When . . . one and the same conceptual feeling is derived impartially by a prehending subject from its analogous, simple, physical feelings of various actual entities in its actual world, then, in a subsequent phase of integration of these simple physical feelings together with the derivate conceptual feeling, the prehending subject may transmute the *datum* of this conceptual feeling into a characteristic of some *nexus* containing those prehended actual entities among its members, or of some part of that nexus" (PR 40).

system, other bodily systems and organs, and ultimately from the external environment. We are dealing therefore with historic chains of objectifications stretching from the external environment to the final percipient or regnant monad—chains of transmission of feelings, routes of sensa. Depending on the subjective aim of the regnant occasion and also upon conditions in the environing societies, certain parts of this route—certain links in the chain—are enhanced, and others reduced to trivial relevance. The important links—the external region and the end organ—enter the experience of the final percipient as significantly objectified. The " 'eye as experiencing such and such sights' " (PR 180) is the intensely felt objectification in visual perception; the route to and within the brain and the route through the external environment is de-emphasized. Therefore, "the predominant basis of perception is perception of the various bodily organs, as passing on their experiences by channels of transmission and of enhancement" (PR 181). The "human body is to be conceived as a complex 'amplifier' . . ." (PR 182) of signals from within and without. What is being enhanced and amplified in the bodily route is vector feeling-tone—i.e., sensa, the causal objectifications of past occasions in the external and internal routes.

The enhancement consists in the supplementation of the data by means of the intensification of the transmitted sensa accomplished through transmuted feelings and through the explosion of novel, reverted sensa resulting from the operations of living occasions in the route. Thus, the route through the animal body exemplifies *both* the transmission of vector feeling-tone from the environment *and* its own additions to the inherited data, e.g., the "datum transmitted from the stone becomes the touch-feeling in the hand, but it preserves the vector-character of its origin from the stone" (PR 183). The living occasions in the hand experience the multiplicity of causal influences from the corpuscular stone-society, conform to them, transmute that experience to an experience of the stone-nexus-as-one, to which is attributed the stone-causality. They then revert the stone-feeling to a touch-feeling with which they objectify themselves to subsequent members of the bodily route. These occasions further enhance the relevance of the reverted touch-feelings. The final percipient in the brain inherits these enhanced sensa, transmutes them as objectifications of the hand-nexus-as-one, vividly experiences the hand as experiencing the touch-sensum while derivatively and vaguely experiencing the stone as environmental source of the reverted sensum to which it is genetically related. The novelty which enters via this reversion is the sensum "touch feeling," an eternal object relevant to but not identical with the original sensum transmitted from the stone region. There is, thus, both repetition and origination going on in the route from the stone to the percipient occasion: (*a*) the conformation of each occasion in the bodily route to its immediate bodily past and to the more remote past of the ambient environment; and (b) the origination of transmuted and reverted feelings in the living occasions of the route, whereby the inherited sensa are enhanced and translated into terms relevant to the organism. Perception in the mode of causal efficacy emerges as "perception of the settled world in the past as constituted by its feeling-tones, and as efficacious by reason of those feeling-tones" (PR 184). It is present functioning as limited and conditioned by the environmental past, yielding the sensitivity to environmental influences noticeable in low-grade organisms.[19]

On the human level, where causal efficacy is derivatively illumined by the light of ordinary sense perception, it constitutes the vague fringe surrounding the vivid perceptual display. It is experienced as an emotionally charged feeling of the presence and pressure of the bodily and external environments: "the terrifying sense of vague presences, effective for good or evil over our fate" (S 43); "insistent, ... haunting, ... unmanageable," ... "heavy with the contact of the things gone by, which lay their grip on our immediate selves" (S 43–44).

> In the dark there are vague presences, doubtfully feared; in the silence, the irresistible causal efficacy of nature presses itself upon us; in the vagueness of the low hum of insects in an August woodland, the inflow into ourselves of feelings from enveloping nature overwhelms us; in the dim consciousness of half-sleep, the presentations of sense fade away, and we are left with the vague feelings of influences from vague things around us [PR 267].

It is the same sense of looming, overpowering presences which terrified Wordsworth in his youthful night voyage on the lake (see *The Prelude*, I.355–400). The feeling presents no sharply defined geometric arrangement of the causal presences felt, no discrimination into clear-cut objects with determinate spatial positions; it gives merely a sense of the vague yet controlling "aroundness" of the environment with vague, vector regions from which stream important influences. The causal feeling of the bodily environment is less vague, discriminating itself into clearer feelings of efficacious bodily organs with their general spatial location and relationships. It is this sense of the "withness" of the body, of the fact that we touch *with* the hand, see *with* the eye (these organs having been significantly objectified in the route), which will ultimately ground the objectivity of sense perception. We perceive because we receive, and know that we receive because we are vaguely aware of receivers and of the reception.

Despite the vagueness of perception in the mode of causal efficacy, it

---

[19] For example, heliotropism in plants and reflex behavior in lower animals represent an "awareness" (not in the fully conscious sense of the term) of the relevant causal influences in the organism's past.

is the perception of what is the dominant focus of our interest, of the important factors in the environment which spell survival or destruction to the organism. Without these vague, peripheral yet inescapable feelings, sense perception could have no more objectivity than that of a dream or of the flickering images on a television screen:

> these controlling presences, these sources of power, these things with an inner life, with their own richness of content, these beings, with the destiny of the world hidden in their natures, are what we want to know about. As we cross a road busy with traffic, we see the colour of the cars, their shapes, the gay colours of their occupants; but at the moment we are absorbed in using this immediate show as a symbol for the forces determining the immediate future [S 57].

The show, taken in itself, leads nowhere, leaving us locked in an isolated present; the vague feeling of past agencies leads us from the causal past into a future-directed present, in which adaptive responses can be forged to modify that future creatively. Causal efficacy permits a present enjoyment of past agency, whereby that agency can become effective in the future. It is "our general sense of existence, as one item among others, in an efficacious actual world" (PR 271).

b. *Perception in the Mode of Presentational Immediacy*
The second mode of perception—the mode of presentational immediacy —is difficult to isolate in its pure state, for, with the exception of certain instances of illusion or hallucination, it never exists in its purity but always as integrated with the causal mode. By the same token, pure causal efficacy is difficult to isolate in human experience because of the importance presentational immediacy has assumed for man. The mixed state —symbolic reference—is the ordinary component of human consciousness. But since, in ordinary sense awareness, the "show" is vivid (the gray shape), and the causal influx vague and ill-defined (the felt influence of the stubborn, factual stone-nexus), philosophers tend to overlook causal efficacy and to identify sensory awareness with presentational immediacy, thereby opening the door to the host of epistemological problems which beset philosophy from Descartes to Kant.

When this form of Misplaced Concreteness prevails, it is quite logical to equate perception with the subjective entertainment of universals whose origins are unknown. As a result of the mis-equation of presentational immediacy with conscious experience and of the more fundamental mis-identification of experience with conscious experience, the experient becomes permanently locked in the movie theater of the mind, endlessly watching a parade of images essentially unconnected either with each other or with an external, active world. *Esse est percipi* and nothing more. Locke's vague notion of "power" was an attempt to bridge the gap between conscious experience and reality, but it fell victim to Hume's assault. In asserting that sensory awareness is a budding of a more primordial physical experience shared by all actual entities, Whitehead overcomes the phenomenon–noumenon bifurcation and objectively grounds human awareness, recognizing that although it may be the most primitive form of judgment,[20] it is nevertheless an abstract modality of experience. In the subsequent discussions of presentational immediacy, it must be continually borne in mind, therefore, that Whitehead is deliberately isolating this mode of perception from its existential context as an outgrowth of causal efficacy, but that this isolation is methodological and not ontological.

When presentational immediacy is examined, the first characteristic which becomes apparent is that a different mode of objectification is at work here. Causal efficacy concerns itself with causal objectifications of the antecedent world, with past facts considered as operative in the present and as leading to a future. Presentational immediacy, on the other hand, is singularly indifferent to past and future alike. It concerns itself with the present world—the world contemporaneous with the percipient. However, as advances in relativity physics have shown, "the present" is a term with as many meanings as there are "presencing" occasions. The only possible universal meaning of contemporaneity is causal independence. For Whitehead, occasions are contemporaries when they *do not* enter into each other's constitutions, when they *do not* physically prehend each other. Thus, every occasion enjoys its drop of experience alone. This is not to say, however, that "nothing is going on" in the world contemporaneous with a concrescent occasion. This world is a multiplicity of self-actualizing activities, each involved in creating its own drop of private enjoyment. The past is populated with factual occasions of experience; the present, with potential, "about-to-be" occasions. Therefore, the past is incurably particulate; the present, only potentially divisible: a continuum of possible perspectives yet to be specified. Both are extensive, but in different ways. The past is a network of concrete, interlocked, spatio-temporal facts—the extensive continuum as atomized by mutually implicated, satisfied occasions. The present, as not yet atomized, is the extensive continuum considered as the abstract schema of possible extensive relations which could be atomized. In other words, the present is the pure unbroken continuity–possibility of spatio-temporal extensity. When a concrescence objectifies its present, it does so as a locus of *possible* relations, as a continuum of interlocked, *possible* perspectives—as a continuous, spatio-temporal region.

Whereas in causal objectification the eternal objects involved are the

---

[20] Inasmuch as symbolic reference, the taking of one modality of perception as symbol of the other, is a proto-judgment.

sensa (the vector feeling-tones of past agencies), in presentational ob-jectification the eternal objects are those pertinent to spatio-temporal, extensive relations. An occasion for which the present is significant—that is, an occasion which achieves *novel* immediacy in its satisfaction, which appropriates its past *for itself* in a personal "now" which is important to it rather than merely passing along that past to the future—spatio-temporalizes its world, displaying its present as a continuum of spatial and temporal relations, thus lifting the past into its present. For vaguely social occasions, such as those constituting a physical field in empty space, subjective immediacy and intensity do not have any relevant import; hence "no intelligible definition of rest and motion is possible for historic routes including them, because they correspond to no inherent spatializa-tion of the actual world" (PR 269). They are victims of the geometry of whatever societies with significant presented duration happen to wander through them. Thus, the sun can alter the structure of its environing space, as evidenced in the bending of light waves which pass close to it. Geom-etries are relative to the mode of spatialization important to varying so-cieties. Hence, no one geometry can be absolutized. The extensive continuum is not geometric in the strict sense of the term, but merely the schema of possible extensive relations of the most general sort, those of "extensive connection," "overlapping," etc., described in Part IV of PR.

What is felt via the spatio-temporal eternal objects accomplishing pres-entational objectifications is the past *as present to* the concrescent occa-sion, *as enjoyed in* the present of its drop of experience. Presentational objectification is therefore found only in those occasions whose environ-ment and subjective aim promote the subjective enjoyment of experience, occasions for which the "now" is important.

In perception in the mode of presentational immediacy, something more than mere presentational objectification is taking place. It is not simply the case that the conscious occasion is displaying the past in its present; it is further interpreting that display as a display of the con-temporaneous world: of "a contemporary spatial region, in respect to its spatial shape and its spatial perspective from the percipient" (PR 185). But pure extensity cannot be displayed in itself. A circle is given in the equation $x^2+y^2=r^2$, but the equation does not *display* circularity unless it is plotted on a set of coordinates in ink of a determinate color. The visual sensum allows the circular shape to be seen. Extensity must be "decorated" with sense data before it can enter into conscious perceptual experience. The so-called secondary qualities illustrate (make visible, audible, etc.) the extensity of the contemporaneous world, allowing the stone, for instance, to enter into experience as a gray shape contempora-neous with the perceiver.

An adequate theory of presentational immediacy must therefore give an account of the two sets of eternal objects through which the objectification of the contemporaneous world takes place. One set—the spatiotemporal eternal objects—is contributed by the region perceived from the standpoint of the perceiver; the other set—the perceptual qualities —is contributed by the historic route through the animal body, as it enters into the composition of the percipient occasion. Both sets are universal, abstract eternal objects functioning as relational between perceiver and perceived. Both lack the insistent particularity and causal relevance of the past region which they represent. In one sense, therefore, perception is the entertainment of universals, but they do not float into consciousness from nowhere. The extensive set have their origin in what Whitehead calls "strain feelings"—complex physical feelings of the geometric relations latent in the datum[21] and given for the concrescence. The qualitative set is given by the past functionings of the animal body and is "an adventitious show, a show of our own bodily production" (S 44), conceptual reversions resultant from the physiological imbalance caused by the strain feelings. Thus the bodily produced percepta exhibit the contemporary environment as an extensive set of important regions systematically related to each other and to the percipient[22] and shading off into extensive backgrounds of less and less importance.

As opposed to the indistinctness of causal efficacy, the display produced in presentational immediacy is a vivid and geometrically precise rendering of the manageable elements in experience, a show which is totally barren as far as meaningfulness to the perceiver is concerned. It reveals nothing about the "thing" perceived, not its past or its importance to the perceiver and for the relevant future, or its causal relations to other "things" and to the percipient. Hume was quite correct: pure impressions merely come and go, succeeding each other without any genuine internal connection. Presentational immediacy is a total absorption in the "now." "The present moment is then all in all" (S 42): a total, self-contained solipsism. The value of presentational immediacy lies in the fact that its vivid display of the contemporaneous world in no way violates the mutual independence of contemporary occasions. It reveals the present solely in its potentialities: as a systematic locus and a presented duration undergirding the extensive togetherness of possible occasions arising within it.[23] It is perceived in quasi-independence of those actualities growing within it—as a mirror image illustrates the space "behind" the mirror. But the presented

---

[21] These are discussed at length in Chapter 5.

[22] "Focal regions" and "seats," in the language of Part IV of PR.

[23] To make this discussion a bit more concrete: what Whitehead is saying is that the white rectangular area one sees when looking at this page—an area which is an unbroken continuum as far as the visual image is concerned—is a region within which entities are concrescing and which they will atomize into discrete facts when they have reached satisfaction. It is where actual entities will be, not where they are.

locus is not in complete independence of actuality. It bears a perfectly definite, systematic, geometric relatedness to the body of the percipient, which relatedness is definable in terms of straight lines.[24] This fact necessitates, however, that the traditional understanding of straight lines in terms of events[25] be replaced by more fundamental and purely formal definitions.[26] The presented locus likewise bears a relation to past societies in the region, a relation which can be explicated only in the context of the integration of presentational immediacy and causal efficacy which Whitehead calls "symbolic reference": the ordinary form of human sensory awareness.

c. Perception in the Mode of Symbolic Reference

For Whitehead, the "human mind is functioning symbolically when some components of its experience elicit consciousness, beliefs, emotions, and usages, respecting other components of its experience. The former set of components are the 'symbols,' and the latter set constitute the 'meaning' of the symbols" (S 7–8). The ability to make the transference from symbol to meaning is not necessarily a high-grade activity proper to man alone. Blind transference—symbolically conditioned action—characterizes all vertebrates, certainly the more complex invertebrates, and perhaps all life forms as well. The tendency to take the present as a symbol of a past agency which can lead to the future weal or woe of the organism appears to be one of the indicators of the presence of life. To be more precise, the specifically human capacity seems to be the ability to *inhibit* the transference: to remain on the level of the symbol (e.g., the artist, the geometer, the algebraist, the lexicographer, etc.). Very young children (and primitives as well) appear to have difficulty with pure symbols. They want them to stand for *some thing*, not an irrelevant unknown.

The symbol-to-meaning transfer is not to be interpreted as an activity performed by an already constituted entity. It is an element in the constitution of the percipient occasion, a synthesis of earlier prehensions in its self-creative process. By means of the synthesis, the percipient defines its actual world, vividly delineating features in its immediate past which have import for its future. The colored shapes, the sounding, odor-full spaces represent other, more primitive elements in its experience, toward which its future behavior must be adapted. The symbols do not, therefore, create the physical bodies in the external environment which they represent; they *dis*cover them as already having been causally felt in earlier

---

[24] The lines utilized in the construction of a perspective in art are instances of this relatedness.

[25] E.g., the shortest distance between two points; the path of an unimpeded moving body.

[26] This is part of the purpose of Part IV of PR.

phases of its self-production. By means of the transfer, the colored shapes, etc. which are projected in the continuum of extensity of the present are taken to be indications of genuine causal presences in the regions into which the sensa are projected. Past agency is extrapolated as emerging agency in the present.

This transfer is a learned response: "nature taught [its] use" (S 57) through the pragmatic interactions of enduring, living organisms and their environment. Furthermore, which environmental influences are presentationally objectified is likewise pragmatically determined.[27]

Since symbolic reference is a learned response, it is fallible. In fact it is only with respect to symbolic reference that truth talk has any relevance. The other perceptual modes are infallible: causal efficacy, because it *is* the constitution of a percipient arising from the causal influx of its past; presentational immediacy, in that the display simply is what it is—a gray shape, a sour taste, a flowery odor. Truth and error come about in the synthetic activity referring the shape, the taste, the smell to an environmental agency. Human perception, therefore, is a complex inference, a "judgment," which can go wrong for lack of experience or as a result of pathological conditions within the organism. Symbolic reference "may induce actions, feelings, emotions, and beliefs about things which are mere notions" (S 6), i.e., which are not exemplified in the actual world of the concrescence.

To identify symbolic reference as the seat of error is neither to downgrade the activity nor to make error seem a cardinal sin to be avoided at all cost. One function of reason—a subsequent refinement introduced by high-grade occasions—is to pass judgment on the blind transferences which take place earlier in the concrescence, thereby purging them of possibly erroneous meanings.

The "evolutionary use of intelligence is that it enables the individual to profit by error without being slaughtered by it" (PR 256). Error is not therefore to be construed as a totally destructive agency. Rather it promotes imaginative freedom, a liberation from the given which enables mind to soar into realms not exemplified in the concrete. As Whitehead succinctly puts it, "in the real world it is more important that a proposition be interesting [i.e., opening up novel vistas] than that it be true [conforming to the given actual world]" (PR 395–96). The half-submerged stick which appears bent, the apparent lowering of the pitch of a sound emitted by a moving object, the reflection which deceived Narcissus—all are erroneous transferences which opened up new areas of truth. The entire human mythopoetic faculty, in its creation of art, religion, literature,

---

[27] See Bergson's theory, as expressed in *Matter and Memory* and *Creative Evolution*, that perception consists in the tracing in advance of an organism's potential action in and on the environment.

music, etc., reveals in its "errors" a world of possibilities not exemplified in actual fact, and frees man from slavery to the concrete. But even prior to the activities of both critical reason and deliberate myth-making, symbolic reference is purged of its more blatant mistakes through interplay with the environment, in the dialectic between symbol use and its pragmatic consequences.

If, however, there is to be any validity whatever to symbolic transfers, there must be some ontological ground to symbolic reference, some objective communality between meaning and symbol which provokes the synthesis, which makes the diverse elements apt for synthesis. This communality cannot be of the sort which would intrinsically specify which components can be symbols and which can be meanings without at the same time bifurcating reality into experienced things *vs.* things unexperienced, thought things *vs.* things as unthought: the dilemma bequeathed by the history of philosophy from Descartes to Hume, which compelled Kant to divorce phenomena from noumena irrevocably. For Whitehead there can be neither pure symbols nor pure meanings; which component of experience (causal efficacy or presentational immediacy) assumes each role is decided in the concrescence: "symbolic reference holds between two components in a complex experience, *each intrinsically capable of direct recognition*" (S 10; emphasis added). Nor can the communality making transference possible guarantee that it will be free from error. As in any judgment—any synthetic activity conjoining elements given as separate or separable—the percipient assumes "moral responsibility" for the truth of perceptual inferences, maintaining a watchfulness for physiological or environmental abnormalities which might so distort appearances that their reference to reality is unjustified.

That which is common to both perceptual modes is a twofold set of structures directly recognizable as identical in both: a set of eternal objects with a two-way functioning. The first of these is the set of sensa given for presentational immediacy as derived from the actual world of the conscious percipient: from the functioning of the sense organs in the immediate past, not directly from the perceived object. By means of these eternal objects, the organ region is objectified (via a transmuted feeling) as the contributor of the sense data.[28] The "sense-data functioning in an act of experience demonstrate that they are given *by* the causal efficacy of actual bodily organs" (S 51). The implications of this statement need careful clarification. Our language is too steeped in Aristotelian categories for Whitehead's notion of a sensum to be grasped readily. Quality words are adjectives—states of either objects or subjects[29]—which accidentally modify objects or subjects. In an Indo-European language, "blue" in-

---

[28] Even a dog experiences the fact that he smells odors *with* his nose.
[29] Depending on whether one is a sensationalist or a subjectivist. See PR 239.

variably ends up qualifying a noun (the "name of a person, place, or thing"); in Whitehead's conception, it is the subjective form of a relational activity: a vector feeling-tone not a bare passive quality, an adverb not an adjective. "Blue" cannot be abstracted from the eye's functioning in response to an environmental stimulus; it has *no* meaning apart from an eye. It is the eye's activity of grasping into itself the causality of a light wave objectified by an item in the wave's definiteness: its energy structure or frequency. The illustration is, of course, oversimplified. A more correct physiological account would include several intermediate objectifications between the eye and the percipient occasion. The frequency of the light wave is objectified by the rods and cones in the retina as a determinate bleaching of their included pigments. This bleaching itself is objectified as a burst of electrical energy of a certain frequency, which is transmitted via the central nervous system to the visual cortex in the brain, where further objectifications eventually lead up to the blue-experience. All these different yet related objectifications are accomplished by conceptual reversions in the route. The causality of the light wave, and, for that matter, the causality of the environmental object reflecting it, are thus transmitted through the route by means of the reverted sensa. Because of the reversions, the sensum-as-experienced—the structure the causality ultimately assumes—is contributed by the bodily occasions in the route; but, despite the reversions, the ultimate objectification to the percipient occasion retains the vector feeling-tone of its origination in the eye region: a feeling of the sensum as *impressed* on the eye.

In presentational immediacy, the sensa given by the bodily route and felt in the conformal and aesthetic phases of the percipient's concrescence are projected on a contemporaneous region, thus objectifying and illustrating its extensity via sense qualities. The conscious-awareness-of-a-blue-area—the sense impression—is the last link in this chain of objectifications. Hume is totally wrong. The causes of impressions *are* known.

> If Hume had stopped to investigate the alternative causes for the occurrence of visual sensations—for example, eye-sight, or excessive consumption of alcohol—he might have hesitated in his profession of ignorance. If the causes be indeed unknown, it is absurd to bother about eye-sight and intoxication. The reason for the existence of oculists and prohibitionists is that various causes *are* known [PR 259–60].

Be it genuine external stimulation, myopia or martinis, the functioning of the eye is the cause of the blue-seeing experience.

In presentational immediacy, diverse regions are illustrated and objectified: the object region and the eye region; but at the same time there is an identity of sensa involved. The sensa contributed by one region (the past functioning eye) are used to illustrate the contemporary object region. The eye region is causally objectified by the vector feeling-tone, "blue-seeing," which eternal object, stripped of its vector origin, and enhanced, is projected on the contemporary object region. The contemporary eye region is presentationally objectified as well, via a different yet related eternal object—the feeling-of-functioning: "eye strain" as a conscious phenomenon projected on the eye region to illustrate it more precisely. This double objectification of the eye as both past and present serves to identify further and to locate more precisely the cause of the given sensum.

Therefore, as a result of the same sensum felt as characterizing the past activity of the eye region in causal efficacy and hence projected into the contemporary object region in presentational immediacy, the symbolic reference can take place. The two prehensions can be synthesized into a unity of feeling, the feeling of a contemporary blue wall in the external environment. Yet the two-way functioning of the sensum is not sufficient fully to ground symbolic reference, for there remains a diversity of regions involved: (a) the past object region which was the vector origin of the causality received by the eye, and the eye as the vector origin of the transmitted sensa; and (b) the contemporary object and organ regions as presentationally objectified. If the illustration of (b) by sensa derived from (a) is to be legitimate, there must be some felt communality between the two sets of regions.

One fairly obvious intersect of past and present is the human body presentationally objectified as the geometric focus of both external and internal regions.

> . . . the animal body is the great central ground underlying all symbolic reference. In respect to bodily perceptions the two modes achieve the maximum of symbolic reference, and pool their feelings referent to identical regions. Every statement about the geometrical relationships of physical bodies in the world is ultimately referable to certain definite human bodies as origins of reference [PR 258–59].

> . . . the spatial and temporal relationships of the human body, as causally apprehended, to the external contemporary world, as immediately presented, afford a fairly definite scheme of spatial and temporal reference whereby we test the symbolic use of sense-projection for the determination of the position of bodies controlling the course of nature [S 56].[30]

---

[30] This point was underlined in a set of experiments in which subjects were fitted with lenses that inverted the visual image projected on the retina, making everything appear upside down. When allowed to move through their environment, using their kinesthetic and tactual senses, the topsy-turviness of the environment soon disappeared. The pragmatic check on the illusion by the other senses caused it to disappear, despite the fact that the physical cause remained (Irvin Rock and Charles S. Harris, "Vision and Touch," *Scientific American*, 216, No. 5 [May 1967], 96–104).

The centrality of the human body in the perceptual field is not sufficient, however, to ground metaphysically the projection of data from a
past "place" onto a present "place," for the two "places" are ontological-
ly different in character. The vector origin of the sensa—proximally the
bodily region and ultimately the environmental region—is the incurably
atomic, factual plenum of discrete, satisfied occasions of the immediate
or more remote past. It is the extensive continuum as *ruptured* by actualization. The contemporary place is the extensive continuum as unrup-
tured, as divisible yet undivided—pure extensity considered as the locus
of possible relations of future occasions. It is a "duration" in the spatio-
temporal sense of the term detailed in SMW, the extended present in its
potentiality for subdivision. If symbolic reference is to be legitimate, this
presented locus must also be felt in the earlier causal feelings. It cannot
be directly felt, for this would violate the causal independence of contemporary occasions. However, it is felt indirectly and objectified vaguely
in causal feelings of the antecedent world. Although each occasion contemporaneous with the percipient occasion is "alone" in its enjoyment of
its own unique actual world, those actual worlds are practically identical
as far as their important elements are concerned. Social occasions share
an *almost* common world, with an *almost* common real potentiality.
Therefore, in the percipient's causal feelings of its own actual world, of
its own real potentiality, it is simultaneously grasping the important aspects of the real potentiality given for its contemporaries. In grasping the
causal influx to which it is subject, it grasps at the same time the important causal past of its neighbors concrescing in the present. It is therefore
physically feeling the presented locus indirectly, by extrapolation. This
feeling is vaguely defined in causal efficacy as (*a*) feeling of the "aroundness" of the environment—an "aroundness" incapable of more precise
elucidation—and of the vague "thereness" of contemporary occasions;
and (*b*) the "withness" of the contemporaneous body, whose geometry
is felt with a bit more precision because of the greater shared importance
and degree of coordination of the data. Causal efficacy gives, therefore,
a vague sense of important contemporary regions with, however, no clear-
cut geometrical relations and structure.

When presentational feelings grow out of these indirect causal feelings
of the presented locus, it is then directly felt: that is, the presentational
feelings are feelings of the causal feelings as objectified by an aspect of
themselves—the vague feeling of the presented locus. The subjective
forms of these presentational feelings are the precisely and vividly displayed geometric eternal objects of presentational immediacy. These are
directly illustrated instead of vaguely felt, and constitute the display of
the contemporaneous world, a geometry decorated with sense data. "Thus
the presented locus, with the animal body of the percipient as the region

from which perspectives are focussed, is the regional origin by reference to which in this perceptive mode the complete scheme of extensive regions is rendered determinate" (PR 257).

The past world, directly objectified in causal efficacy, gains only indirect objectification in presentational feelings, an objectification grounded in its extensive relations to the presented locus. Pure presentational immediacy yields, therefore, a pure phenomenology of appearances with existence bracketed, "direct observation . . . purged of all interpretation" (PR 257). It illustrates the set of geometrical relations unexplicated in the indirect causal feelings of the presented locus—of the regions in the body, of regions to the body, of regions to other regions from the perspectival standpoint of the body, and of the systematic divisibility of all regions. The presented locus, as indirectly prehended in causal efficacy and directly grasped in presentational immediacy, undergirds symbolic reference and permits past sensa to be projected on a present world, as a vision of "what the nexus really *is* in the way of potentiality realized" (PR 411).

In the doctrine of symbolic reference, Whitehead gives his definitive critique of Hume and Kant, demonstrating their position to be an inversion of experience. He sees them as asserting that perception is the most concrete element in experience, and that causality is either an *a priori* form of the perceiver or an unwarranted inference from perceptual data. Both are therefore maintaining the primacy of presentational immediacy as the only source of information about the present world, a source which reveals no ties to past or future. It was quite logical for them to infer, therefore, that causality was either a category of pure reason or a mere invariable sequence among impressions, one "learned" through habit. If their doctrines are correct, however, to dim perception would be likewise to dim causal feelings; whereas precisely the reverse occurs.

Whitehead takes the position that causal feelings are primary, being the basic physical, conformal feelings out of which the percipient constitutes itself,[31] that such feelings characterize even the most primitive occasions, and that presentational feelings are derivative. Occasions can be separated into four categories on the basis of the importance of presentational feelings in their satisfactions: (*a*) those with minimal presentational feelings because the order in their environment is so trivial that their common world is virtually non-existent, thus rendering whatever vague feelings they have of the presented locus almost absolutely irrel-

---

[31] "The first phase is the phase of pure reception of the actual world in its guise of objective datum for aesthetic synthesis. In this phase there is the mere reception of the actual world as a multiplicity of private centres of feeling, implicated in a nexus of mutual presupposition. The feelings are felt as belonging to the external centers, and are not absorbed into the private immediacy" (PR 323).

evant (hence such occasions do not spatialize their present); (b) occasions for which presented durations are important but not clearly discriminated into regions (occasions in personal threads in inorganic societies, for example); (c) living occasions for which the present is vitally important and which hence enhance presentational feelings and perform symbolic references, thus making possible self-preservative activity; and (d) human percipients, who can transcend the necessity of presentational display of the *actual* past, imaginatively display what is unexemplified in the world, reorganize the given, adjust given values, and critically judge their own operations. Humans can likewise expand symbol use beyond the limits of perception, in language, art, science, mathematics, social custom, etc., enabling them not only to live and live well, but to live better (see FR 8).

V · PROLEGOMENON TO A THEORY OF JUDGMENT: PROPOSITIONS

The epistemological difficulties besetting modern philosophy were not restricted to those directly connected with misconceptions of the nature of perception. They pervaded analyses of the higher modes of human conscious activity as well: specifically the activity of judging, and its truth value. Whitehead's theory of propositions is an attempt on his part to circumvent such problems by grounding his epistemological theories in ontology. Just as sense perception is interpreted as a more complex integration of the primitive feelings initiating a concrescence and not as a feeling radically discontinuous with and ungrounded in earlier feelings, so the act of judging, as an element in the constitution of an act of experience, is seen as a further integration of earlier feelings—in this case, as a "comparison" of a "propositional feeling" and an initial physical feeling.[32] The former is itself a complex feeling having as its datum a "proposition"[33] given for it in the definiteness of the data. Since the data and the series of feelings by means of which they are integrated *are* the act of experience of the judging actual occasion, Whitehead need admit of no ontological bifurcation of nature into experience and things experienced. The former *is* the togetherness of the latter: "togetherness in experience" is the only type of togetherness in the philosophy of organism.

Since this is the case, the affirmation of the truth or falsity of a proposition (the act of critical judgment) is an affirmation of the togetherness or non-togetherness of elements in the constitution of the judger, which in

---

[32] The genesis of these complex, synthetic feelings will be laid out in Chapter 4.
[33] ". . . Matters of Fact in Potential Determination" (PR 32–33); ". . . a proposition is the unity of certain actual entities in their potentiality for forming a nexus, with its potential relatedness partially defined by certain eternal objects which have the unity of one complex eternal object" (PR 35–36).

turn is the togetherness or non-togetherness of the ideal and real worlds from the judger's perspective. An affirmative judgment is not, therefore, the conjugation of a logical subject and predicate given as disjoined; it is the affirmation of a more primordial togetherness in experience, which is togetherness in the actual world the felt synthesis of which is the experient occasion.

The togetherness affirmed or denied in a judgment is the togetherness of an eternal object (the predicate) and an actual entity or nexus of actual entities (the logical subject). This togetherness, as given in the actual world of a concrescence, is what Whitehead terms a proposition. Therefore, propositions not merely are data for logicians to exercise their wits on, but are hybrid *entities* which are elements in the definiteness of the universe out of which an occasion arises. Furthermore, it must be remembered that no artificial separation exists between a proposition and the feeling of a proposition. Such a separation is an abstraction with no concrete exemplification in the world. There are neither mere concrescent subjects with mere subjective activities, nor mere objects with mere objective propositional characters. To be a proposition is to be a proposition *for* a concrescent subject (actual or potential) and entertained (or entertainable) by that subject.

Prior to an analysis of the judging activity, it is therefore necessary to examine that peculiar modality of togetherness between actual entities and eternal objects which can be termed propositional. Not every conjunction of actual entities and eternal objects constitutes a proposition. Some are merely the lower grade of prehension which Whitehead calls "physical purposes." These are indeed grasps of the togetherness of a nexus and an eternal object, but the eternal object in question is grasped not in its transcendent character—i.e., as a possibility for *any* actuality —but merely as a possibility exemplified in *this* nexus, as "tied to the datum." For example, the appetitive grasp of the "warmth" of a particular fire, the "safety" of one's home, the "thirst-quenching wetness" of this glass of water are physical purposes. The eternal objects are grasped only *as exemplified* in the fire, the home, the glass of water, not as potentialities for exemplification in other actualities. Furthermore, the grasp is emotive–appetitive: a "desire" for the datum as exemplifying the eternal object. The "could-be *vs.* is," potentiality *vs.* actuality, contrast is missing. Hence, for reasons to be explored later, physical purposes are unconscious elements in the aesthetic supplement of an actual occasion, lacking the affirmation–negation contrast which Whitehead sees as central to consciousness and intellectual supplementation.[34]

In a proposition, it is the "could-be" of the eternal object which is important—the "*germaneness* of a certain set of eternal objects to a cer-

[34] See Chapter 4.

tain set of actual entities" (PR 286; emphasis added). The togetherness of the logical subject and predicate, the nexus and the eternal object, is *potential*; it is a togetherness *proposed* as *realizable* within the concrescent subject, not *given* as *already realized*. Whether the eternal object is actually realized in the nexus or not is an additional qualification differentiating true from false propositions, but not an essential characteristic of propositions as such. In either case it is the potential relevance of the eternal object to the nexus—their potential togetherness—which distinguishes a proposition from a physical purpose.

The object of a propositional feeling is this potential togetherness; hence a propositional feeling is a hybrid feeling—one which involves a synthesis of a prior transmuted feeling of the nexus-as-one and a prior conceptual feeling of the eternal object in terms of which the transmuted feeling was possible. To clarify this obscurity by a simplistic example: if the nexus is a society of actual entities each of which inherits and exhibits the defining characteristic "stone," the multiple physical feelings of the members of the society are transmuted into one feeling of the nexus as unified by the defining characteristic "stone." The original feelings are "simplified" in their transmutation into one feeling. The eternal object making the transmuted feeling possible is then felt in a pure conceptual feeling.[35] The synthesis of these two feelings in one hybrid feeling constitutes the propositional feeling "This nexus could be a stone." That the eternal object proposed as a predicate relevant to the nexus is exemplified in it as well is the additional qualification rendering the proposition true.

If the proposition is false—i.e., if the proposed predicate is not realized in the nexus physically felt—the unexemplified eternal object does not float into subjective experience from nowhere. Rather, the concrescent subject performs a conceptual reversion upon the eternal object felt as actually exemplified in the nexus, a reversion grasping another eternal object related to that structuring the nexus as a relevant and alternative way in which that nexus could be realized as an element in the constitution of the emerging subject. In the preceding example, the pure conceptual feeling of "stone"—the eternal object both exemplified in and possible for the nexus—could be reverted to "weapon," an eternal object relevant to "stone" but not exemplified in the stone society, and the reversion integrated with the nexus feeling as "This could be a weapon."[36] False propositions are thus the lure for novelty in the world. Without their possibility, the present could only endlessly re-echo the forms realized in the past.

[35] The origination of pure conceptual feelings out of physical feelings will be elaborated in the genetic analyses of Chapter 4.

[36] The reader is urged to take the examples solely as aids to understanding, not as explications of conscious, judgmental processes.

Just as a propositional feeling is a hybrid prehension, a proposition is a hybrid entity in the actual world for the propositional feeler. It is the togetherness of a nexus and the penumbra of possibility which surrounds its factuality. It quite literally takes the "S is P" form: the subject being the actual entities in the nexus; the predicate being the eternal object, the complex pattern, in terms of which the factual entities could be structured for the concrescent occasion. In Whitehead's words, a proposition is "particular facts in a potential pattern" (PR 295), the particularity resulting from the past satisfactions in the nexus, the potentiality from the relevance of eternal objects to the nexus from the perspective of the propositional feeler.

Propositions are not given to an occasion primarily for purposes of judgment; they are proposed as "lures for feeling": as possible values to be *entertained*, not to be judged as to past exemplification. They offer themselves for intrasubjective realization, for a private enjoyment which may be followed by critical evaluation but need not be. Propositions therefore initiate feelings which can transcend the givenness of the past and open the door to novel futures. In more complex feelings, when the "S could be P" of the proposition and the "S is objectified by P" of the basal physical feelings are felt together in the affirmation–negation contrast, consciousness arises as the subjective form of the synthetic feelings. It is to be noted that the contrast relates the actual and the potential exemplification of the eternal object in the nexus, a contrast absent from physical purposes, which concern only the eternal object *as embodied*.

In still more complex feelings, the "S could be P" is grasped as a genuine novelty because of its contrast with the non-exemplification of P in the nexus. With such feelings, arising from the entertainment of false propositions (the togetherness of a nexus and predicates possible for it but not exemplified in it), novelty enters the world: novel individuals, new facts, genuine creativity as opposed to merely more complex and hence "new" modes of feeling. The "interesting" proposition has infinitely more evolutionary worth than the merely true proposition.

This description of a proposition as the potentiality of a nexus makes more concrete the discussions of the primordial nature of God which have preceded, for the reason *why* certain patterns are relevant to a nexus whether or not that nexus factually exemplifies them lies in the protean ordering of eternal objects on which finite process depends. Without an order among eternal objects which is independent of the relevance imposed by joint exemplification, novel advance would be impossible, and process would be an endless re-enactment of the past—a symphony embodying one chord and its inversions. Given the togetherness of the divine ordering and the world of fact, a togetherness manifested in propositions, finite process is drawn forward on the road to novelty. The divine ordering, logically expressed, is the "if p, then q, r, s, t, . . ." which enables a reverted feeling to grasp t when only p is given.

The propositions in the world "grow" with the advance of the world. Some are already "in" the world, in the actual entities "whose actual worlds include the logical subjects" (PR 283): others are not realized as yet for any actual occasion or in any actual world. These latter are the unrealized potentials of the universe, "await[ing their] logical subjects" (PR 287), pure, abstract hypotheses as yet ungrasped and ungraspable.

If a proposition is to be felt as "particular facts in a potential pattern" (PR 295), these facts must be stripped of their own pattern—of the objectification by which they were physically felt at the inception of the concrescence—in order to be integrable in the potential predicative pattern. The subjects of a proposition, though fully definite actual occasions, do not bring their full determinateness into the predicative relation. In a proposition they function as bare relata, variables whose relations are those assigned to them by the predicate. As such, they can only be indicated in the proposition, and can have no character of their own. (Whitehead is ontologizing what is a common property of subjects of logical propositions: i.e., that in the context of the proposition, they have no intelligibility other than that assigned them by the predicate.) Indeed, the propositional subjects must be indicated if the scope of the proposition is to be made determinate. Hence, quantifiers in logic serve to restrict the locus of the predicate to *just these* members, be they particulars, kinds of particulars, or kinds of sets.

Whitehead sees two modes of "ontological" indicators: (*a*) a simple variety—position indicators such as "this," "here," "now," "that," "there," "then," etc., functioning in propositions like "this set of actual entities (the S's) could be a chair (P)"; and (*b*) more complex indicators such as the italicized in "*John* bought *the tickets* from *Jim* for *$10*," which point to the sets of actual entities involved in the "bought-from-for" relational pattern.[37]

The former are the ontological, spatio-temporal indicators which are verbally symbolized in demonstrative pronouns and their correlatively implied positional adjectives. Such indicators cannot function, however, unless they are enmeshed in an overarching indicative system; otherwise the absolute, isolated, barren abstractness of "here," "now," "there," "then" as described in Hegel's *Phenomenology* destroys any possibility of synthesizing the subjects via the predicate. This indicative system is an eternal object of the order of a general principle—a complex eternal object exemplified through instances of itself which are eternal objects

---

[37] In both examples, it is the ontological state of affairs which constitutes the proposition and its indicators, not the verbal expression.

themselves.[38] The instances necessarily embody the general principle, but the realization of the general merely necessitates *an* instantiation, not *which* instantiation. (In fact, the various instances of a general principle are mutually exclusive.) The indicative system unifying individual indicators is such that it concerns itself solely with direct unmediated and hence dyadic relations between pairs of propositional subjects[39] related by the eternal objects which are its instances. An example of the simplest variety of this type of indicative system is the directional system of compass coordinates, whose instances are the eternal objects "east of," "west of," "north of," "south of." Let us consider an actual entity, X, whose actual world is defined by the actual entities A, B, C, and D.

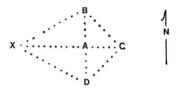

From the standpoint of A, the following dual relations hold: B is north of A, C is east of A, D is south of A. From these relations it follows that B is northwest of C and that D is southwest of C. From the standpoint of X, if X feels its relation to A (as west of A) and feels A's relations to B, C, and D (which in feeling A it must also feel, because A *is* its relations to B, C, and D), then X likewise feels its own relations to B, C, and D, and all the interrelations of B, C, and D. The system—the general principle of "compass relationship"—makes it possible to indicate the position of each member from the standpoint of any other. In other words, this is an *objective* indicative system, one not dependent on the idiosyncratic characters of the perspectives realizing it. The experient can be eliminated, while the system still stands. This type of system permits the precise "location" of the subjects of a proposition with respect to each other so that as thus indicated and mutually coordinated they can be enmeshed as variables in the predicative pattern.

Indicative systems not specifying dual relations are less precise in their indication of the propositional subjects. They are vague in the nexus itself, being rendered determinate by the perspective of the experient occasion. In Whitehead's example, the proposition "Caesar has crossed the Rubicon,"[40] what is indicated by "Caesar" and "Rubicon" depends on whether the experient is a legionnaire in Caesar's company or a twentieth-

[38] Thus, "triangle" is a general principle, having scalene, isosceles, equilateral, etc. as its instances.

[39] Note that, as Charles Sanders Peirce points out, all spatial and mechanical relations are dual, involving pairs of particles (*Collected Papers*, edd. Hartshorne and Weiss, 1.325, 1.457).

[40] Again, the state of affairs, not the verbal expression.

century historian, being a function of the direct perceptual experience of the experient. For the legionnaire, Caesar is an historic route of experienced Caesarian occasions culminating in the experienced Rubicon-crossing, and the Rubicon is the perceived river. For the historian who has never seen the Rubicon, both it and "Caesar" denote *types* of nexuses, not actual nexuses. The legionnaire affirms a particular proposition; the historian, a general one. It is obvious therefore that between the propositions asserted by the legionnaire and the historian there lies a continuum of other propositions all assuming the same verbal form but whose "objective content" as denoted by the "Caesar" and "Rubicon" indicators is quite diverse. Hence, though position indicators may supply an objective spatio-temporal reference system, beyond that, any proposition has indeterminations to be rendered determinate by the functioning of the prehending subject from its relativistic perspective. No verbal statement can completely exhaust the possibilities of a proposition because of this inherent indefiniteness. A proposition is "the *potentiality* of the objectification of certain presupposed actual entities via certain qualities and relations, the objectification being for some unspecified subject for which the presupposition has meaning in direct experience" (PR 299; emphasis added). The actual objectification solves the indeterminancy, because the specification of the feeler, and consequently of its actual world, determines what will be the real "meaning" of the proposition *for* this feeler. The indicators may point to the logical subjects of the proposition, but the perspective of the emergent feeler ultimately decides what they are for it. Thus, "Caesar has crossed the Rubicon," as the potentiality for objectifying Caesar and the Rubicon via the relation "has crossed," means (when taken in abstraction from a concrete feeling subject) "a Caesarian type of route has crossed a Rubiconian type of route," in which expression the Caesarian route is located in the Roman world of 49 B.C. and the Rubiconian route, in Italy. How the potentialities of "Caesarian" and "Rubiconian" are further specified is a function of the actual world of the experients entertaining the proposition: of the legionnaire or of the historian. Their past experience has determined the objectifications under which both routes have entered into their self-constitutive process. Therefore, as additional indicators, "Caesar" and "Rubicon" are vague and indeterminate.

A proposition thus has both the particularity of actuality in its indication of the actual logical subjects to be conjoined in the predicative pattern, and the generality of possibility in its general reference to indeterminate experients.

A proposition becomes metaphysical when its predicative pattern is capable of relating all possible actual entities as its logical subjects and is in the actual world of all experients. As such, any true proposition of the requisite generality is metaphysical; in addition, any fully general false proposition is metaphysical if and only if it is not only false in itself, but false in any possible specification of itself to particular circumstances.

VI • THE THEORY OF JUDGMENT

Although the illustrations in the previous discussions have been cast in the structure of the logical judgment, it must be borne in mind that "judgment" is one of the rarer ways in which a proposition is admitted into feeling. The same must be said of the conscious grasp of propositions. Both are more advanced integrations of propositional feelings and earlier feelings arising in a concrescence. The more common subjective forms whereby a proposition is realized in an experient is "entertainment": appropriation via emotional or purposive subjective forms. Thus propositions function in the actual world of any concrescence, given that the actual world, and hence the resultant occasion, have the minimum of order necessary to make originative, non-conformal response possible.

As already seen, a propositional feeling is the actual enjoyment of a proposition—the actual integration in feeling of the subjects and predicate proffered as integrable. The judgment is a further integration—a feeling together of a propositional feeling and an earlier physical feeling. In Whitehead's words, it is "a synthetic feeling, embracing two subordinate feelings in one unity of feeling" (PR 293). Judging is the integration of the "S could be P" of the proposition and the "S as objectified (or not objectified) by P" of the basic conformal feeling in which the S nexus is grasped. It is the togetherness or non-togetherness, the consistency or inconsistency, of two elements in the self-formative experience of the judger which is the "object" of judgment: whether the propositional and physical feelings correspond and cohere. Judgment thus evaluates a proposition with respect to its relevance in the constitution of the judger, enhancing or playing down its role. If propositions are lures for feeling, judgments are the critics of their allurement.

Since judgments concern themselves with "real fact[s] in the constitution of the judging subject" (PR 291), truth talk, with its implications of objectivity, is entirely inappropriate with respect to judgments. They may be correct, incorrect, or suspended in their affirmation of facts in the judger's constitution, but never true or false, since the primary content of the affirmation does not deal with what the universe is in independence of the act of judging. Only propositions are *given for* a concrescence and hence can be true or false. The judgment remains entirely within the realm of appearances, and can be criticized only by subsequent occasions.

The overt "S is P" declaration of a state of affairs in the objective world is not, therefore, the primal affirmation of a judgment but one derivative from it by an abstraction which separates S and P from S-as-felt and P-as-felt and their propositionally felt togetherness. It is this derivative affirmation—the affirmation of the truth value of the propositional feeling—which is subject to error, for it is an affirmation made in abstraction from the constitution of the judging subject. Hence, there are in fact two modalities of judgment: (a) the intuitive affirmation of appearances; and (b) the affirmation of an objective, external state of affairs derived from (a) by a further comparison and integration of feelings. In the intuitive judgment, the full detail of the felt proposition—the totality of the relational pattern—is felt in its contrast with the nexus-as-felt. Such a judgment is the "consciousness of what is" in the full awareness of what it could-be-and-is, and could-be-and-is-not. It is experience compelled to affirm itself, the judgment of consciousness affirming its content. Since the intuitive judgment is a "summing up" of the concrescence, it is always correct.

Error enters with the derivative judgment, since it abstracts from the full detail of the proposition and of the nexus, dealing only with aspects of that totality. Thus, "the wall is green" indeed compares the felt possibility of being-a-wall and being-green with a segment of physical experience, but it eliminates the totality of other relations and causal influences (e.g., green lights in the room) which might make the wall *appear* green. The judgment of appearances is categorical and correct; the judgment of reality is hypothetical and possibly incorrect, and must be validated pragmatically through further experience.

Thus, derivative judgments can attain only degrees of probability—never truth or falsity. However, to speak of probability opens the door to the problems with probability theory to which Whitehead had become sensitized by his earlier immersion in the philosophy of science. The difficulty, as elaborated in layman's terms, takes the form illustrated in the following example. If the question is to determine the relative proportion of red and green marbles in a container, and a rubric forbids emptying the container out so that the marbles can be counted, the only recourse possible is the sampling technique. The red–green proportion as evidenced in each of a number of samples will eventually cluster around a mean—e.g., 3:5. We can therefore make the statement that the red–green proportion is probably 3 to 5. However, is this statement of probability (or the derived statement that the probability of any drawn marble's being red is 3/8) certainly true or only probably true? Naturally, the latter is the correct alternative, and the probability of truth of the statement of probability is a function of how randomly the samples were taken, the number of samples, etc. But the validity of the sampling technique itself is grounded in statistical probabilities. To escape the infinite regress which opens up, some non-statistical, non-probabilistic ground must be found to undergird probability statements, a ground neither needing further grounding nor asserting itself as an arbitrary ultimate. In its broadest form, the basic question is of the truth value of human judgment; in its restricted form, of the ultimate justification of induction and of the intuition of probability.[41]

With this simplified version of the problem as backdrop, Whitehead's exposition can be more meaningful. As he sees it, if probability is the proportion of favorable to unfavorable cases in the set chosen as the ground, the question as to why the ground set was selected immediately arises. If the response is that this ground is probably superior to other grounds, a second-order probability and the very real possibility of an infinite regress enter. The response must be that the selected ground has an equiprobable character (that it not be a skewed ground) and that this equiprobability must ultimately have a non-probabilistic meaning. For example, in a coin-tossing experiment, the probabilistic ground is the run of throws; but its equiprobable character is grounded in the indifferent two-sidedness of the coin, which ultimately guarantees the probability of any throw (case) turning up a "head" to be one-half.

The necessary finiteness in the statistical ground further complicates the issue, for probability has no meaning in a denumerably infinite set.[42] The purpose of the sampling technique is to overcome this difficulty, given an infinite ground set. But sampling can do so only if the sampling procedure is absolutely random—purely chaotic and lawless—an impossible rubric. In any sufficiently long run of cases, patterns will appear which result from the minuscule quantum of order latent in the sampling procedure and not from the order sought in the statistical ground. Furthermore, the sampling technique cannot overcome the problem of the novel case (the case not part of the ground) to which the probabilities determined for the ground are to be applied (for example, the extrapolation of the general laws of nature from particular observations). Other evidence is necessary in order to argue from the statistical ground to the novel case, and how is this evidence to be grounded? In fine, must it be the case that science, in its search for the predictable regularities of the universe, must choose between the anti-scientific acceptance of unverifiable probabilities on the one hand, and on the other, the postulation of nebulous "powers" in the things of the world as causative of their regular behavior, an attitude brilliantly burlesqued by Molière in the last *intermède*

---

[41] Note that, as Peirce points out (ibid., 6.476), this "intuition of probability" is also a factor in our selection of hypotheses. Man seems to have an uncanny "sense" for the right hypothesis. Without such a sense, science could never advance, given the quasi-infinite plurality of possible hypotheses.

[42] The ratio of heads to throws in an infinitely long run of throws is $\infty : \infty$ or $1:1$ —a meaningless probability.

to the *Malade imaginaire?*[43] And in the wider framework of human judgment in general, must the judger be locked irrevocably in the prison of appearances with no access to statements about reality? Whitehead's response to both questions is a natural consequence of his theory of actual entities as prehensive unities. Granted: "the data upon which the subject passes judgment are themselves components conditioning the character of the judging subject" (PR 309); nevertheless, the appearances seized in the intuitive judgment are outgrowths of the actual world given for the concrescence, so that the extrapolation from appearance to reality is not entirely without foundation. The togetherness in appearance is the subjective appropriation of the togetherness in a reality of which appearance is a further ordering. The derivative judgment is the final ordering of data given *as ordered* for the concrescence. Hence the solution to both the objectivity of judgment and the validity of induction lies in the general social character of the region to which the judgment or induction relates.

This social character is given for the judging occasion as an element in the actual world out of which it creates itself, and hence is reflected in its experience and felt in the intuitive judgment. The inductive judgment, since it "has regard to the statistical probabilities inherent in [the] given [social] order" (PR 311), is and can only be the prediction of a *particular* future on the basis of an observed past, a prediction assuming (*a*) the environmental stability requisite for the survival of the observed social order, and (*b*) an analogy between the social order in the environment of the predicted occasion and that in the observed environment. If the future and past societies are to be analogous, the situation can come about only as a result of their having arisen out of analogical data, which can only be given by wider analogous environments. The widest environmental analogies are those provided by the society dominating the cosmic epoch: the so-called "laws of nature." Thus Whitehead is not reduced to postulating either a mechanism of externally imposed law or a crude Aristotelianism of internally determining substantial forms. Regularity is

---

[43] The M.D. candidate is asked:
> Si mihi licentiam dat Dominus Praeses
> Et tanti docti Doctores,
> Et assistantes illustres,
> Tres scavanti Bacheliero,
> Quem estimo et honoro,
> Domandabo causam et rationem quare
> Opium facit dormire.

and answers:
> Mihi a docto doctore
> Domandatur causam et rationem quare
> Opium facit dormire:
> A quoi respondeo,
> Quia est in eo
> Virtus dormitiva,
> Cujus est natura
> Sensus assoupire.

spawned by regularity; ordered environments tend to propagate themselves analogically, because regularity in the past is prehended into present occasions which form the social environment out of which future occasions will grow. (Hence the particularity of inductive judgments.)

The analogy between past and future environments is not to be taken as an identity, however. The social universe is not locked into a wooden order. Societies *dominate* an environment; they do not totally pervade it. There are chaotic occasions, anarchists, in any society and in any cosmic epoch. Therefore, absolute predictability is impossible. Sampling is necessary and inductive judgments depend for their probability on the size of the set considered and the "amount" of social order observed in it. The primordial sampling and probabilistic judgment is the experience of the judging occasion as it arises out of its actual world and its contained order. Its experience, as intuitively grasped, provides the basis for its vague judgment of "more or less" with respect to favorable and unfavorable occurrence in that actual world, which in turn gives the judging occasion a vague and imprecise intuition "as to the statistical basis of the presupposed environment" (PR 315) from which the future environment can be extrapolated by analogy. There is also an intuition of the "intrinsic suitability of some definite outcome from a presupposed situation" (PR 315), derived from the judger's prehension of the primordial nature of God, in which eternal objects are graded in degrees of relevance to actual occasions. Such an "intuition of suitability" provides the basis for the probabilistic prediction of novel occurrences in the future and for man's uncanny sense for the right hypothesis. "There will be nothing statistical in this suitability. It depends upon the fundamental graduation of appetitions which lies at the base of things, and which solves all indeterminations of transition" (PR 315).

Thus, by refusing to separate the experimenter from the experimental situation, the judger from the data judged, Whitehead can objectively ground both inductive and derivative judgments without losing sight of their subjectivity and fallibility.

VII · PROCESS: AN OVERVIEW

To put the complexities of the previous analyses in proper perspective, the various functionings described must be reinserted in the fundamental model of the concrescence of an actual occasion, of a drop of experience. An actual entity arises out of its actual world via a process in which objectivity is gradually transformed into subjective immediacy, which is to say, into the final integration of every element in the ideal and real realms and of every element arising in the concrescence. The data originally felt as alien are integrated in the conformal phase of this process by means of selective objectifications whereby they become a unified (but still not private) datum susceptible for further integration. Thus the initial phase of any concrescence is characterized by receptivity, re-enactment, reiteration. In the various phases of the supplemental stage, this public datum is met with private feelings arising in accordance with the private ideal of the occasion. The scalar overwhelms the vector; physical feeling loses its pre-eminence to the burgeoning conceptual feelings. In the aesthetic portion of the supplement, emotional and purposive subjective forms transmute the objectively given into the subjectively appropriated: the alien becomes the personal; the datum is appreciated, enjoyed; its elements are adjusted in importance through intensifications and inhibitions. But the phase is "blind." Pure intellectuality—the pure grasp of eternal objects in themselves—is not as yet functional. The conceptual feelings in the aesthetic supplement grasp the eternal objects as tied to and exemplified in the particularity of the datum. Hence physical purposes may arise but neither propositional feelings nor consciousness. But this "blindness" itself must be integrated into the concrescing subject. The occasion must take a determinate stand with respect to its blindness: either by ratifying it and thus reaching satisfaction as a personal, subjective re-enactment of objectivity, or by refusing to ratify it and thus opening up the possibility of intellectual supplementation, with its inrush of propositional and comparative (conscious) feelings. When these intellectual feelings have exhausted the possibilities of integration and comparison (which are a function of the order–disorder in the data), the concrescence "closes up," reaches the satisfaction of a fully determinate drop of novel, private experience, and perishes to be a new datum for further synthesis. In its process, it has both satisfied the urge of the creativity that "all may be one," and provoked a transition to future creative activity.

4

THE STRUCTURE
OF A CONCRESCENCE

(PR, Part III)

THERE ARE TWO MODES OF PROCESS operative in the universe: concrescence and transition, micro-process and macro-process. In concrescence, the many elements in the universe given for an occasion achieve the private, subjective unity of a perspective, transforming the efficient causality of the past into the final causality of an emerging viewpoint functioning with respect to its own determinateness. Transition, on the other hand, represents the functioning of an actual entity in the future—its pragmatic afterlife as causally objectified in subsequent occasions. Since both modes of process are different translations of the same entity (concrescence—in terms of its genesis from the world; transition—in terms of its efficacy as a stubborn fact for the future), they cannot be torn apart. But they can be analyzed in isolation from each other, provided each analysis is viewed as an abstraction from the twofold functioning of a concrete entity. Thus, each analysis will yield quite different sorts of information about an actual occasion. In genetic analysis, the self-creative process of the subject is traced as it grows from phase to phase. Coordinate analysis, focusing on the fully determinate satisfaction achieved in concrescence, takes as its object the spatio-temporal standpoint in the extensive continuum which the entity has actualized. The former mode divides an occasion into prehensions, underscoring its final causality; the latter mode yields space–time regions through which chains of efficient causality are propagated.

Both modes are possible because the occasion, though essentially undivided, whether as separate subject with separate prehensions or as separate superject divided into separate regions, is yet divisible, in that its process, and hence its satisfaction, possess a complex and therefore composite unity. However, this composition is not to be viewed as additive. It is not the case that process proceeds by a linear succession of prehensions each complete in itself, or that the satisfaction thus represents a distinct multiplicity of independent feelings externally conjoined. Since the subjective aim realized in the satisfaction is immanent in all phases of the process, each phase and each prehension are necessarily incomplete, depending for their full determinateness on the final decision giving them their determinate value in the satisfaction. For example, a conformal physical feeling originating in a high-order entity is further involved in aesthetic, propositional, and comparative feelings in subsequent phases and does not attain its significance in the concrescence—its full determinateness—until those "later" phases are completed. A phase or a prehension reaches "completeness" only in the satisfaction, when it has attained its perfectly definite relation to all other phases and prehensions in the one, fully determinate, and subjective feeling-of-the-universe which is the satisfied occasion. Only at this point is it a "proper entity"[1] with its own character; but that character is its own because of its place in the unity of the whole. Prehensions and phases are thus separable but not separated. The separateness which seems to accrue to them stems from our inability to conceive process in other than spatio-temporal terms. For Whitehead, though process results in the superjection of a quantum of space–time, it does not *run through* that quantum in its "succession" of phases. Thus, in Whitehead's conception, the subject is immanent in all incomplete phases of itself, luring on its own realization. The lure, or subjective aim, forms a proposition with each incomplete phase, a proposition whose subjects are the feelings in the phase and whose potential predicative pattern is the aim at the concrescent subject—the lure for further integration. But since the concrescent subject aimed at is one unified feeling of every item in the universe and in the concrescence, its immanence in each phase makes the phases undivided from the whole although potentially divisible from it.[2]

II · THE NATURE OF FEELINGS IN GENERAL

With the foregoing clarifications in mind, it is possible to "divide" an occasion into stages and separable feelings, thereby "tracing" its nontemporal genesis and enabling finite statements to be made about it. Whitehead's genetic account of an actual occasion enters a spiral of complexity so dizzying that it is all too easy for the reader to lose sight of its purpose and central theme: namely, to give a metaphysical account of the self-creative process of an occasion, of its experience. What is to be explicated in the account is the core of the philosophy of organism: that

---

[1] "Proper entity" is not to be confused with actual entity. The former is a "completed" *aspect* of the latter, and hence an abstraction.

[2] Analogously, a half is a half only because it is half of some whole. But if it is a *real* half, i.e., really divided from its other half, the whole is no longer real and the half is no longer a half but a new whole. For halves to be genuine halves of a whole, they must be actually undivided but potentially divisible structural elements in the whole.

out of the sheer multiplicity of the past, new subjective unities emerge. Past chapters of PR, and indeed all of SMW, speak of "intertwined prehensive unification," of "the many becoming one and being enriched by one," of the subject's emerging from its actual world as a novel, aesthetic synthesis of that actual world. However, if this romantic insight is to become metaphysics rather than mere poetic metaphor, it must achieve the precision of exact formulation, a formulation meeting and answering the metaphysical problems latent in the romantic insight. Through what mechanism can objectivity become subjectivity without destroying either or both in the process? How can novelty in the present arise when perforce it must arise within the context of a causally efficacious past? How are the primary feelings in a concrescence related to subsequent feelings so that phenomena such as the various modes of perception and the higher forms of consciousness do not lock the conscious and judging subject into a phenomenal world hopelessly divorced from the unattainable noumenon? How can freedom be a meaningful world, given the inescapability of past fact? In a word, what is the fine-grained rendition of process, of concrescence and transition, of the actual entity as subject–superject, which fills in the interstices in the coarse-grained account to make it more than a "likely story"? Whitehead's response is the labyrinth of detail which constitutes his genetic and coordinate analyses of Parts III and IV. But the two techniques of analysis must not be taken as merely philosophical tools. If they are only that, if they are not specifications of more general analytic techniques involved in the self-formative activity of any occasion of experience, then the metaphysics of organism fails the foundational test of self-reference and is incoherent despite its protestations to the contrary. The following chapters must be read, therefore, on two levels: (a) as philosophical "divisions" or analyses of the complex structure of an actual occasion; and (b) as modalities of "division" which any actual occasion exercises on the data which constitute its past so that it may synthesize them into the unity of its subjectivity. The divisibility of an occasion therefore serves a metaphysical function over and above its epistemological value, being the condition for the possibility of one entity's entering into the composition of other entities in its pragmatic afterlife. Specifically, the divisibility of an occasion grounds the theory of feelings; it makes possible the "eliminations" whereby what Whitehead calls "initial data" can become an "objective datum."

The total satisfaction of one entity cannot enter into the composition of another entity in its full complex unity without that entity's quite literally *becoming* the entity absorbed. Any satisfaction is a unique, one-of-a-kind, unrepeatable perspective on the universe. Thus the initial data for any concrescence are the sheer multiplicity of past facts, each in its own self-sufficient unity: integr*able* because of the primordial relevance of eternal objects and of the systematic interrelations of the extensive continuum, but not integrated. To be felt into the concrescent unity of feeling of a subject, the elements in the complex unity of each past satisfaction which are inconsistent with other elements in the other satisfied occasions in the actual world relative to the concrescence must be negatively prehended, i.e., eliminated from feeling. The initial data are "felt under an abstraction" (PR 353), each objectified by means of an aspect of its definiteness —one of its component feelings—which is compatible with aspects or component feelings of the others.

What precisely is eliminated in the transition from data to datum requires explication. The sheer multiplicity of data given for an occasion is a multiplicity of satisfied (or completed) actual occasions, each of which is a subjective unification of its many feelings of its actual world. There is, therefore, a multiplicity of actual worlds: not such that each excludes the other, but such that each is included as a subordinate nexus in the other. This involves, therefore, that the satisfactions of the entities felt in the initial data are composed of feelings, many of which feel the same items. Thus, to use Whitehead's example: when A arises from an actual world containing B, C, and D, it may be the case that A feels not only D as directly given for it, but also D as felt by B and C. The three feelings cannot be identical, for each is a *subjective* grasp of the publicity of D; nor can they be entirely diverse (inconsistent), inasmuch as the possibility for the three objectifications was "decided" *by* D in its own concrescent process, and hence must manifest the unity of D as subject–superject. In order for the three feelings of D to be integrated by A into one feeling of D, all aspects of the totality of D's feelings as felt by A which are not consistent with D's feelings as felt through the mediacy of B's and C's feelings must be eliminated—i.e., negatively prehended—so that the multiple D-feelings (D as initial data) can be integrated into one D-feeling (D as objective datum) playing one self-consistent role in A's process. D is felt under an abstraction from its full determinacy, under an objectification decided by it in its own concrescence and superjected along with other possible objectifications to the future as mutually consistent elements in D's satisfaction and hence as alternative ways in which D could be felt. What is eliminated from feeling is not D as a causative agency but those of D's feelings which cannot be meshed with A's actual world, which includes the D-feelings incorporated into B and C.

The objective datum is thus a harmony of "mutually adjusted abstraction" (PR 321). The multiplicity of the past grows together into an actual world: "a nexus whose objectification constitutes the complete unity of objective datum for the physical feeling of that actual entity" (PR 351), "a realized pattern of the initial data" (PR 352). Since what is going on in the outgrowth of the objective datum from the initial data is a process in which one feeling out of the manifold of feelings integrated in each satisfied occasion in the data is detached to become the abstraction under which that entity is felt into the concrescent occasion, "A feeling . . . is essentially a transition [i.e., a superjective functioning] effecting a concrescence" (PR 337).

For a feeling to be thus detached from the aesthetic complex of a satisfied occasion, the component feelings in that satisfaction must be determinate, i.e., separable; for such a component feeling when grasped into a subsequent occasion to be felt as the causality *of* the satisfied entity and not as "just itself," the component feelings in the satisfaction must be inseparate; otherwise the unity of the satisfied occasion explodes into a diverse multiplicity of essentially unrelated aspects. Thus, the divisibility of an occasion grounds not only the possibility of genetic analysis and finite truth, but, more fundamentally, the possibility of an occasion's intervention into processes transcendent to itself; it is the condition for the possibility of transition. Any occasion of experience, not merely an occasion of philosophic thought, performs genetic analyses of the satisfied entities in its actual world.

The initial phase of a concrescence, that in which the objective datum is growing out of the initial multiplicity, is difficult to describe because it marks the transition between the satisfied occasions of the past and the concrescent occasion in the present. From one point of view, the objectifications of the initial data are the causal functionings of the satisfied occasions, growing together under the impetus of the creativity to elicit the self-actualization of a new perspective. From the alternative point of view, the objectifications mark the initial prehensions in the concrescence of the new entity, lured toward subjectification by its ideal of itself received from God by way of the real potentiality of the initial data. Neither point of view is complete in isolation from the other, since process intertwines the objectification of subjectivity and the subjectification of objectivity in the ongoing, organic development of the universe. Therefore, though the language used in Whitehead's descriptions of the primary feelings is "slanted" from the side of the subject and its purposive activity, the objective efficient causality of the satisfied past must be seen as correlatively operative. Each past actual occasion decides the way*s* in which it could be objectified; the present decides the *way* in which it is to be objectified, given its immersion in the medium of the actual world of the concrescence.

The transition from initial data, with their possibilities for objectification, to objective datum, with its actual objectification, is a decision which is part of the concrescent process of any occasion; for in actualizing itself as a synthetic experience, it superjects the elements of that experience in their relevance to the future. Thus, an actual entity is "responsible" both *to* and *for* the future use to which its achievement may be put. Herein lies the genesis of both good and evil, seasonable and unseasonable birth, sensitivity and insensitivity to the future. The disruptions which irrelevant novelty can produce provoke painful effort in the future to overcome disharmony by incorporating it into a wider harmonic pattern. Evil is not totally destructive, therefore; it may proximately hinder intensity of satisfaction, but in the long run it promotes the aesthetic growth of the universe.

The necessity for a social environment to ensure in advance some minimum of harmony among superjected decisions now becomes more obvious and adds a new dimension to the role of society in macro-process. In a social context, the initial data for a concrescence share common feelings—the inherited feelings of the defining characteristic—and hence have an aptness for synthesis not found in a disorderly environment. In a social context, even non-social occasions can be felt—not *in se*, but in their contrast with the sociality of their neighbors: as faint, chaotic, and irrelevant influences, if the social pole of the contrast is emphasized; or as significant suggestions for future change, if the chaotic pole is enhanced. In a *purely* chaotic environment, no concrescence could occur, because all objectifications would be mutually inhibiting.

Furthermore, the concrescence from initial data to objective datum cannot occur unless the "possibility for the subject" is a relevant item in the real potentiality of the actual world. If the positive feelings are to satisfy the Category of Subjective Unity[3] by being integrable, they can be integrable only from a standpoint whose possibility itself is felt. The eliminations from feeling, arising so as to prevent duplication of feelings or of the roles played by objectifications, demand that the concrescence initiate from a vague grasp of the final unity of those feelings and roles in the satisfaction. Furthermore, the eliminations themselves must be mutually consistent, for any entity's refusal to admit an inimical factor into its constitution is itself a factor in its constitution and must be integrable with all other refusals and admissions. Therefore, any concrescence must originate from an initial grasp of its own possibility: the potential pattern, as yet vague and indeterminate, in terms of which its public data can be felt together into a private unity. This feeling of subjective aim is a feeling of the possibility of definiteness, the possibility-for-a-subject, given in the world for the perspective: of that aspect of God's initial ordering of the possibles "which is immediately relevant to the universe 'given' for that concrescence" (PR 343). It is therefore a hybrid physical feeling of God as objectified by the "segment" of his conceptual feelings propositionally

---

[3] "The many feelings which belong to an incomplete phase in the process of an actual entity, though unintegrated by reason of the incompleteness of the phase, are compatible for integration by reason of the unity of their subject" (PR 39).

related to the actual world for the perspective. This is to say that the real potentiality of the universe from a perspective is a set of eternal objects graded in degrees of relevance to that universe, the set being a subset of the primordial ordering of eternal objects. In any universe, therefore, God is objectified by aspects of his conceptual valuation of eternal objects—those eternal objects embodied in or relevant to that universe. An actual entity arising in that universe physically prehends God under that objectification, thereby seizing its relevant potential for self-realization, or subjective aim.

The subjective aim thus envisioned directs the positive and negative prehensions, ensuring that the Categories of Subjective Unity, Objective Diversity, and Objective Identity[4] are unviolated in the subjectification of the data, thereby safeguarding both the unity of the subject and the unity of its objects. "The oneness of the universe, and the oneness of each element in the universe, repeat themselves to the crack of doom in the creative advance from creature to creature, each creature including in itself the whole of history and exemplifying the self-identity of things and their mutual diversities" (PR 347–48).

The transition from the public character of a datum to the private character of a prehension is accomplished through the rush of private feelings with which the datum is met: the subjective forms of feelings—how the feelings feel. The subjective form of a feeling, when it reaches full definiteness in the satisfaction, bears within it the history of its origination within the subjective process. "The way in which the feeling feels expresses how the feeling came into being. It expresses the purpose which urged it forward, and the obstacles which it encountered, and the indeterminations which were dissolved by the originative decisions of the subject" (PR 354). The fully matured subjective form of any component feeling in a satisfaction, therefore, embodies the genesis of that feeling in the process, from the time the subject encountered the data, eliminated any inconsistencies, and, through a series of integrations, decided the role the feeling should play in the satisfaction and for the future. The subjective form is both the private *and* the pragmatic aspect of a feeling: "the datum is felt with that subjective form in order that the subject may be the superject which it is" (PR 355). It is therefore the seat of novelty for the subject–superject, the private appropriation of objectivity which becomes a public possibility for objectification in the future.

"The subjective form is the ingression of novel form peculiar to the

---

4 "There can be no 'coalescence' of diverse elements in the objective datum of an actual entity, so far as concerns the functions of those elements in that satisfaction" (The Category of Objective Diversity, PR 39). "There can be no duplication of any element in the objective datum of the 'satisfaction' of an actual entity, so far as concerns the function of that element in the 'satisfaction'" (The Category of Objective Identity, PR 39).

new particular fact, and with its peculiar mode of fusion with the objective datum" (PR 356). It is an eternal object structuring the datum into the private unity of the subject. But the datum itself is a feeling with its own novel subjective form, which form cannot be lost in the transition to the new subject. The novelty in any emergent subjective form consists, therefore, not in its content (the subjectively formed feeling felt) but in its subjectification of that content. What begins as subjective re-enactment acquires patterns of emotional quality and intensity derived only in part from the feeling felt and assuming more and more importance as the concrescence advances from stage to stage—always under the aegis of the subjective aim, which is the ultimate determinant of subjective forms. The subjective form of a fully matured feeling in the satisfaction is a synthesis of the re-enactment and emotional supplementation it has undergone in the concrescence.

Thus, in summary, any feeling is analyzable into five elements: (a) its subject—immanent in the feeling and that at which the feeling aims; (b) its initial data—the insistent "stuff" out of which it arises; (c) its elimination of incompatibilities through negative prehensions in order to make the initial data capable of further synthesis, which negative prehensions add their own traces to the developing emotional complex; (d) its objective datum—the actual world as a unity for feeling; and (e) its subjective form—"how" the datum is felt. With this generalized discussion of feeling as a backdrop, the more specific kinds of feelings can be explicated more clearly.

III · THE PRIMARY FEELINGS

Primary feelings are distinguishable from subsequent feelings in a concrescence in virtue of the fact that their object is an element in the actual world of the concrescence and not a "prior" feeling in the concrescent process. Via simple physical feelings, the efficient causality of a past occasion is incorporated into the concrescence under an objectification. As seen before, one of the aspects whereby the object made itself to be what it is becomes one of the aspects whereby the subject makes itself to be what it is becoming. The subject is conditioned by the object as a result of the subject's initial physical functioning, and past-to-present-to-future continuity is grounded. The primary phase of a concrescence, the phase dominated by simple physical feelings, "constitutes the machinery by reason of which the creativity transcends the world already actual, and yet remains conditioned by that actual world in its new impersonation" (PR 362).

The re-enactive subjective forms of simple physical feelings guarantee the effective transfer of energy from past to present. The feelings felt are felt *as alien*—as originating, vector-like, from the there–then of the object —and do not lose their alien character when initially felt into the here– now of the subject. The same eternal object structures the subjective feeling as structured the objective feeling, thereby effectively transferring the causality of the object into the subject. Since the object is felt under an abstraction from its own definiteness, physical feelings of an object will differ as a function of what sort of element in the object is serving as its objectification. If the objective feeling felt is itself a physical feeling, the subjective feeling is purely physical—a simple case of energy transfer. If, on the other hand, the objectification is one of the object's conceptual feelings, the subjective feeling is termed "hybrid." But in both cases the feeling felt is an abstraction from a past, satisfied occasion which is being re-enacted in the concrescence.

In contradistinction to a physical feeling, a conceptual feeling is a direct grasp of an eternal object as a pure potential selected for realization in the concrescence. In no way can a conceptual prehension be likened to a passive "vision" of the eternal object. Just as a physical feeling is the incorporation of the causality of a satisfied entity into the constitution of a subject, so a conceptual feeling is the admission of an eternal object as a structural element. Conceptual functioning is appetition, not contemplation. The subjective form of a conceptual feeling is therefore valuation, concerned with *how* the eternal object is to be utilized in structuring the data of the physical prehensions and with what importance it will have in the resultant structure. As a function of their relevance to the nexus physically felt and to the subjective aim of the subject, eternal objects will be "valued" (either admitted into the concrescent subject or negatively prehended) and valued "up" or "down," as important or insignificant structural elements. The subjective form of a conceptual prehension is therefore not a re-enactment as it is in the case of a simple physical feeling—it is not object-conditioned. The valuation of an eternal object given as relevant to a concrescence is a function sheerly of the subjective aim of concrescence.

But "where" are the eternal objects which are conceptually felt? Whitehead is not maintaining a crude Platonism of direct vision of a world of forms by finite occasions. This can occur just once—in God's primordial envisagement which structures the eternal objects into gradations of mutual relevance. For a finite occasion, all conceptual feelings are derivate from physical feelings. *Nihil est in intellectu quod non prius fuerit in sensu.* The hybrid physical feeling of a datum elicits a conceptual feeling of the eternal object whereby the datum is objectified. The subject derivatively feels the same eternal object the datum is objectified as feeling, but with a different subjective form, for the valuation of the eternal object is proportionate to the perspectival aim of the subject.

Thus, in accordance with the Category of Conceptual Valuation,[5] every physical feeling initiates a conceptual feeling of the eternal object exemplified in the datum felt.[6] This initial activity of the mental pole of any occasion is its "conceptual registration of the physical pole" (PR 379). Through conceptual feeling, the brute causality of the actual world is overcome, for the question answered by conceptual valuation has to do with the possible role of the felt eternal objects in the constitution of the subject. Conceptual feeling introduces purpose into the concrescence; eternal objects can be grasped as lures for a self-creative activity which is not mere re-enactment of objective functioning. "The mental pole introduces the subject as a determinant of its own concrescence. The mental pole is the subject determining its own ideal of itself by reference to eternal principles of valuation autonomously modified in their application to its own physical objective datum" (PR 380). Thus, the original physical feelings, whose subjective forms were reiterations of the subjective forms of the feelings felt, can, by integration with the conceptual feelings, acquire subjective forms determining the importance of those physical feelings for the concrescent subject. It is not so much the case that new subjective forms have arisen, as that the forms re-enacted have been valued up or down relative to the ideal of the emergent subject. Genuinely novel forms enter initially through conceptual operations subsequent to these initial valuations.

Because the eternal objects are ordered in a relevance independent of the relevance introduced by joint exemplification in the concrete, an occasion can have what Whitehead calls "reverted feelings" of eternal objects which are relevant alternatives to those which it conceptually registers, and thus can admit new forms into its constitution. In order for a conceptual reversion to take place, however, a ground of identity must exist between the registered eternal object and the reverted eternal object. Since any concrescence aims at an aesthetic unity, a totally novel form—one completely "disconnected" from and irrelevant to the objective datum —would be an incoherent element diminishing that unity or rendering it impossible to attain. Novelty can be admitted only on the basis of its relevance to and contrast with the given. "All aesthetic experience is feeling arising out of the realization of contrast under identity" (RM 111). It

---

[5] "From each physical feeling there is the derivation of a purely conceptual feeling whose datum is the eternal object determinant of the definiteness of the actual entity, or of the nexus, physically felt" (PR 39–40).

[6] At first glance, this would seem to preclude the emergence of novel (unexemplified) forms in the universe. However, if it be remembered that according to the principle of relativity God's primordial nature is a datum for every finite concrescence, then the appearance of novel forms can be seen as justifiable. Unexemplified eternal objects are ideally together in the primordial nature, and graded in degrees of relevance to finite perspectives through the integration of God's conceptual and physical feelings.

is the deepening of intensity provoked by contrast which lures reverted feelings.

Intensity in satisfaction is further enhanced through the combined width and narrowness of its formal structure. If the sheer multiplicity of initial physical feelings is to be overcome so as to rescue the satisfaction from triviality, those feelings must be simplified: the many feelings of elements in a nexus reduced to one feeling of the nexus. This simplification is achieved through transmuted feelings. If it is the case that a plurality of physical feelings are "registered" as analogously exemplifying the same eternal object in the initial conceptual valuation, the manifold can be synthesized under the unity of the eternal object. Through the integration of the physical and conceptual feelings, the many physical feelings of the many actual entities in the nexus are transmuted into one physical feeling of one actuality—the nexus. Without the intervention of conceptual feelings, all that could be felt in the multiplicity is the mutual implication of its contained members—a vague many-in-oneness. Because of the intervention of transmuted feelings, the many-ness disappears, leaving only the unity of the nexus as the datum for physical feeling. If the eternal object making the transmutation possible is initially grasped in a reverted feeling rather than in a valuation, pathways both to novel integration of the nexus and to possible error are opened.

An entity in which transmuted feelings achieve a degree of importance is on its way toward consciousness, for it is already simplifying its world via abstraction. No longer is it a low-grade organism, "merely the summation of the forms of energy which flow in upon it in all their multiplicity of detail" (PR 389). It has introduced order and intelligible system into its actual world—the right kind of vagueness which makes further integrations possible. Note how transmutation is the basis of perception in the mode of presentational immediacy. Perception is never the reception or display of an actual entity functioning in the past or present; it concerns itself always with a nexus unified by the analogous exemplification of an eternal object among its members. In some cases, the total nexus is characterized by an eternal object derived from a segment of its constituency; in others, an eternal object derived from one part is used to characterize another part. In both instances, the "generalization" of the partially shared characteristic is justifiable on the basis of the mutual implication of the members of the nexus. When a transmutation leads to a physical feeling of a nexus-as-one, the qualifying eternal object is felt as the sensum received from the past nexus (this is the basis of causal efficacy). However, the nexus includes by implication members which are not experienced because they are contemporaneous with the concrescing subject. The same eternal object is integrated with the contemporary "part" of the nexus and displays it in presentational immediacy. Furthermore, it is only because of this sort of transmutation that symbolic reference can take place: that it can be "affirmed" that the unexperienced part of the nexus (the present) is analogous to the part experienced (the past).

Out of this interplay between physical and conceptual feelings, an interplay in which simple physical feelings give rise to conceptual feelings which in their turn give rise to further physical feelings all concerned with the same datum, the types of decision characterizing the aesthetic supplement arise. The conceptual feelings arising from the initial physical feelings adjust the importance of the physical feelings for the concrescence, valuing them up or down. If they are valued up and transmuted into a physical feeling of a nexus, the subjective form of that feeling is intensified as adversion. If valued down, the transmuted feeling is either attenuated or eliminated from the concrescence with a subjective form of aversion. A further categoreal obligation is laid upon the complex of valuations which constitutes conceptual functioning: the Category of Subjective Harmony.[7] Just as the Category of Subjective Unity controls the process of objectification whereby the past is enabled to enter the present with no loss of identity to either, so the Category of Subjective Harmony norms the valuations so that they are compatible for synthesis into an emotional complex with a maximum of aesthetic intensity. The subject is therefore responsible for both the matter and the forms out of which it creates itself, while, at the same time, both are derived from the settled world. Whitehead's view of micro-process as the subjective appropriation and structuring of what is objectively received enables him to view an occasion as both determined and free, objectively conditioned and subjectively functioning—as a union of efficient and final causality.

However, the ultimate determinant of the latitude of autonomy open to a concrescence is a function of its environment. The complex order given for an occasion is the basis for the simplifications and intensities of conceptual feeling achievable in transmuted and reverted feelings. Hence consciousness as the subjective form of more autonomous feelings can arise only in the environment of a bodily organism providing highly ordered data for the conscious monad. In a disorderly environment, the inconsistencies among its members dominate and must be negatively prehended, leaving only trivial aspects to be used as objectifications. In such a situation, the maximum intensity open to a concrescence is that of a mere subjective summation or reiteration of the objectively given.

IV · PROPOSITIONS AND FEELINGS

It is unfortunately all too easy to slip back into a non-process understanding of the nature of a proposition, thereby hopelessly muddying White-

---

[7] "The valuations of conceptual feelings are mutually determined by the adaptation of those feelings to be contrasted elements congruent with the subjective aim" (PR 40–41).

head's genetic analysis of propositions and propositional feelings. It cannot be emphasized too strongly that a proposition is *not* a fact given for prehension the way an actual entity or a nexus is given: as a state of affairs which *must* be grasped into a concrescent subject under an objectification of itself. A proposition is, rather, a way in which a nexus *could be* felt; it is a potential type of entity, *proposed for* feeling as a lure for feeling, differing from an eternal object because it has a determinate reference to a set of actual entities, differing from an actual entity or a nexus in that it is realizable rather than realized. It is "the potentiality of the eternal object, as a determinant of definiteness, in some determinate mode of restricted reference to the logical subjects" (PR 393). Its realization is indeterminate: i.e., a proposition need not be prehended into the constitution of a subject; whereas a nexus, by the principle of relativity, must be felt.[8] Furthermore, the mode of a proposition's realization is indeterminate. Is it to be realized imaginatively? Perceptively? Intuitively? This is left to the decision of the concrescent subject feeling the propositional lure, a decision which is a function of the "past history" of the concrescence. Moreover, a proposition is indeterminate as to its truth or falsity. *In fact*, it is true or false (i.e., realized in the members of its locus or not), but its truth or falsity is not relevant to its propositional status. In itself, that is, in abstraction from a concrescent occasion, it is merely "particular facts in a potential pattern" (PR 295), the "germaneness of a certain set of eternal objects to a certain set of actual entities" (PR 286).

In the concrete, propositions are both *given for* and *created by* the concrescent occasion entertaining them. As "given for," they are elements in the actual world of a concrescence—hybrid entities; but their givenness is not the sort describable in terms of a simple location metaphysic. It is not the case that propositions are independent realities, over against a concrescent subject which grasps them as "others," as objects in the classical sense of the term. They are "given for" the concrescence precisely because they are "created by" the subject. But again, the "created

---

[8] The obvious implication of this statement is a denial of the possibility of negative physical prehensions—a position I tend to hold. However, my position can be readily misinterpreted if read simplistically. I am *not* implying that all causal agencies in the settled world are efficacious in each concrescent occasion. On this reading, I would be hard put to justify Whitehead's insistence on the uniqueness of an occasion's actual world. As I see the situation, each element in the initial multiplicity ("the universe disjunctively") is initially grasped as a causal element in the initial physical feelings. When the subjective forms structuring the causal feelings felt are conceptually registered and undergo conceptual valuation, that valuation can result in the negative prehension of those forms and in the consequent elimination of the causal feelings vis-à-vis subsequent efficacy in the concrescence. I am maintaining, therefore, that while there can be no negative prehensions of initial data, through the intervening mental operations involved in the concrescence of initial data to objective datum, derived negative physical prehensions (hybrid prehensions) can and do occur. A total denial of negative physical prehensions would result in the tacit affirmation of a block universe—an intolerable assertion.

by" is to be interpreted not as a pure subjective origination—a figment of the subject—but rather as an aspect of the process whereby the subject, via the elimination of incompatibilities through negative prehensions and selective objectifications, transforms the multiplicity of fully determinate facts which constitute the past world (the initial data) into an objective datum, an actual world, apt for subjectification. This process produces both the worldliness of the world and the uniqueness of the perspective, so that it is true to say that, although all actual entities arise from the same universe, no two entities share the same actual world. Each entity can rightly proclaim "This actual world is mine." Yet, at the same time, the uniqueness of each actual world and of each actual entity does not spell their absolute isolation. There can be no "simply located" actual worlds or actual entities, for the ground of all world construction—the patterns for worldliness—is to be found in God, who for that reason can be called "creator" of each actual world and of each actual entity. In virtue of his primordial valuation of eternal objects, they are graded in relevance to every possible finite perspective, which infinity of gradations is synthesized into an overarching harmony of finite possibilities—the Whiteheadian analogue of Plato's Form of the Good. Each finite concrescence initiates from a hybrid physical feeling of God objectified via the primordial valuation relative to its perspective—feels the subjective aim whereby it begins the subjectification of the initial data.

With these qualifications in mind, Whitehead's genetic account of the origination of propositions and propositional feelings becomes less subject to misinterpretation. To take the simplest case as a paradigm: consider the situation of an actual entity's arising out of an actual world containing only one satisfied entity—X—which constitutes the initial datum for the concrescent entity. In order to admit X into its own constitution, the complete determinate pattern achieved by X's synthesis of its many feelings (for the sake of illustration, a, b, and c) must be abstracted from. The concrescent occasion, under the lure of its subjective aim as received from God, negatively prehends X's b and c feelings and objectifies X by a, one aspect in its determinateness, one separable yet inseparate feeling in its final aesthetic unity of feeling. X_a is then the objective datum which the concrescent occasion feels via a simple physical feeling which grasps a sheer matter-of-fact—what Whitehead calls an "indicative feeling." But the fact felt is not a bare fact but a formed fact —a, the objectification is one of X's feelings, felt by X with a subjective form consonant with X's other feelings because of the Category of Subjective Harmony. Consequently, the indicative feeling of X_a develops into a "physical recognition" of the eternal object structuring a—A. This derivative feeling is a further physical feeling of a hybrid type—i.e., a physical feeling which objectifies its datum by one of the datum's conceptual feelings. By the Category of Conceptual Valuation, every physical feeling gives rise to a pure conceptual feeling of the eternal object structuring the objectification; therefore, the physical recognition leads to pure conceptual prehension of the eternal object A. The concrescent subject feels A as a pure potential; it "conceptually registers" its physical pole in a "predicative feeling." The predicative feeling may limit itself to reproducing the A-ness of a, or, by the Category of Conceptual Reversion, may originate a new eternal object, relevant to but diverse from A. In either case, the valued or reverted eternal object is the proto-predicate of the evolving proposition. Its proto-subject is X_a as felt in the indicative feeling. (This is the same as saying that the indicative feeling is proto-subject and the valuation or reversion is proto-predicate, for the object felt is not concretely separable from the feeling which feels it.)

In order for X_a and A to achieve the unity of a proposition, their incompatibilities must be overcome. With respect to A, this incompatibility is the universality of A's relevance to realization. In X_a's case, it is the predicate already inscribed in it by the initial objectification—i.e., its a-ness. Both incompatibilities are overcome in a double elimination which negatively prehends the "any-ness" of A, limiting its possibility to possibility-for-structuring-X (A_x) and negatively prehends the a-ness of X, its actual predicate, rendering it a bare fact, an "it," an X, with the potentiality for realizing the predicative pattern. The potential togetherness of this "naked X" and A_x (the predicative pattern) is a proposition, a lure for the concrescent occasion to realize that togetherness in its own constitution by a propositional feeling which feels X and A_x together in one feeling.

The ideally simple case used for purposes of illustration is unexemplifiable in fact, for one-member actual worlds are non-existent and propositions normally concern the togetherness of an indicated *nexus* and a predicative pattern. In the more realistic cases of propositional prehension, the initial data are a multiplicity of occasions mutually implicated in the unity of a nexus. In this instance, a transmutation occurs whereby the nexus is physically prehended as one fact because the multiplicity of actual entities within it exemplify the same eternal object in their definiteness. In place of the simple indicative feeling described above, a plurality of X's is felt in the unity of a determinate pattern. The determinate plurality must be stripped of its determinations and must become an indicative system (then–there, Caesar–Rubicon) which is subject of the proposition before the further phases of propositional prehension can emerge.

The feelings whereby propositions are grasped may take one or the other of two subjective forms: they may be perceptive feelings or imaginative feelings, depending on the past histories of their subjects, specifically (a) on the relation between the indicative feeling and the physical recognition, and (b) on the presence or absence of significant reversions in the predicative feeling. Note that in neither of the two cases does the subjective form involve consciousness.

In the case of perceptive feelings, the indicative feeling and the physical recognition are the same feeling (i.e., their objective datum is the same); hence this form of propositional feeling "predicates of its logical subjects a character derived from the way in which they are physically felt by that prehending subject" (PR 400). If the predicative feeling has involved no significant reversions, then the perceptive feeling is authentic: i.e., the predicate of the proposition is realized in the nexus of actual entities which are its subjects. This is not to say, however, that the propositional feeling is de facto true. If a transmuted feeling has intervened, the subjects in the nexus have been synthesized into the unity of a nexus physically felt on the basis of a shared eternal object in the definiteness of each, which eternal object is felt initially in a hybrid physical feeling and then in a pure conceptual feeling. But the resultant perceptive feeling does not reveal the manner in which the eternal object was felt by the members of the nexus. It could have originated via a hybrid physical feeling on the part of the members, and hence be a physical fact in the nexus. On the other hand, it could have originated as a conceptual reversion in the subjective processes of the members of the nexus. In the latter case, a perceptive feeling may wrongly attribute to the propositional subjects the physical enjoyment of what was in fact only conceptually entertained. It may exemplify mere concept as physical fact. (For example, a nexus characterized as utopian in a perceptive feeling may consist not of citizens ideally happy in an ideal state, but merely of utopian theorists in a less-than-perfect society. Concept has been transmuted into physical bond.[9] If no such reversions have taken place in the perceived nexus, the perceptive feeling is both authentic and direct: authentic, in that no subjective distortions have intervened; direct, in that a genuine physical bond in the nexus has been seized. When a reverted feeling in the members of the nexus has been transmuted to characterize the nexus, the perceptive feeling, though authentic, is deemed indirect. But when the reverted feeling arises from the predicative feeling in the concrescent subject, the perception is inauthentic: imaginative, in the sense that a novel eternal object has entered the universe; inauthentically imaginative, in that it enters as tied to an object in the actual world. Thus a subjective distortion of the genuine state of affairs in the nexus has occurred.

A propositional feeling of the authentic imaginative species (as opposed to the inauthentic) does not necessarily introduce an objective distortion of the nexus felt, because the predicative feeling derives its eternal

---

[9] The example should be taken as illustrative only, not as an instance of a perceptive feeling.

object not from the indicative feeling, but rather from a physical recognition which has a different datum. This is to say that two distinct physical feelings originate the genuinely imaginative feeling: one, the indicative feeling grasping the nexus of logical subjects; the other, a prehension of a nexus in some sense different from the indicated nexus. It is this latter physical feeling which spawns the physical recognition and the consequent conceptual registration and valuation which yield the predicate. The S–P unity is therefore felt as imaginatively realized (i.e., realized in the concrescent subject), not as a fact in the nexus of the factual past. It cannot be said categorically that an imaginative feeling is always false, however. Its truth or falsity depends on the presence or absence of analogous similarities between the two nexuses physically felt. Even if the proposition is false, it has introduced a novelty into the world, a proposition which may have to "wait" for its logical subjects, but which may further the creative advance of the universe: "in the real world, it is more important that a proposition be interesting [luring the world onward to embody new forms] than that it be true [reiterating what has already been factually achieved]" (PR 395–96).

V · COMPARATIVE FEELINGS[10]

With the appearance of propositions in an actual world and of propositional feelings in concrescent subjects, the way is paved for higher forms of synthesis, more complex integrations, and consequently more intense and immediate satisfactions for concrescent occasions entertaining them. These modes of integration concern not so much new modes of togetherness of items in the actual world as more complex unifications of prior phases in the concrescent subject. Their data are not entities (actual entities, eternal objects, or propositions) per se, but generic contrasts between or among feelings in the concrescence.

To speak of a contrast is to speak of the antithesis of incompatibility. A contrast is a unity achieved in a multiplicity, which unity does not eliminate the multiplicity of the unified items but rather joins those items in a higher unity. A proposition itself is a contrast—a hybrid entity, a new existential type, resulting from the contrasted unity of its subjects and the potential predicative pattern. Such unities, such "new creatures," may themselves enter into contrasts with other unities, yielding structures whose structural pattern reveals depth as well as breadth, intensity rather than triviality, a deepening of the aesthetic character of the result. In order for contrast to overcome incompatibility, however, some ground of congruence must be present—some common element must play a role in each of the opposites to be contrasted. This element may either be an actual

[10] See Figure 4.

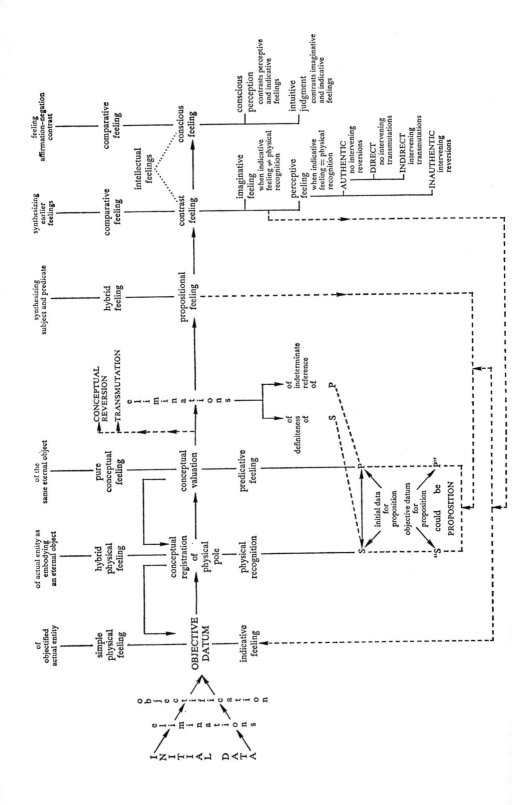

entity or a nexus (as in the case of "this is a dog" and "this is black" integrated in the contrast "this is a black dog,"[11] where the contrast is between two eternal objects functioning in the same nexus) or an eternal object (as in "a gorilla is an anthropoid ape," "an orangutan is an anthropoid ape" integrated in the contrast "gorillas *and* orangutans are anthropoid apes," where the contrast is between two nexuses sharing the same eternal object). By the principle of objective identity, however, one element cannot play two roles in a concrescence without violating the unity of the universe; therefore Whitehead must speak of the common element as one element with a two-way functioning in the contrast—which is not to say that the common element is *felt* twice in the concrescence, but to say that it is felt once initially, and that the feeling has undergone various modifications which reveal its two functions.

The nature of such two-way functioning is revealed most clearly in Whitehead's analysis of the genesis of intellectual (conscious) feelings. In such feelings, the contrasted items are (*a*) the propositional feeling (resulting from the synthesis of the indicative feeling and the predicative feeling derived from the physical recognition as conceptually valued or registered) and (*b*) the original indicative feeling. The common element in both feelings is the actual entity (or entities) whose causal functioning in the prehended nexus provoked the indicative feeling and which was stripped of all character save "this-ness" in the eliminations which produced the subject of the propositional feeling. It is the *same entity* (or entities) in both feelings. The contrast lies in the twofold functioning of that actual entity: as *realized* in the nexus and as a *potential* item integrable in the predicative pattern. This contrast between the facticity and possibility of the same entity (or entities) is termed the affirmation–negation contrast: between what is and what is not but might be.

It is the contrast between the affirmation of objectified fact in the physical feeling, and the mere potentiality, which is the negation of such affirmation, in the propositional feeling. It is the contrast between "*in fact*" and "*might be*," in respect to particular instances in *this* actual world [PR 407].

For Whitehead, the subjective form of feeling this contrast is consciousness. Note here the close analogy to Bergson's analysis of consciousness in *Matter and Memory*. Bergson sees conscious perception as the moment of hesitation between causality received and causality exercised, a hesitation brought about when more than one response is appropriate to the stimulus, when there is a juncture of actuality and possibility. Perception thus delineates for him the outlines of possible actions in the

---

[11] Although verbal propositions will be used as illustrations throughout this section, the reader is reminded that they are to be taken as representing propositional feelings and contrasts in the constitution of a concrescent subject.

world. Whitehead's notion of conscious perception, though less pragmatic than Bergson's, supplies the ontological basis lacking in Bergson's psychological account. It is the "feeling of what is relevant to immediate fact in contrast with its potential irrelevance" (PR 409).

In general terms, perception is the integration of a perceptive feeling and an indicative feeling. As we have already seen, however, perceptive feelings fall into two species, only one of which is always factually true—the direct authentic species. In the instance that such a perceptive feeling undergoes integration (or is "compared") with the original indicative feeling, the factual nexus is confronted "with the potentiality derived from itself, limited to itself, and exemplified in itself" (PR 411). In a word: perception in the mode of symbolic reference has arisen—the vivid display in the present of eternal objects felt as derived from past functionings, the vision of what *could be* because *it was*, of "what the nexus really *is* in the way of potentiality realized" (PR 411). Conscious perception is, therefore, the synthesis via contrast of *was* and *could be* into the immediacy of *is*—the experience of the present as confluence of past (affirmation) and future (negation).

This same character marks conscious perceptions arising from indirect authentic and inauthentic perceptive feelings as well, leaving as an open question how such perceptions, whose truth value is at best uncertain, can be discriminated from direct perceptions, whose truth is infallible. An absolute test is impossible, leaving all conscious perceptions open to fallibility. However, certain criteria are available to enable the perceiver to place relative confidence in those of his perceptions which satisfy the norms. In the first place the "force and vivacity" of a percept—its compelling character—provides some testimony as to its directness and authenticity. This in itself is not, however, sufficient to separate an authentic experience from an experience which is the result of subjective pathology, for delusions can at times feel overpoweringly real. This difficulty can be partially overcome inasmuch as the "insistence" of a percept is a result of its derivation from more primitive feelings within the concrescence, notably the indicative feelings and physical recognitions which initiate and supply the data for the later propositional and perceptual feelings. The vivid consciousness of presentational immediacy indirectly and vaguely illumines these earlier phases, revealing at least the causal efficacy of the end organ as an intensification of the causality of the environment; but even this vague awareness does not vitiate the possibility of a reversion of the sensum transmitted from the environment through the end organ to the conscious occasion. Nor does it raise to consciousness any evidence for the possibility that the entity provoking the indicative feeling may lie within the nexus of the organic body rather than within the external environment, or that the end organ itself is victim to some pathology. The ultimate test of the authenticity of a perceived pink elephant is the oculist, Alcoholics Anonymous, or the plaster cast on an elephant-tromped foot. The ultimate test, in serious terms, is pragmatic: i.e., whether future experience bears out present expectations. From the standpoint of the perceiver, a percept is an hypothesis to be verified inductively in a future occasion of his historic route.

The defining characteristic of conscious perception is, as has been earlier analyzed, the felt unity of the indicative feeling and the physical recognition which initiate the proposition, which, in its turn, is integrated with the indicative feeling to form the percept. The "this" indicated and objectified is the same "this" from which the propositional predicate is derived. In the case of an intuitive judgment, the second species of comparative or intellectual feeling, such an identity is not present. The data integrated in such a judgment are an indicative feeling and an *imaginative* feeling whose datum is a nexus in some degree different from the nexus seized in the indicative feeling. The predicate of the imaginative feeling, that pattern in which the subjects of the indicative feeling are integrable, has been derived from the physical recognition of a different nexus. For example, in the intuitive judgment "this appears to be a platypus," the "this" is an index of the nexus physically felt in the past environment. By the category of conceptual valuation, a complex eternal object is grasped: "furry, duck-billed, oviparous, etc." From the integration of this eternal object with the indicative feeling, a perceptive feeling emerges, which when integrated with the indicative feeling yields a conscious perception of a curious creature swimming around in its zoo environment. In another physical feeling, a signboard on the wire enclosure is grasped, which, via a physical recognition, is conceptually registered as a picture of a furry, duck-billed, etc., animal with the word "platypus" lettered beneath it.[12] A predicative feeling is formed: an eternal object "platypus" is grasped as a possible pattern exemplifiable in a nexus of actual entities. The resultant propositional feeling of the imaginative species integrates the predicate derived from the sign with the "this" (or indicative feeling) of the furry creature in its pool. It is this initial disconnection—of the logical subjects of the indicative feeling as involved in their factual pattern, and of the predicative pattern derived from the sign—which must be overcome; otherwise two sets of actual entities are playing identical roles in the intuitive judgment and the Category of Objective Diversity has been violated. The indicative feeling and physical recognition of the sign are negatively prehended, and replaced in the intuitive synthesis by

[12] Obviously, several intervening steps are skipped over here for the sake of simplicity: those which would evaluate the picture as a representation or symbol of a kind of animal, and the configuration of letters as a word conventionally signifying the pictured animal.

the indicative feeling of the animal, potentially unified by the predicate "platypus." Like any negative prehension, the negation of the sign-feeling adds its subjective form to the synthesis: the platypus-watcher–sign-reader knows that the eternal object "platypus" did not float into his mind *ex nihilo*. Therefore, there is again a two-way functioning of actual entities in the intuitive judgment: the prehended nexus is also subject of the predicative pattern of the imaginative feeling; hence the two feelings are integrable. The affirmation–negation contrast is manifested in the twofold function of the nexus: as actually involved in the furry animal pattern, and as potentially structurable in the "platypus" pattern. In the case that the indicated nexus and the nexus from which the predicate is drawn are virtually identical (e.g., the platypus recognized *vs.* the platypus presentationally objectified) the intuitive judgment approaches a conscious perception. On the other hand, when in conscious perception there are significant reversions in the perceptive feeling integrated with the indicative feeling, conscious perception approaches intuitive judgment.

A similar two-way function of an eternal object is possible in certain modalities of intuitive judgment. In the instance that the pattern exemplified in the prehended nexus (and conceptually registered via a derived physical recognition) and the predicative pattern derived from the physical feeling and recognition of the alternative nexus are identical (e.g., the eternal object "platypus" grasped yesterday and today), the proposition (imaginative feeling) is felt as cohering with the nexus physically felt in the indicative feeling. The absence of any contrast between the two eternal objects over and above the exemplification–potentiality, affirmation–negation contrast renders the intuitive judgment a "yes-judgment" characterized by the subjective form (emotional pattern) of belief.[13] In the event, however, that additional material contrast exists between the two eternal objects, a pseudo-contrast without a concomitant ground of identity, the judgment is a judgment of the "no" form. "This animal in the platypus pool is not a platypus." The subjective form of the "this is a platypus" judgment in this case is disbelief—a feeling of the falsity of the proposition, its lack of coherence with the primary feelings in the propositional feeler. The feeling of explicit negation, of "what might have been and is not," restores to the propositional predicate what had been eliminated from it in the negative prehension which had rendered the original valuation (e.g., "platypus") apt for synthesis in a proposition: namely, its full scope of potentiality as unbound by the exigencies of par-

---

[13] It should be carefully noted that "truth" and "falsity" are in no way characteristics of intuitive judgments. As has been remarked earlier, only propositions can be true or false: true if the predicative pattern is actually exemplified in the nexus of propositional subjects; false if it is not. The "yes"-judgment judges "S is P" believingly; the "no"-judgment disbelievingly. In both cases, the result is heightened intensity in experience and heightened importance for elements in the data.

ticular modes of ingression. To express this phenomenon in the language of classical logic: whereas the predicate of an affirmative proposition is particular (that is, the subject set is part of the predicate set), the predicate of a negative judgment is always universal (the subject set having been excluded from any coincidence with the predicate set). The eternal object is seized in its full, abstract, indeterminate potentiality: not as having been derived from a physical feeling as in conceptual valuation, not as potentially exemplifiable in a physical nexus as in a proposition, but in its pure character as an eternal object. Thus, the negative judgment, the judgment of propositional falsity, constitutes the peak operation of the conceptual pole of an actual entity.

In the more common case, the instance that the nexus pattern and imaginative predicate exemplify both partial identity *and* partial diversity in their compared structure, judgment is suspended. This is not to say that no judgment is made, for then the concrescence would reach the stalemated situation of an unresolvable opposition between physical and conceptual feelings. An affirmative judgment cannot be made because of the elements of diversity in the two eternal objects; a negative judgment cannot be made because of the identical features in the two patterns. What confronts the concrescent subject is the ground for a compatible contrast between the two patterns and an opportunity for grasping additional information about the nexus pattern, the seed ground for novel hypotheses: "Could this be a female platypus? An immature animal? a mutant?" etc. The suspense forms allow knowledge to grow beyond the hard and fast limits imposed by the objectivity of conscious perception.

The subjective form of all variants of the intuitive judgment is characterized by "*attention* to truth" (PR 419; emphasis added); that is, by attention to the coherence, incoherence, or partial coherence of the nexus pattern and the imaginative predicate. Not all judgments need to be so preoccupied with the world; if they were, then a concrescence could never escape its bondage to the facts, could never initiate novelty. If, however, "belief," "disbelief," "suspense"—the subjective forms of "attention to truth"—are not the relevant qualifiers of a judgmental feeling; if, instead, it is qualified by "*inattention* to truth" (PR 419; emphasis added), the concrescence takes flight on the wings of imagination. In the imaginative judgment, a break with nature as exemplified in the actual world is effected, a readiness to negatively prehend the patterns in the actual world enters the concrescent subject as a result of its subjective aim, and the wellsprings of genuine creativity are opened, a creativity not rigidly controlled by objective data and given free reign to fathom the depths of limitless possibility. In the imaginative judgment, the universe moves forward in creative advance, new forms luring new data to exemplify them—genuinely creative, non-imitative art which elicits new universes, new concrete values, new civilizations, theoretical breakthroughs. The readiness to break with the past, with tradition, and to envision what could be even though it is now impossible, draws the advancing cosmos toward richer and deeper satisfactions of the creative urge. Without such untied imagination, progress is merely the better mousetrap, the more thoroughly explicated theory—elaborated traditionalism, with its ultimate consequences of staleness, boredom, and triviality.

Intellectual feelings generally characterize high-grade organisms, those in which the flickerings of consciousness assume important roles in their satisfactions. As has been seen already, that which makes such feelings capable of being grasped with the subjective form of consciousness, or, to put the matter in an alternative mode of expression, that which *presences* such feelings, making them reveal a contemporary world rather than record past facts, is the functioning of significant affirmation–negation contrasts in the concrescence, by means of which the illumination of past fact by future possibility consciously realizes the present nexus.

Less sophisticated comparative feelings characterize lower-grade organisms, actual entities lacking sufficient complexity in their actual worlds to elicit affirmation–negation contrasts and yet capable of grasping contrasts of a less abstract modality. Such comparative feelings are termed "physical purposes": "physical" because of the more important role played by physical feelings; "purposes" because intellective function, in its integration with physical functioning, intensifies the degree to which the concrescent subject becomes a private, self-creative creature rather than a perspectival re-enactment of the environment.

The principal differentiation between the mode of functioning in any of the sorts of physical purposes and that characterizing intellectual operations of the conscious variety lies in the manner in which the valued eternal object is grasped. As analyzed earlier, in the conceptual valuation propaedeutic to propositional feeling, the eternal object is stripped of its determinate reference to the data exemplifying it and seized in its full indetermination as a form for *any* possible fact. It is this elimination of the particularity of the eternal object which renders the affirmation–negation contrast possible between the eternal object as exemplified and as a germane form-of-definiteness. In the conceptual functioning which initiates physical purposes, this negation-of-exemplification is absent, leaving only a pure affirmation of the eternal object *as* exemplified in the data, its indeterminate aspects valued as negligible or insignificant to the concrescence. Note the functioning of the Category of Subjective Harmony here. A more abstract seizure of the eternal object would be inconsonant with the subjective aim of the concrescence, and would vitiate the emergent superjective value, in the same manner as blatant incompatibilities in the initial data and resultant physical feelings would, according to the Category of Subjective Unity, yield a trivial satisfaction.

In the conceptual feelings involved in physical purposes, the eternal object is prehended as a pure potential *in this mode of ingression*: as the warmth of *this* fire, the thirst-quenching character of *this* glass of water, etc. With this understanding of the mode of conceptual operation involved, the schema of integrations in physical purposes becomes easy to trace.

Two principal modes are implicated, determined by the absence or presence of reversions in the conceptual feelings. In the most primitive sort of physical purpose, no conceptual reversion intervenes. The nexus is physically felt, its pattern grasped in a hybrid physical feeling of the eternal object constituting the pattern; the pattern itself is conceptually felt as the pattern-in-the-fact, and this conceptual feeling integrated with the original physical feeling. As an integration of two feelings, some ground of unification, some identity (contrast), must be present; otherwise the integration would be an incoherent summation. The contrast lies in the two-way functioning of the eternal object: as felt in the physical feeling and as valued in the conceptual feeling. The subjective form of the integration (its value in the concrescence and its pragmatic value to be superjected to the future) can be either adversion or aversion. If adversion, the integration has been valued up as a result of its contribution to the "fleshing out" of the subjective aim of the concrescence, and that valuation tends to secure the propagation of like integrations in future occasions of the same historic thread. But if the integration has been valued down, if its subjective form is aversion, the propagation of like integrations is weakened for the future; change is called for. Aversional purposes might therefore seem to serve a valuable function for an historic route of occasions. They do not, however, because the change called for is of a negative sort—one characterizable as a loss of data for the future, an impoverishment of the environment which abandons relevant possibilities—rather than the creative momentum introduced by negative or imaginative judgment which lures the world onward toward novelty.

The second species of physical purposes serves the function of deepening the intensity of satisfaction in lower-grade entities, because such feelings introduce additional levels of conceptual functioning: namely, reversions. Two categories are operative here: (*a*) the already mentioned Category of Conceptual Reversion whereby the valuation of the exemplified eternal object generates a grasp of an eternal object relevant to but not embodied in the data;[14] and (*b*) the Category of Transmutation, whereby what is merely conceptually entertained in a superject is physically felt by subsequent subjects. By the Category of Subjective Intensity, any subject's aim is at intensity: in its own satisfaction and in the relevant future, particularly in future occasions of its own route. Such intensity is gained through the integration of data via contrasts and lost when incom-

---

[14] E.g., the instinctive reversion of the valuation of water-as-thirst-quenching to water-as-soothing-a-burn.

patibilities must be negatively prehended. When eternal objects can be felt together in contrasted unity, intensity deepens; hence the subjective aim of any concrescence is at the realization of more and more complex contrasts, which themselves can be synthesized into systematic structures of contrasted contrasts, yielding aesthetic satisfactions evidencing both balance and complexity.

The appearance of reverted feelings in physical purposes provides the data for such complexity even on the level of relatively low-grade occasions. When a reverted feeling is derived from a conceptual valuation, the two feelings have a common ground which makes their contrasted unification possible, and have as well the conceptual diversity which makes the contrast significant for the concrescence. The integration of the initial physical feeling and the contrasted eternal objects deepens the intensity of the comparative feeling. Furthermore, for actual occasions involved in the historic routes termed personal orders, what is felt as a conceptual reversion in one occasion of the route is physically felt by its successor, which, upon conceptually registering the prior reversion, initiates its own reversion: a conceptual grasp of the physically recognized eternal object grasped by the initial occasion. The result of this repeated "swing" from physical grasp of an eternal object as factually realized to a conceptual reversion of a related eternal object, which reversion itself becomes fact for future physical feelings, introduces a periodic character into the route, an overarching rhythmic pattern of "vibrations" between the two eternal objects in the contrast. The rhythmic pattern itself provides additional contrasts for occasions in the route, and hence additional intensity and complexity in the individual satisfactions composing the personal order. It serves the same function as meter in poetry or rhythm in music—deepening the aesthetic experience through unity in diversity, diversity in unity. The occasion has

> the weight of repetition, the intensity of contrast, and the balance between the two factors of the contrast. . . . An intense experience is an aesthetic fact, and its categoreal conditions are to be generalized from aesthetic laws in the particular arts. . . . "All aesthetic experience is feeling arising out of the realization of contrast under identity" [PR 426–27].

5

THE THEORY OF EXTENSION

(PR, Part IV)

I · COORDINATE DIVISION

AS SEEN IN THE PREVIOUS SECTION, the genetic analysis of an actual entity reveals a non-linear succession of feelings and phases growing out of and integrating with each other until they reach the fully determinate unity of feeling which is the satisfaction. "The problem dominating the concrescence is the actualization [of a spatio-temporal] quantum *in solido*" (PR 434), a solution made possible by the immanence of the subject in all phases of its self-creation. Therefore, despite the fact that an actual occasion realizes an *extended* temporal duration, that quantum of time is indivisible. The same must be said of the spatial region actualized in a concrescence. It is an indivisible unit of real space, interlocked with all other regions because of its actualization of the general schematic relations of the extensive continuum it atomizes. The concrescence presupposes the region in the same way as any perspective on a spatial region presupposes the interlocked geometric relations of the perspective. But the region does not elicit the concrescence, which is to say that, in any given spatial extensity, not all possible perspectives must be realized. Which are and which are not realized is contingent upon the possibilities for subjectification in the region, derived from God as initial subjective aims. In abstraction from actualization, any region is divisible; when, however, it becomes the perspective for a concrescence, it acquires the same actual undividedness as the concrescence itself, an undividedness derived from the unity of the subjective aim. However, given the *abstract* divisibility of a region as extended, this potential for division carries over into the perspectively actualized region and is reflected in the potential divisibility of the satisfaction. The plurality of interwoven physical feelings patterned into the unity of feeling of the superject is still a plurality: i.e., the many feelings are separable, yet they are inseparate. They are separable in that the aspects which make each feeling itself and not other can be described without explicit reference to the entire concrescence.

Coordinate division is therefore the isolation of the separable elements in the inseparate unity of the satisfaction. In genetic analysis, which is likewise an analysis of these separable elements, the emphasis is placed on the feelings themselves: their arising, structure, subjective forms, integration, and comparison. Coordinate division, as an analysis of the concrete superject emergent from the process of feeling, concentrates on the fully determinate, unified space–time region actualized in the concrescence and distinguishes in it the sub-regions, extensive quanta, and standpoints which *might* be. Therefore, it is primarily the data from the physical pole of an entity which are susceptible to coordinate analysis.

It is imperative to realize that an actualized region is not merely spatial, despite the fact that all the language which perforce must be used to describe extensity is based on spatial imagery. A concrete region has both spatial and temporal extensity, both of which are defined in the process whereby the actual world is created by the joint activities of the past, the concrescent occasion, and God.

Whitehead's conception of the actual world as a "medium" is an explication of this understanding of extensity. When a region is considered as having "time-depth," and particularly when it is populated by enduring objects and strands of personal order, the causal influences physically felt by a concrescent occasion multiply to an unimaginable degree. Perhaps the simplest analogue is to be found in Bergson's description of memory. For Bergson, the totality of the relevant past is funneled into and operative in the present moment. Thus the past is not past in the dead, sterile sense in which it is normally viewed. It is agency having been lifted into the present to meet the exigencies of the "now."[1] For Whitehead, this becomes the vector reception of the past in the present, whereby the past is present as determining, operative agency pregnant with possibilities for novel synthesis. The actual world is the spatio-temporal medium through which this agency is conducted.[2]

If we take Whitehead's example of a simplistic actual world, one in which X, the concrescent occasion, feels the personal order A–B–C, X feels not only C, the most recent member of the chain, but A and B as well: A as objectified in B, and A–B as objectified in C. What is given as the decided conditions for X is not, therefore, merely C's contribution to the actual world, but A's and B's as well, through the mediacy of C. If A, B, and C are previous moments in the personal order of X, they "exist" *in* X as the active memories out of which X creates its present.

An actual world is therefore filled with chains of objectifications, chains

---

[1] The difference between Bergson and Whitehead lies in Bergson's exclusion of spatiality from his analyses, since "space" for Bergson is a product of the intellect.

[2] That I use the language of agency with respect to the functioning of the past in the present is the other face of the same bias which prompts me to use "superject" as a verb. I see the past not as an inert welter whose formal structures are re-enacted in the present, but as a multiplicity of vectors, of trajectories, of thrusts, attaining the unity of a novel subject in the present.

of time, so to speak, so that the present is a summation of the world history decided for it. As pointed out in the discussions of SMW, it is fatal to conceive these chains via a linear, "beads-on-a-string" model. Each link subsumes the previous ones, lifts them into itself as part of its own constitution. Time is perpetually growing in "extensity," not in "length," in the same manner as that in which memory is continually growing in the richness of its content.

As has been stressed before, this wealth of data decided for a concrescence does not leave the concrescent occasion decisionless—without any leeway for subjective functioning. The aspect of this leeway already analyzed in the treatment of genetic division has to do with the subjective appropriation of decided data, an appropriation personalized through a rush of private emotional feeling consonant with the subjective aim. The other aspect of this leeway, that relevant to a discussion of coordinate analysis, has to do with an emergent occasion's choice of the quantum to be actualized.[3] Unless the crude, Newtonian, absolutist notion of space and time as containers is abandoned, this doctrine is absolutely meaningless. There can be no notion of absolute spatio-temporal positions haunting the background of understanding: no homogeneous space with absolute coordinates, no homogeneous time ranging its contents in absolute and rigid sequences. What is at issue here is the relativity of time and of position in time, of space and of position in space, a relativity stemming from the fact that the rate of transmission of vector feeling-tone from past to present is not necessarily uniform for all types of feeling-tone, and that the "speed" of transmission has an upper limit in our cosmic epoch (the speed of light). Every entity in a very real sense "decides" its own time and space, is not bound to a universal schema, decides what will be past for it—i.e., operative in its constitution.[4]

The basis for the possibility of coordinate division is that aspect of the genesis of an actual entity which concerns the reception of vector feeling-tone—the operations of its physical pole, for only with respect to the physical pole is it legitimate to speak of a genuine multiplicity of initial feelings. It is not appropriate to speak of a discrete multiplicity of con-

---

[3] It is important to note the self-referential character of Whitehead's doctrine at this point. It would be all too easy to view both genetic and coordinate division as analyses performed by philosophers in their search for the ultimate metaphysical structures of the real. This view is, indeed, correct. But philosophical analysis is authentic rather than mythological only because it is a further refinement of an analytic activity performed by any entity in its self-creative process. In arising out of an actual world, any occasion, be it an occasion of highly reflective philosophical thought or an occasion of brute, non-conscious energy transfer, performs genetic and coordinate divisions upon the entities in its past.

[4] In Whitehead as in Bergson (see his *Matter and Memory*), memory funnels into the present—i.e., literally, makes present—those aspects of the past which are relevant to the present situation of the organism.

ceptual feelings, for each is a specification of the subjective aim qualifying the appropriation of the initial data. In abstraction from conceptual feeling, there are as many physical feelings as there are efficient causalities to be felt. Therefore, it is legitimate to consider each physical feeling as though it had its own subject,[5] as though the satisfied entity were a synthesis of a plurality of physical feelers. Therefore, the extensive region actualized in a concrescence can be viewed as divisible into a plurality of sub-regions, each the "object" or actual world of a distinct physical feeling. For entities in which conceptual feeling never achieves significant importance, physical feelings *almost* assume the character of independent entities.

In its structure, a coordinate division is a contrast—the unification of a diversity on the basis of a communally shared element. One pole of the contrast is the satisfied entity felt into the concrescence; the other is a proposition whose subject is a physical feeling in that entity and whose predicate is that aspect of the total geometric pattern exemplified by the satisfied occasion supplied by the potentially divisible sub-region which is the actual world of the physical feeling. Before the contrast can be effected, all the physical data from the other sub-regions must be eliminated through negative prehensions, as must any valued eternal objects derived from those sub-regions. With these eliminations and negative prehensions, the subject of the proposition is the physical element in the satisfied occasion which is derivable from the sub-region in question. Thus, the subject is a potential actual entity—the entity which would emerge from the concrescence of *just* that sub-region; the predicate is the potential way of patterning that abstracted subject. The communality which makes the contrast possible is that existing between the satisfied entity functioning as a whole and under an aspect of itself, and between the subjective form of the fully unified feeling and the abstracted feeling.

Since the propositional pole of the contrast does not cohere with the actual world of the satisfied subject (inasmuch as its subjective aim has been negatively prehended and with it the unity of both concrescent subject and actual world), the proposition is false—which is to say that the mental operations under the hypothesis of the proposition (which considers *one* of the physical feelings of the propositional subject as if it were the total subject) are not those of the parent entity from which the propositional subject was abstracted. However, with qualifications, the proposition is a matrix from which true propositions concerning the sub-regions can be deduced.[6]

---

[5] Since in the abstraction from conceptual functioning, the unitary subject is precisely what is abstracted from.

[6] In the example used earlier, to claim that, given X feeling the actual world B,

What arises from the process of coordinate division is the ability to keep irrelevant physical extensity out of the appropriation of an important region. By analogy, it is impossible to do plane geometry without eliminating the extra spatial and temporal dimensions. Historical study would not be possible unless an epoch could be isolated from the world-historical mesh. The point being made is that reality is incurably atomic, an interweaving of unbreakable nets of actual worlds, extensive standpoints, and perspectival regions. Through the abstractions of coordinate division, that solidity can be indefinitely divided into spatial and/or temporal sub-regions—isolated systems—about which qualified true statements can be made.

What keeps the coordinate divisions performed by any concrescent occasion from fragmenting the universe into as many regions and sub-regions as there are perspectives and physical feelings is the fact that the entire atomic yet abstractly divisible multiplicity of regions and sub-regions is enmeshed in the systematic interconnections of the extensive continuum, which both ground the possibility of indefinite subdivision and at the same time keep potentially unified the plurality of spaces, times, and space–times the division effects. Thus, the extensive continuum not only ensures a common worldliness for concrescent occasions, preventing them from degenerating into windowless monads linked only through a divinely pre-established harmony, but provides as well the primal unity which makes abstract divisibility possible. In other language: it is the condition both for the possibility of the formation of internal relations and for the laying out of external relations. Finally, the phenomenon of extensive connection between regions explored in a coordinate division makes possible the unification of the manifold threads in a nexus into the experience of *one thing*, be it man or moon or mountain.

In summary, therefore, extensive connection—the public interlocking of regions and sub-regions revealed in coordinate division—is the primary relationship among physical occasions and makes all other relations, both internal and external, possible. Indefinable in itself, it manifests certain formal properties which can be analyzed, although which of these properties are metaphysical and which are idiosyncratic to our four-dimensional space–time is a moot point. Certainly, coordinate divisibility, with its relationships of connection, inclusion, overlap, etc., is metaphysi-

---

C and D, C is northeast of D is false, if "northeast of D" is taken to express the

$$
\begin{array}{cc}
\text{B} & \text{\textit{A}} \\
\text{x} \cdots \text{A} \cdots \text{C} & \text{N} \\
\text{D} & \text{I}
\end{array}
$$

full determinateness of C. If, however, it is taken as an abstraction, it is a true statement of a limited relation between B and C.

cal; but the more precise geometrical relationships are more than likely provincial.[7]

Coordinate division reveals the public character of the world, its routes of causal transference, its mode of extensive connection. The privacy of the world is manifest only in genetic division. The necessary interdependence of both modes of analysis overcomes the foundational subject–object, private–public bifurcation which has plagued philosophy since Descartes. It is the public world which is extended, quantifiable, measurable, determined; the private suffers alone, creates alone, enjoys alone, in its subjective autonomy. But what is suffered, created, and enjoyed in privacy becomes a public contribution to the universe, a condition imposed on all future creativity. Neither pole can be stressed at the expense of the other. If all is public, then B. F. Skinner's theory of operant conditioning is the ultimate metaphysical generalization, but one which cannot account for the origination of publicity. If all is private, then the laurels go to Leibniz, who in turn cannot account for publicity without reducing God to an overworked secretary, eternally inscribing worlds within worlds. All is *both* public *and* private, *both* objective *and* subjective, *both* autonomous *and* determined.

The world of fact is not alone in displaying the dialectical unity of the public and the private. It is likewise manifest in the prehensions which are ingredient in fact. Every prehension, be it physical or conceptual, initiates from a public datum which is then privatized through emotive or valuative subjective forms. A prehension *is* the making private of what is public, for only then can it be republicized, which is to say that public and private have no meaning apart from their conjugation. Without the public data, no private assimilation could come about; without the private assimilation, no new public data could come about. Each is for the sake of the other and cannot be torn from the other. Each is what the other makes it to be.

The same wedding of public and private is manifest in the world of eternal objects. Forms have a threefold function in the world of fact: (*a*) they are the public patterns, the public relations and connections, displayed in actual entities or nexuses; (*b*) they are the private emotional elements clothing feelings with subjective forms; and (*c*) they are the objects of pure conceptual or propositional feelings, grasped either in their generality or as relevant to an indicated nexus. This latter mode of implication is, however, the valuation of either the public pattern grasped or of the subjective form of the grasp with respect to its importance in the con-

---

[7] ". . . this planet, or this nebula in which our sun is placed, may be gradually advancing towards a change in the general character of its spatial relations. Perhaps in the dim future mankind, if it then exists, will look back to the queer, contracted three-dimensional universe from which the nobler, wider existence has emerged" (MT 79).

crescent subject. The three functions thereby reduce to two: (a) objectively functioning eternal objects—exemplified forms, vehicles of objectification, relational patterns; and (b) subjectively functioning eternal objects—emotional, evaluative, purposive, comparative forms personalizing prehensions. The former are the mathematical Platonic forms: the patterns structuring the public world into a medium through which causality is transmitted, the forms discoverable in a coordinate division. The latter, although transferred from object to subject in feeling (for prehension is feeling the *feeling* in another), enhance the intensity of feeling in the feeling subject; the objective forms structure the causality received.[8]

What precisely happens in a coordinate division is that all eternal objects of the subjective type are negatively prehended, and the entire analysis proceeds "objectively"—on the basis of objective, Platonic, mathematical forms:[9]

the subjective forms of feelings are only explicable by the categoreal demands arising from the unity of the subject. Thus the coordinate division of an actual entity produces feelings whose subjective forms are partially eliminated and partially inexplicable. But this mode of division preserves undistorted the elements of definiteness introduced by eternal objects of the objective species [PR 447].

The objective forms most fundamental to coordinate division, and hence those most significant to the metaphysician, are those structuring the most basic modes of extensive connection in the present cosmic epoch: i.e., the ways in which the extensive regions realized in the concrescence of occasions are systematically interconnected.

II · EXTENSIVE CONNECTION

The point of Whitehead's foray into geometry is at first totally obscured by the intricacies of his exposition. The goal in his analysis of the possible relations among regions is to prepare the way for the construction of purely formal definitions of the basic geometric elements such as point, line, plane, surface, and volume, definitions which do not have to refer illegitimately to existents or metric elements for their definiteness. If mathematical forms are the public structures of the world, then they must be "prior" to the world in the sense that they do not depend on either existential or epistemic events for their definition. They thus must be comprehensible in total abstraction from actuality. They must be purely

[8] For example, given a thread of conscious occasions experiencing anger as a result of an insult: the present occasion feels the objectivity of the insult and the angry appropriation of that insult by occasions in its past; hence it feels the insult (objective eternal object) angrily (intensified subjective form inherited from the past).

[9] As B. F. Skinner once put it, "Physics did not advance by looking more closely at the jubilance of a falling body" (*Beyond Freedom and Dignity* [New York: Bantam, 1972], p. 12).

formal: given *in* experience as its structure and not defined *through* experience.

The basic elements of geometry as Euclid construed them are a hopeless muddle of formal and quasi-existential definitions. His definition of a point as "that of which there is no part" is clearly formal, but when in his first postulate he states " 'Let the following be postulated: to draw a straight line from any point to any point' " (PR 460), the point suddenly becomes an existent of a very curious sort to be the term of the "from–to" relationship. This strange intermixing of "ultimate physical things of a very peculiar character" (PR 461) and purely formal structures pervades Euclidean geometry. The straight line is another instance. For Euclid, it is a line which " 'lies evenly with the points on itself' " (PR 460), yet the non-metric notion of "evenness" is vague and inexplicable in purely formal terms. The modern attempt at clarification, which defines a line as "the shortest distance between two points," introduces a metric term (shortest distance) when no purely formal basis for measurement has been established, and virtually implies a route of occurrences in the "space" between the points.

Since Whitehead's ultimate goal is to give a purely formal account of the interrelations of actual worlds in general and in particular of the geometric relations between regions which are displayed in presentational immediacy and undergird the objectivity of symbolic reference, he must commence by doing a meta-geometry to place the science of extension and its basic geometric elements on a purely formal footing. No admixture of formal and physical definitions is allowable, because the abstractions of coordinate division have to do solely with the formal structural relations of regions, inasmuch as the negative prehension of subjective functioning has left behind only purely objective structures—undifferentiated regions with their possibilities for subdivision and interconnection.

Whitehead's earlier attempt to found geometry on basic definitions derived from the fundamental relationship of "extending over" (see PNK 101)—which in ordinary language is the whole–part relation—had led to theoretical difficulties in the definition of basic geometric elements. If one is to use the whole–part paradigm, one must introduce the notion of exact boundaries delimiting the part; but to do this is to introduce surreptitiously precisely the geometric element one wishes to define on the basis of the whole–part relation: the line. Hence Whitehead's gratitude to Professor de Laguna's notion of extensive connection as a more advantageous starting point, for through relations of inclusion the necessity for exact boundaries can be circumvented and implicit circularity avoided in the resultant definitions.

Whitehead's meta-geometric analysis of the modes of connection between regions has metaphysical as well as mathematical import, for in describing the ways in which abstract regions can relate to each other, he is giving the formal basis for the ways in which entities can be objectified in each other and for the character of the actual world as a medium across which physical disturbances can be propagated. Since Newtonian space–time and its physical counterpart, the ether, had fallen victim to the Einsteinian ax, it was imperative that a new schematization of energy transfer be constructed to overcome the specters of *actio in distans* on the one hand and Zeno's paradoxes of motion on the other. The metaphysical question as Whitehead sees it reduces to this: If it is the case that each actual occasion arises out of an actual world unique to it, how can actual worlds enter into subsequent concrescences as subordinate nexuses in the actual worlds of those entities? The question, as proposed in coordinate analysis, translates: How can the atomic region actualized in a superject be connected with other such regions? The question itself requires clarification. Granted: an actual world is always unique to the entity whose concrescence it is; however, since in doing coordinate division the subjectivity of the entity (and hence the emotional appropriation and valuation of the items in that actual world) is abstracted from, the abstraction (which is an abstraction of the superject from the subject–superject) leaves as representative of the actual world an atomic region.[10] For example, if the original physical situation was one in which entity *a* arising from the concrescence of actual world A, which actual world "contained" *b* and its actual world B as a datum for *a*'s feelings, a coordinate analysis would negatively prehend the subjectivity of both *a* and *b*, leaving only two extensies, one somehow "contained" in the other. The question central to coordinate analysis becomes "What are the universal and formal properties of extension which yield such relationships and hence are the condition for the possibility of energy transfer from one spatio-temporal quantum to another?" Furthermore, since the physical sciences have to do with the *measurement* of such transfers, and since measurement is always performed within the presentational immediacy of the measurer,[11] how

[10] To speak of *atomic* regions seems to imply, however, regions which are external and unrelated to each other, like an assemblage of monads. It is precisely this misinterpretation of Whitehead's notion of atomic which must be overcome if the logic of extensive connection is to be comprehensible. Each region *is* the totality of space–time realized for the perspective. It must be continually borne in mind that an actual entity and its actual world cannot be torn apart as subject and object. From one perspective, the actual entity *is* its actual world as having grown together. From the alternative perspective, an actual world is the spatio-temporal totum which superjects the actual entity. Therefore, the regions analyzed in coordinate division are not extensive frameworks *in which* actual entities are inserted, but the extensity of the actual entity itself.

[11] It is important to remember that presentational immediacy is the sheer display of the as yet unatomized, unfactualized present as a continuum in which actualization *could* occur, and that hence presentational immediacy does not measure facts which are, but facts which could be.

does science escape being the private dream of an individual scientist "with a taste for the daydream of publication" (PR 502)? To ground (a) the possibility for the transfer of energy from event to event (the objectification of the past in the present), (b) the systematic regular interconnections of events, and (c) the objectivity of the sorts of symbolic reference performed in the scientific endeavor (where the sheer display of geometrized regions decorated with sense data is taken to have genuine causal facts as its meaning), Whitehead is compelled to develop a purely formal account (i.e., in terms of public eternal objects alone) of the systematic interconnections of things—indeed, of systematic interconnection as such—an account which excludes the intrusion of any eternal objects of the subjective variety and hence prescinds from the experience of the concrescent occasion (be it electron or scientist) as subject. In other words, he must develop a theory of extensive relations which depends for its explication, not upon experienced facts, but merely upon purely formal notions of the utmost generality.

Whitehead begins his derivations with only two indefinables or "primitive" notions: "region" and "connection." The former contains no implication of precise boundaries circumscribing regions, for these could only be lines, surfaces, or volumes—eternal objects of the public objective sort which are discovered *in* experience (in presentational immediacy), and experience is bracketed in coordinate analysis. Nor is "region" to be considered as having spatial, temporal, dimensional, or metric connotations. It is to be taken as denoting mere "spread"—extensity is its most general form. Regions are merely "the relata which are involved in the scheme of 'extensive connection'" (PR 449). The second primitive notion, "connection," has no intrinsic meaning other than regional relationship. Its formal properties are what are to be deduced in the subsequent analyses. The goal of the entire endeavor is to develop a purely formal account of the connections between regions and of the geometric elements given in perception which will undergird the organic character of process and demonstrate the objectivity of the scientific enterprise by showing that modes of connection and geometric elements are themselves objective— being what they are in total independence of their inclusion in any experience. In the language of geometry, Whitehead is searching for invariants, for formal structures which retain their identity under various sorts of transformations.[12]

---

[12] An interesting analogy appears when Chapters 2 to 5 of PR are compared with the four major levels of geometry. Whitehead's chapter "Extensive Connection" seeks topological invariants; "Flat Loci" concerns the formal character of straightness (and flatness) which is preserved through a projective transformation; "Strains" can be related to the invariants of affine geometry (where in its early years the term "strain" was used); "Measurement" concerns the least general invariants, those

The first step beyond the primitive notions is accomplished in the definition of mediate connection. Presupposing no information save that already contained in the primitive notions, Whitehead can affirm that "two regions are 'mediately' connected when they are both connected with a third region" (PR 450). The definition says no more than what it says: i.e., it does not specify *how* the two regions are connected with the third or whether the relation is transitive.

A second elementary type of connection is what in ordinary language would be termed the whole–part relation—a relation of inclusion such that if A includes B, every region connected with B will also be connected with A. Thus, in Figure 5, C and D, as regions connected with B, are also connected with A. The language of inclusion, although conveying the same idea of asymmetrical connection found in the whole–part relation, avoids

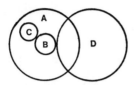

FIGURE 5

the problematic inherent in the language of the latter, for whole and part have meaning only in terms of precise boundaries, and, as mentioned earlier, the types of elements which can serve as boundaries have not been formally defined as yet (nor can they be, given only the primitive notions and the derived notion of the mediate connection).

From the definition of inclusion as a derivative type of connection, Whitehead can proceed to define a specification of inclusion which he terms "overlapping"—a situation occurring when a third region is included in both of two regions (see Figure 6). In the two instances illus-

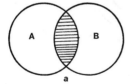

FIGURE 6

trated, the shaded region (the shared element in 6a or the totality of B as included in A in 6b) is termed the intersect of the two regions. It is ob-

---

forming the object of the metric geometries. (I am indebted to Paul Shields, currently a doctoral candidate at Fordham University, for pointing these correlations out to me.)

vious that regions can overlap with any number of intersects (6a and 6b illustrate unique intersects; Figure 7 is an instance of multiple intersects).

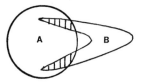

FIGURE 7

Using the notion of overlap, Whitehead is able to define a third type of connection: external connection. "Two regions are 'externally' connected when (i) they are connected, and (ii) they do not overlap" (PR 453). Figure 8 illustrates two types of external connection. Within the context of the notions already derived, it is not possible to distinguish 8a from 8b

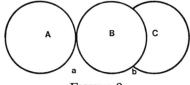

FIGURE 8

formally. However, the formal content of external connection, as contained in the definition, makes it possible to specify further the kinds of inclusion. In Figure 9, B is non-tangentially included in A because there is no third region externally connected to both A and B. All regions connected with B are *included* in A.

FIGURE 9

However, in both cases in Figure 10 there are regions externally connected with B (region C for instance) which are externally connected with A as well.

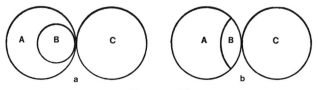

FIGURE 10

From these preliminary examinations of the possible modes of connection between regions, Whitehead proceeds to what is the main point at issue for him: the attempt to construct purely formal definitions of the principal elements of geometry, definitions which do not lock geometry into any metric and hence possibly idiosyncratic framework relative to a particular cosmic epoch or region of a cosmos. The entry point is through the notion of an abstractive set: "A set of regions is called an 'abstractive set,' when (i) any two members of the set are such that one of them includes the other non-tangentially, (ii) there is no region included in every member of the set" (PR 454). Some type of model is necessary to clarify this fundamental notion if the further analyses which yield the definition of point, line, etc., are to be comprehensible to the non-mathematician. For the sake of simplicity, I will use a one-dimensional set (although dimensionality is as yet a notion to be clarified) with no specification as to whether the set is one dimensionally "straight" or "curved," since these notions have not been differentiated. For purposes of illustration, although the set may be infinite, concentrate on a finite portion of it, viz. a, and isolate within it a subset AB (see Figure 11). AB has the properties (1) that it is non-tangentially included in a and (2) that there are regions included in a not included in AB. But still another set, CD, can be isolated as non-tangentially included in AB. It becomes apparent (1) that a con-

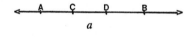

a

FIGURE 11

tains an infinity of included subsets—i.e., it is a dense set—and (2) that as a is progressively "shrunk," the included sets infinitely converge on an ideal limit. It must be stressed that the limit is *ideal* (as indicated in the second part of Whitehead's definition: "there is no region included in every member of the set") and *not actual*. If it is construed as actual, all the problems associated with actual infinitesimal quanta intrude to destroy the elegance and exactness of the subsequently derived definitions. To prevent the intrusion of spurious, real limits into abstractive sets, Whitehead stresses in PNK that in an abstractive set "there is no event which is extended over by every event of the set" (PNK 104). The series indefinitely converges to a "nonexistent ideal" (IS 59). In this convergence, the set may ultimately go beyond any real event, but the ideal, non-extensive terminus remains infinitely distant. Any property of the set which remains constant despite the diminution of the set is taken as a characteristic of the ideal limit: "the series itself is a route of approximation towards an ideal simplicity of 'content' " (PNK 104).

If another set, *b*, can be found, such that every member of *b* contains members of *a*, *b* is said to "cover" *a*. When *a* and *b* cover each other, they are said to be equivalent (insofar as they share the same ideal limit). For an example of mutual covering of sets and hence their equivalence, consider the nest of squares and circles of Figure 12. Each circle is covered by the square in which it is inscribed and covers the square it includes.

FIGURE 12

Both converge toward the same ideal limit—a point—and hence are equivalent despite the other characteristics rendering them different.

The set of all equivalent sets is considered a geometric element. The shared convergent tail defines the geometric element "associated with" each of the equivalent abstractive sets. Note that covering relations, though transitive, are not necessarily symmetrical.[13] If geometrical element X covers geometrical element Y, and Y does not reciprocally cover X, Y is said to be "incident" in X. The difference between the incident element and the covering element is that the member sets in the former have a "sharper convergence" than those in the latter. For example, a line covers the points it includes but is not equivalent to *a* point, inasmuch as its ideal limit of convergence always includes *two* points: i.e., is less "sharp."[14]

With these definitions as background, it is now possible to give a completely formal definition of a point. It is, quite simply, a geometric element with no other geometric elements incident in it (see PR 456): "without parts," in Euclid's phraseology, a geometric element absolutely

---

[13] A transitive relation is of the form, A implies B, B implies C, therefore A implies C. Symmetry is expressed in the instance that if A=B, B=A.

[14] For an intuitive example: in the following figure,

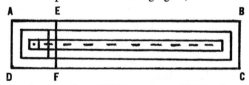

the abstractive set of rectangles, ABCD, covers AEFD, the abstractive set of squares. Yet the covering relation is not symmetrical since AEFD has a point as its ideal limit of convergence and ABCD converges to a line (which is always defined by a *pair* of points). As a result of this sharper convergence, the set of squares is said to be incident in the set of rectangles.

prime.[15] A word is in order on the curious character of this definition of a point. The oddity is not the condition that no other geometric element can be incident in a point—this is fairly straightforward and obvious— but the conception of a point as an abstractive *set* rather than as an ultimate, indivisible unit (a notion ruled out by Whitehead's assertion that in an abstractive set there cannot be one region shared by all members of the set). An examination of what goes on in processes of measurement intuitively reveals the reason for considering the point as a set of regions converging on an ideal limit. Does the statement "New York City is 95 miles from Philadelphia" imply that the precise geometric center point of both cities has been determined, and that the specified distance is measured from one point to the other? Of course not. The geographic "center" of each city is taken as the "end point" of the measurement, e.g., Times Square and Broad and Market. The distance from Jupiter to the sun, or from the sun to Alpha Centauri takes even larger "points" as its termini. When the distances between smaller and smaller entities are measured (e.g., between two cells or between two atoms) the end points of the linear stretch shrink. A point is being construed as an abstractive set of indivisible "volumes," prime to the condition that no other geometric element is incident in it (under the hypothesis of the particular measurement being performed) and progressively converging toward a non-voluminous ideal limit. To say "point" is not therefore to imply a smallest indivisible unit, so small as to be extensionless. The same *caveat* must be heeded with respect to Whitehead's understanding of the other geometric elements— lines, planes, surfaces, etc. They are *not* metric; they are concerned not with *how much* extension they involve but with the purely formal character of that extension.

III · FLAT LOCI

Although armed now with the definition of a point, it is not possible for Whitehead to move directly to the definitions of the other geometric elements without introducing non-formal notions such as the *path* of a point, etc. Intermediate definitions must be introduced to avoid such illegitimate introductions. The first such notion is that of a segment. In Whitehead's words, "A geometrical element is called a 'segment between two points *P* and *Q*,'" when its members are prime in reference to the condition that the points *P* and *Q* are incident in it" (PR 457), which is to say that the set includes P and Q but is not equivalent with them (is not included in P and Q) because of the difference in the sharpness of the converging

---

[15] The notion of a geometric element being prime with respect to certain conditions means simply that only the members of its associated abstractive sets satisfy those conditions: no other elements incident in it can satisfy the same conditions.

tails involved. Note that, as shown in Figure 13, A is not the only segment prime to the incidence of P and Q. So also are B and C; hence no more

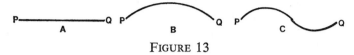

FIGURE 13

content can be placed in the notion of a segment than that given in Whitehead's definition—it is not a straight line, merely a linear stretch. Thus, "there can be many geometrical elements which are prime in reference to some given conditions" (PR 457). What Whitehead seeks are the conditions so basic that only one geometric element can be prime in reference to them. One such condition he has already discovered: the condition satisfied by a point. His search for the definition of a straight line, as well as that for flat loci (planes and volumes), is a search for the conditions to which only these elements will be prime and which at the same time will open the way to a purely formal definition of "straightness" and "flatness." It might be well at this point to situate the discussion within the framework of the kind of geometry Whitehead had concerned himself with during his association with Bertrand Russell and thereafter, inasmuch as the term "geometry" signifies to most lay readers one of the metric geometries with all its implications of constructions, congruence theorems, and the like. The sort of geometry Whitehead was involved in is of a less limited scope, being, in Russell's words, "the study of series of two or more dimensions,"[16] or, as Whitehead put it, "the science of cross classification" (ESP 245). It is immediately obvious that the subject matter of the science is not points, lines, planes, etc., considered as determinate types of entities, but "any entities for which the axioms are true" (ESP 245), provided those axioms are consistent, applicable to *some* determinate entities, and independent of each other. Geometry is therefore "the theory of the classification of a set of entities (the points) into classes (the straight lines), such that (1) there is one and only one class which contains any given pair of entities, and (2) every such class contains more than two members" (ESP 246). Spatial intuition is therefore logically irrelevant to geometry itself, despite its occasional helpfulness in geometric study. At times, spatial intuition can be a positive hindrance to the geometer, as a result of the limitations imposed by four-dimensional space–time on geometric imagination. Therefore, most especially in Whitehead's discussions of "straight" and "flat" loci, it is imperative that the reader not rely on Euclidean images of straightness or flatness in searching for meaning, for more often than not these images, drawn from one species of metric geometry, cloud the issue. Whitehead is not involved in metric geometry of

16 *The Principles of Mathematics* (London: Allen & Unwin, 1937), p. 352.

any variety: Euclidean (parabolic), hyperbolic, or elliptic. In his discussions in Chapter 3, he is following researchers such as von Staudt, Cayley, and others into non-metric, projective geometry, an infant science in the mid-'twenties, whose intricacies lie outside the concern of this work but whose general procedures are critical for an understanding of what Whitehead is doing in Part IV.

Projective geometry is a branch of mathematics spawned by the tendency toward realism and naturalism in Renaissance art, a trend which impelled painters to discover techniques whereby the three dimensionality of the physical world could be reproduced on a two-dimensional canvas. Their researches produced the notion of perspective and the correlative techniques of projection and section whereby paintings with the illusion of three dimensions could be produced. The eye of the beholder was considered to be the point of convergence of light rays projected from all points of the scene viewed. A glass screen, real or imaginary, was placed at a certain distance from the eye—intersecting the converging lines from the scene—and the points marked where each line penetrated the screen, thus producing a "section" of the projection, which was then reproduced on the canvas. The practical theorems respecting projection and section worked out by and for artists do not concern us here. What is significant is a fact soon noticed by geometers: namely, that certain properties of figures remained constant no matter how the figure was deformed by a particular projection or section, while others did not. With the researches of Desargues and others into these properties, projective geometry was born—but born out of season, for as a branch of pure mathematics it was soon dismissed as radical and went into eclipse until its revival in the nineteenth century. Arthur Cayley, in the early-twentieth century, saw it to be the foundation of all metric geometries, Euclidean and non-Euclidean, each of which could be demonstrated to be the study of the geometric properties of special projections. Thus, Cayley could exclaim, " 'Projective geometry is all of geometry!' "[17] Though Cayley's encomium was premature, as evidenced by the emergence of a still more general form of geometry in topology, the significance of projective geometry for the philosophy of organism cannot be overstressed.[18] It enables Whitehead to identify the invariant properties of regions, those remaining unchanged throughout any perspectival transformation or deformation of that region when it is felt into a concrescent subject. The primitive notions from which these properties are deduced—the notions of "region," "connection," and

[17] Quoted in Morris Kline, "Projective Geometry," in *The World of Mathematics*, ed. James R. Newman, 4 vols. (New York: Simon & Schuster, 1956), I 639.
[18] For a readable account of the nature and principal theorems of projective geometry, the reader is urged to consult the excellent article by Kline cited in note 17.

the derivative notions "inclusion," "incidence," "intersect," "equivalence," and the like—are projective (perhaps even topological) properties with no metric connotation. The notions remaining to be derived—straight line, two- and three-dimensional flat loci—are equally non-metric. Straightness and flatness have to do with those properties of lines, surfaces, and volumes which remain unchanged throughout any projection or section.

At this point, therefore, the instinctive tendency of the lay mind to "Euclideanize" the notions to be derived is a positive obstacle to understanding, most especially since the language and diagrams Whitehead perforce must use are Euclidean. A case in point is Whitehead's next step in the derivation of a purely formal definition of a straight line—the step detailing the properties of an ovate abstractive set. That a set is termed "ovate" has no reference whatever to "ovate" as metrically considered—as an oval *shape*. It concerns itself rather with the ordering of the points within the set, specifying that the order be closed and serial (cyclic) rather than open. Only closed serial order remains invariant under projective transformation; open serial order does not. To take a simplistic, intuitive example: in the open series of points A B C (see Figure 14), B "divides"

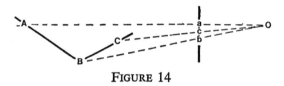

FIGURE 14

A from C. But via projection and section the series can be deformed so that B no longer divides A from C. However, if the series is closed and cyclic, as in Figure 15, no amount of projective deformation will change the fact that in running through the set in *some* direction (either clockwise

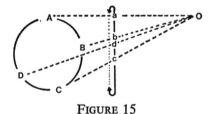

FIGURE 15

or counterclockwise) A and/or C must be passed through in order to reach B and/or D.

The ovateness of a set has to do, therefore, with the type of order it manifests among its elements (that it is defined by closed serial order—

and not by the "shapi-ness" of an oval), which alone is invariant under projection. This is to say, therefore, that there is an intimate connection between elliptical space and the space of projective geometry; in fact, projective geometry *is* the elliptical geometry of Reimann with all metric characteristics removed. Whitehead is being consistent in his aim at defining the basic geometrical elements without recourse to measurement. In effect, he demonstrates that projective space has a positive curvature (i.e., returns upon itself) without having defined "positive" or "curvature" in metric terms.

The next question to be approached is: "What are the unique properties of a set of ovals?" *An* oval is indefinable, save as a closed series, which definition does not distinguish one oval from another.[19] Neither does that definition *define* an ovate set, for it presupposes notions ("closed," "serial," "cyclic") not previously derived from the primitive concepts. Therefore, although Whitehead intuitively grasps the necessity for defining "line," "plane," etc., in terms of ovate sets, and has an intuitive understanding of the nature of a class of ovals, he must deduce a formal definition from the primitive concepts.

He does this by examining the ways in which oval and non-oval regions are connected, seeking the conditions of connection to which *only* ovals are prime, and hence developing a formal definition of a *class* of oval regions, or of an ovate abstractive set (a dense set of ovals). For our purposes, we can consider these conditions as falling into three sets of non-abstractive conditions (two of which are relevant to the eventual formal definition of a straight line) and one set of abstractive conditions. The first set has to do with the way in which ovals overlap each other (overlapping being one of the primitive modes of extensive connection). As can be intuitively grasped in Figure 16, ovals can overlap ovals *only* with a unique intersect, which intersect itself is oval (i.e., positively curved, a closed serial order). Non-ovals, however, overlap *some* ovals

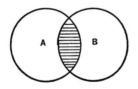

FIGURE 16

with multiple intersects; and all ovals intersect *some* non-ovals with multiple intersects as well. Consider the intersects of an oval such as A in

[19] E.g., does not distinguish an ellipse from a circle, for projectively they are not different.

Figure 17 and a region bounded by two parabolas, such as B. Simple inspection shows that B intersects A with multiple intersects, whereas B

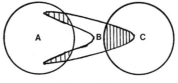

FIGURE 17

intersects C, another oval, with a unique intersect. In neither case can the intersect (or intersects) be called oval.

The second important set of conditions concerns the modalities of external connection between ovals and non-ovals. Ovals can be externally connected with ovals *either* through tangential contact or through a shared interface (linear stretch)—a complete locus of points[20] which itself is oval (18a and 18b illustrate both modes of external connection). Ovals and non-ovals can be connected *only* via single-point contact and never

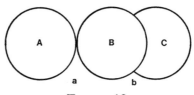

FIGURE 18

by a complete locus of points. If, for instance, the paraboloid B were joined to an oval A via a shared interface (19a or 19b), the continuity of one of the two sets is destroyed. In 19a, the paraboloid is no longer parabolic; in 19b, the oval is no longer an oval.

FIGURE 19

The abstractive conditions, those binding all ovals equally and without exception, and hence being the properties of the ideal limit of an ovate abstractive set, bring us closer to the goal of defining a straight line. It

---

[20] "A 'complete locus' is a set of points which compose *either* (i) all the points situated in a region, *or* (ii) all the points situated in the surface of a region, *or* (iii) all the points incident in a geometrical element" (PR 458).

will be recalled that the point, as a geometric element, was defined as the set of all sets sharing the same convergent tail and prime to the condition that no other geometric element could be incident in it. Among the sets which share a similar convergence and are prime to the given condition are sets of ovals. Therefore, "Among the members of any point [i.e., the sets associated with a point], there are ovate abstractive sets" (PR 464). Now, if a set of two points is considered, *a* and *b*, a dense set of ovals can be constructed, all of which are prime to the condition of covering *a* and *b*. Thus, all ovals are members of points, and all ovals can cover two points. Likewise, sets of three points can be covered by dense sets of ovals (in this case, the ovals are oval surfaces, not oval lines as before[21]). Finally, there are ovate abstractive sets prime to the condition of covering four points—oval volumes. In our cosmic epoch, or, more precisely, in our immediate neighborhood in this cosmic epoch, there are no ovate sets prime to the condition of covering five or more points. Our neighborhood displays only four dimensional determinants—points, lines, surfaces, and volumes. Therefore, our cosmic epoch contains at least one ovate abstractive set of the four-dimensional variety—i.e., a set consisting of points, plus closed, serially ordered lines, surfaces, and volumes.[22]

At this point, the next step in the formal definition of a line can be taken. Two aspects of a line must be formally deduced from the already established assumptions and definitions: (*a*) its "straightness"—i.e., what is the non-metric meaning of straightness; and (*b*) its uniqueness— i.e., that between two points one and only one straight line can be drawn, that all sets of straight lines between two points are projectively equivalent. (These two aspects have been illegitimately collapsed into the Euclidean conception of straightness.) The hinge pin of Whitehead's argument is found in abstractive condition ii:

> If two abstractive sets [their ovateness or non-ovateness being unspecified] are prime in reference to the same twofold condition, (a) of covering a *given* group of points, and (b) of being equivalent to [covering and being covered by] *some* [not necessarily the same] ovate abstractive set, then they are equivalent [again—they reciprocally cover each other] [PR 465].

Two possibilities follow: (*a*) if the two sets are equivalent to the *same* ovate abstractive set, they are co-equivalent; (*b*) but if each of the given sets is equivalent to a *different* ovate abstractive set, they are equivalent as well, as can be seen in the following derivation. The initial two abstractive sets each covered the given group of points and was equivalent to *some* dense set of ovals. If the ovate abstractive sets to which the initial sets are

---

[21] Only the intuitive meaning of line and surface are appealed to in this statement.
[22] For an imaginative model of the latter, consider an ellipse, the surface of an egg, and the volume of a doughnut, respectively.

equivalent are different sets, the points are nevertheless included in their intersect; and that intersect is both unique and oval because, as has already been seen, ovals overlap with unique intersects which themselves are oval. This particular intersecting region is one of an infinity of possible intersecting oval regions covering the points; therefore, there is an ovate abstractive set of such intersects, and it is unique—the only ovate abstractive set prime to the condition of covering the points in question. Thus the possibly diverse ovate abstractive sets of alternative (*b*) collapse into the single set of alternative (*a*). Since a geometric element is composed of all equivalent abstractive sets prime to the specified conditions, it follows that the set of ovate sets prime to covering the given points constitutes a geometric element—one uniquely defined by the set of points.

Now, it has already been demonstrated that two points define a segment or linear stretch. When that stretch is the ideal limit of convergence of a set of equivalent ovate abstractive sets covering the two points, it is a "straight" segment. Therefore, any set which converges to an ideally straight segment manifests the geometric property of straightness. The non-metric meaning of straightness can be intuitively grasped by examining a straight segment—for instance, that formed by the external connection of the two ovals in Figure 20, which connection defines two points,

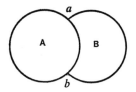

FIGURE 20

a and *b*. The linear stretch *ab* is straight in that its convexity from the side of A is perfectly matched by its concavity from the side of B. It "lies evenly with itself," in Euclidean phraseology. Its curvature is regular. That the line is unique stems from the fact that all ovate abstractive sets covering the two points are equivalent; they cover each other, mutually sharing the same convergent tail and ideal limit. Two points, therefore, uniquely determine a straight line; a straight line is the *locus of points* incident in a straight segment. The formal definition of a complete straight line becomes:

A complete straight line is a locus of points such that, (i) the straight line joining any two members of the locus lies wholly within the locus, (ii) every sub-set in the locus, which is in its lowest terms, consists of a pair of points, (iii) no points can be added to the locus without loss of one, or both, of the characteristics (i) and (ii) [PR 466].

A straight line is therefore the simplest variety of flat locus. If an ovate abstractive set is prime to the condition of covering three non-collinear points, it defines the elementary, two-dimensional flat locus "triangle," from which the formal definition of a plane can be readily deduced (PR 466–67). If the initial set of points contains four which are not co-planar, the three-dimensional flat locus "tetrahedron" is defined, and, derivatively, three-dimensional flat space (PR 467). All the foundational geometric definitions have been formally produced without any recourse to measurement or to experience.

IV · STRAINS

After the dizzying complexities of the last two sections, it would be tempting to paraphrase Peirce and to ask "If there is anyone still reading this besides the compositor, he might rightfully wonder *ad quid?*" "What is the point of this elaborately complicated geometric exposition?" "Won't PR stand without it?"

In the first place, Whitehead himself must have considered the issues as critical to the philosophy of organism on the sheer evidence of the amount of space he devotes to them. But, indeed, are they so critical? In fact, yes; for they are vital elements in grounding the previous epistemological and cosmological discussions. From the cosmological point of view, the geometry provides a coherent framework within which to elucidate notions such as immediate objectification, routes of transmission, and the character of the actual world as a medium. Immediate objectification (i.e., the direct physical feeling of the physical feeling of another actual entity) can come about only between an emerging occasion and past occasions whose spatio-temporalized quantum of extension is contiguous—externally connected—with the standpoint in the extensive continuum which is in the process of actualization by the emerging occasion. In such cases, the objectified spatio-temporal "neighbors" enter into the concrescent subject under objectifications produced by eliminations based solely on the exigencies arising from the synthesis of a manifold of immediately given data into the unity of a perspective. When, however, what is being physically felt into a concrescent occasion is a more remote fact—one not immediately connected spatially or temporally but felt through the mediacy of intervening occasions—the remote fact is felt in a more abstract fashion: it has undergone successive eliminations through the subjective functioning of the intermediate occasions, and hence is not felt in the relative completeness of definiteness which would characterize the feeling of a fact immediately given.[23] Nevertheless, where chains of immediate objectification prevail, physical influence is transmuted through space–time.

[23] In the language of relatives, if ArB and BrC, then ArC; but the C in ArC is more abstract—less fully determinate—than the C in BrC.

Continuous transmission is "immediate transmission through a route of successive quanta of extensiveness" (PR 468), each externally connected with the others, either immediately or mediately. As seen earlier, "any two regions are mediately connected" (PR 451), and yet are still atomic quanta of extension. Zeno has been overcome, because the atomizations of space–time are both discrete (bounded) and continuous (sharing a common interface or a common mediator). Real quanta of space–time are linked so that energy, the transfer of vector feeling-tone, can be transmitted across them and absorbed into the privacy of a new standpoint. Action need not be described in terms of *actio in distans*, nor an ether be created ad hoc; actual occasions actualize their own physical fields, which physical fields are linked in the overarching schema of the extensive continuum, through specifiable relations of inclusion, overlap, external connection, etc.

The schema of extensive relations among satisfied occasions, which schema emerges from their physical feelings of each other, guarantees the possibility of both internal relations and external relations among actual entities, ensuring (a) that each entity creates itself as a unified quantum out of its individual appropriation of an actual world of extensively connected occasions, and (b) that it nevertheless remains other than the world out of which it arises, as a new one added to the given multiplicity. Extension provides "the forms of internal relationships *between* actual occasions [externality], and *within* actual occasions [internality]" (PR 471); "extensive relations mould qualitative content and objectifications of other particulars into a coherent finite experience" (PR 470).

The doctrine of strains represents the epistemological implications of the geometry of extensive connection. The straight lines and flat loci formally defined through the mediacy of extensive connection are not in themselves abstractions suitable only for the manipulation of geometers; they are public facts given in and for experience, public spatio-temporal structures actualized in actual occasions and nexuses and felt with a greater or lesser degree of importance into subsequent occasions. A physical feeling whose datum is the geometric structure interrelating facts is called a strain or strain feeling. It is to be noted, however, that straight lines and flat loci are not immediately given in independence of the causal facts in the actual world. They are felt indirectly in the initial physical feelings whereby past causality, vector feeling-tone, is appropriated in the present. Any entity, like Plato's God, "geometrizes": spatio-temporalizes its world via its process of concrescence. In its satisfaction, it actualizes a strain seat—a set of points defining the volume of the experient's standpoint in the extensive continuum (the new quantum of space–time) and an extensive region defined by projectors from the strain seat (the actual world as geometrized, both by the experient occasion and by the satisfied occasions within it as themselves strain seats, and lifted into the constitution of the experient occasion). In the language of projective geometry, every actual occasion actualizes a projection and section of the extensive continuum in its physical feelings. Just as the geometry already inherent in a scene-to-be-painted is transformed from the standpoint of the painter's eye into the geometry which appears on the canvas, so each actual occasion performs its section of an already geometrized actual world via its strain feelings of that world from its perspectival standpoint. It actualizes a strain in the physical world; it introduces a perspectival geometry of the world from its vantage point and publicly bequeaths it to the future.

When such strain feelings are valued *up* in the concrescence of an actual occasion, through the enhancement resulting from conceptual valuations, the occasion "lifts into importance the complete lines, planes, and three-dimensional flats, which are defined by the seat of the strain [the projection]" (PR 473). It structures its world geometrically. If, in addition, a certain regional nexus in the objective datum is valued up, this region acquires the special status of "focal region" of the strain, being an area of heightened geometric interest and hence more precise geometric structure.

Strain feelings are not to be interpreted as identifiable with the original physical feelings which initiate a concrescence. The geometric character, or actualized strains, of the actual world are latent in the original vector feelings, but only explicated in later feelings. The initial feelings yield sensa, with their geometric relations implicit in the vector character of the feelings. Later conceptual feelings isolate the geometric elements and lift them into importance for the concrescence, so that the sensa are felt as explicitly implicated in geometric structures. The extensive regions of the actual world are geometrically objectified, with the emphasis placed on the seat and/or the extensive region, depending on the subjective aim of the concrescence.

It must not be inferred from the previous discussion that strain feelings necessarily entail consciousness. On the contrary, they arise in any entity whose actual world exhibits sufficient order. They are the geometric basis of the "order of nature" studied by the physicist. "Fundamental equations in mathematical physics, such as Maxwell's electromagnetic equations, are expressions of the ordering of strains throughout the physical universe" (PR 474). Thus, the strains in the physical universe are expressive of the influence of the dominant society in the cosmic epoch: the society of electromagnetic occasions which is environed in and limits the wider geometric society.

Strain feelings acquire particular importance in conscious feelings, however, being the physical basis for the projection of sensa which comes about in conscious presentational immediacy,[24] and for the felt "withness" of the body which makes symbolic reference possible. The geometric pattern of the display as it forms the experience of the final percipient in the animal body is derived from its feelings of states of strain in past entities in the various bodily perceptive organs. The analogous strain feeling in the final percipient feels an extensive region composed of strain seats (the volume of the perceptive organs) and focal regions (the external and/or internal regions defined by projection from the seats) which it integrates into a final seat—the physical body—and a final focal region —the external or internal environment as geometrized by the strain feelings peculiar to the various perceptive organs. This is a feeling, therefore, of the "withness" of the body and of the determinate "aroundness" of the environment, both structured by geometric eternal objects and displayed in the present via inherited sensa. "Thus the [inherited] sense-datum has a general spatial relation, in which two spatial regions are dominant" (PR 476). Either may be lifted into important relevance vis-à-vis the final percipient. If one or more of the strain seats in the body is emphasized, presentational immediacy is predominantly a presentational objectification of the organ in question—e.g., the contemporary eye as dazzled by an exceedingly bright light. If the focal region is emphasized, the final percipient projects the sensa onto the contemporary region defined by the projectors, with little or no objectification of the contemporary organ— as in a dream. In normal perception, both regions are presentationally objectified in the final percipient. In all cases, "The prehension of a region is . . . the prehension of systematic elements in the extensive relationship between the seat of the immediate feeler and the region concerned" (PR 478), e.g., between the eye region and the region upon which the visual sensa are projected.

Via a complex process involving transmutations and propositional feelings, the strain in the immediate feeler (with its seat and focal region) causally felt by the final percipient provides the data—sensa and geometric eternal objects—which are projected by the final percipient to illustrate its contemporary world, a world projectively related to the displayed animal body as the felt synthesis of the various felt strain seats and the contemporaneous environment-display. The basis for the transmutation, which rescues both the display of the body and the display of the world from the possibility of being mere "show" with no relation whatever to states of affairs in the actualized past, lies in the communality of experience between satisfied occasions in the felt nexus and the contemporary occasions arising in the bodily and worldly nexuses. The contemporary occasions illustrated in presentational immediacy are extrapo-

[24] That mode of perception in a high-grade organism in which a region in the contemporary world is vividly displayed via geometric eternal objects and sensa.

lated to be feeling and to be about to transmit the same sensa as those transmitted by the past. Furthermore, as not yet determinate they offer no resistance to the structure imposed on them in presentational objectification. They are viewed as non-discrete potentialities implicated in the geometry elicited from feelings of the past and illustrated by means of sensa derived from the past functionings of the animal body and the external nexus.

One final note needs to be added: namely, an explication of the manner in which the sensum is heightened in importance so that it can become the "flesh" to clothe the geometric bones of projections of presentational immediacy in the final percipient. In the concrescence of the initial percipient (actually, the nexus of percipients in the end organ), they originate as the physically felt objectifications of the antecedent world. However, this bare indicative feeling is subsequently registered as a hybrid physical feeling of the eternal object structuring the datum, which eternal object is then felt in a pure conceptual feeling—i.e., is valued with respect to its significance in and for the concrescence—and reunited with the original physical feeling in that mode of pre-propositional synthesis previously described as a physical purpose. In this way, the sensum gains importance in the satisfaction of the initial percipient and, when felt in the initial physical feelings of the final percipient, is felt *as importantly* relevant to both the initial percipient and the actual world from which this percipient arises. The geometric eternal objects likewise acquire enhanced relevance in the transition between initial and final percipients, although in a different manner. What the final percipient feels is both the strain of the initial percipient *and* the contemporary nexus. The former is felt as the projective geometry of strain seats and focal regions. The latter, although unfelt in causal feelings, as a result of the causal independence of contemporaries, is physically felt as a vague, undifferentiated region—the extensive continuum as not yet atomized by occasions but as the schema of the relational togetherness of possible occasions. This bare extensity of the contemporary world as felt by the final percipient reinforces its feelings of the actualized strains in the initial percipient, and thus gives them heightened relevance. The ultimate synthesis of both sets of feelings results in the propositional unification of geometrized sensa as predicates with the contemporary region as subject, and the body–world complex is presentationally objectified as "conditioned by extensive relations" (PR 494).

As a result of further unification of the final percipient's feelings of the strains actualized in the various bodily regions, the final percipient actualizes a "strain locus" for itself, a "selected locus . . . penetrated by the straight lines, the planes, and the three-dimensional flat loci associated with the strains" (PR 485). Each actual occasion lies in its own strain locus, a three-dimensional flat locus with temporal thickness, in terms of which physical concepts such as rest and motion take their meaning. An actual entity does not "move"; it "rests" in its strain locus. Motion is evidenced in the comparison between the various "rests" of occasions in personal threads.

The strain locus of an actual occasion is not to be confused with a "duration," a term explicated earlier in the analyses of SMW. A duration is a slab of time, comprising all those occasions in unison of becoming with each other. It is a "locus of actual occasions, such that (α) any two members of the locus are contemporaries, and (β) that any actual occasion, not belonging to the duration, is in the causal past or causal future of some members of the duration" (PR 487). A duration is not, however, to be considered in the Newtonian sense of *all* nature at the present instant. As relativity physics has demonstrated, what from the standpoint of one occasion lies in its causal past may be in the causal future of another contemporary occasion. Therefore, there is no *absolute* duration in which *all* occasions share—no unique "now" dividing an absolutely common past and future. The past of a duration consists of whatever is past for *some* members of its locus. Thus it is possible for any given occasion to lie in an indeterminate number of durations depending on the different meanings of past and future for its contemporaries. "The paradox which has been introduced by the modern theory of relativity is twofold. First, the actual occasion M does not, as a general characteristic of all actual occasions, define a unique duration; and secondly such a unique duration, if defined, does not include all the contemporaries of M" (PR 488).

V · MEASUREMENT

A mare's-nest of problems surrounds measurement as performed by the physical scientist, problems very real to Whitehead, given his earlier immersion in relativity physics. They are not so real to the philosopher whose primary focus of concern is metaphysics and not the philosophy of science. Therefore, the following discussions will only highlight the important problems Whitehead grapples with and the conclusions he reaches which are significant to the metaphysician, and will not delve too deeply into either their derivation or their ramifications.

The paradox of measurement for the physical sciences is the fact that measurement is measurement of a strain locus as presentationally objectified, whereas that measurement is assumed to be measurement of a duration—"a complete set of actual occasions, such that all the members are mutually contemporary one with the other" (PR 491), i.e., of contemporary actuality. Measurement in science entails therefore a symbolic reference from a strain locus to a duration, a reference not always justifiable. For purposes of everyday perception, the difference between both poles of the reference is so insignificant as to be irrelevant. When certain sorts of scientific measurement are being performed, however, the Uncertainty Principle intrudes and the measurement (in presentational immediacy) and the measured (the contemporary world) do not cohere, inasmuch as the former disturbs the latter. This paradox is something the physical sciences have learned to cope with. A more fundamental problem remains, however. A strain locus is entirely relative to the extensive standpoint of the observer, "privileged observers" having been excised from the post-Einsteinian theoretical framework. A strain locus is entirely defined by the straight lines (projectors) joining pairs of points in the volume of the observer's extensive standpoint. Is it the case, therefore, that the scientist describes only the perturbations of the physical world produced in and by his private psychological field? Unless the geometry of strains is in some sense objective and immersed in a wider geometric framework, the answer must be cast in the affirmative. Thus, for more than geometric reasons, straight lines and the other geometric elements had to be demonstrated as properties of pure extension and not dependent on physical occasions for their definition. A systematic geometric context must be objective, given for and exemplified in all occasions. In other words, science depends for its validity on the public character of the strain feelings as presentationally objectified.

In a strain feeling, actualities are abstracted from, leaving only their extensive regions with their geometric properties as objects of the feeling. These geometrized regions are what are lifted into the present in presentational immediacy and decorated with sense data—the projected sensa—in total independence of whatever actual entities may constitute the duration as contemporaneous with the observer. Therefore, "the theory of 'projection' . . . requires that the definition of a complete straight line be logically prior to the particular actualities in the extensive environment" (PR 494); "the extensive continuum, apart from the particular actualities into which it is atomized [observing occasions as well as observed occasions], includes in its systematic structure the relationships of regions expressed by straight lines" (PR 496). The perception of extensity—perception in the mode of presentational immediacy—is the perception of the systematic geometry of the unatomized extensity of the presented duration, of "the systematic real potentiality out of which these [contemporary] actualities arise" (PR 498). Insofar as it displays these geometric relationships, perception is objective.

Since all scientific measurement is performed in presentational immediacy, it follows that science concerns itself solely with mathematical relations between physical entities and not with the entities themselves, mathematical relations which are objective "laws" of nature (i.e., pertain to the past and future of the physical world with a high degree of probability) because of the dominance of social order and of a particular social order in this cosmic epoch. The widest social order is that of extensive connection, in whose general properties "we discern the defining characteristic of a vast nexus extending far beyond our immediate cosmic epoch. . . . This ultimate, vast society constitutes the whole environment within which our epoch is set . . ." (PR 148). The geometric society, a specialization of the social order ultimate from our limited standpoint, particularizes the conditions in terms of which the geometric elements of our cosmic epoch are defined, yielding "families" of geometric elements and hence families of metric geometries unified in the overarching geometric system of extensive connection.

Presentational immediacy "exhibits that complex of systematic mathematical relations which participate in all the nexūs of our cosmic epoch . . ." (PR 498), a complex inherited and superjected within the personal orders and enduring objects of the physical world: "a systematic framework permeating all relevant fact" (PR 499). Since the observer, in whose concrescence presentational immediacy is an element, is part of that physical world and hence permeated by the same systematic framework, his objectivity is further reinforced, making the scientific enterprise possible both from the standpoint of the observer and from that of the observed.

When the problem at hand is activities of measurement rather than the possibility of measurement, the objectivity of presentational immediacy assumes still greater import to science. Measurement consists in establishing a relation of congruence between two extensities: (a) that of the measuring instrument, be it rod[25] or some more sophisticated device, and (b) that of the nexus to be measured. The relation is determined by placing the rod in coincidence with the nexus to be measured and "counting" the number of measuring units along the rod which coincide with the extensity of the nexus. What is presupposed is that the rod remains congruent with itself during its translocations—i.e., that its length remains the same. This is not to say that the rod *does* remain congruent with itself at all times, that it *does not* vary in response to physical conditions. What is required is that self-congruence have a determinate meaning, for unless the notion of "exactness" has a content, deviation from exactness is meaningless. How are such deviations to be measured? By comparing the conditions under which the suspect measurement is made with some standard set of conditions—in other words, by another activity of measurement. The measurer is ultimately driven back to a fundamental "intuition" that no important condition has changed, without which intuition he would be locked in an infinite regress of measurements to test measurements to test

---

[25] Note that what is said of rods in the following discussion is applicable to clocks as well.

measurements. . . . This "intuition" is given in presentational immediacy's display of the contemporary environment as compared with past environmental displays. Unless it is objective, science says nothing about the physical world and describes merely the perceptual vagaries of scientists. Is Whitehead naïvely taking this intuition of permanence, either with respect to the rod or in regard to relevant environmental conditions, to be absolute? Infallible? Exact? Hardly. It is subject to indefinite refinement; it always approximates, is asymptotic to the "exact." But unless there is an "exactness" approximated, measurement approximates nothing. And unless the intuition of permanence or of congruence is *really* asymptotic to a real objective permanence or congruence, it is a daydream.

What would that real permanence, that real congruence, be? As real, it would have to do with actualized strains in the strain locus of the percipient, ultimately in the object and the rod as having geometrized themselves through the strain feelings of their member actual occasions and contributing those feelings as data for the strain feelings of the percipient through the mediacy of strain feelings in the perceptual organs of the animal body. Since strain feelings are physical feelings of the objective geometric character of nexuses, the root meaning of congruence is geometric. However, at this point, the geometry alluded to is not the general, non-metric geometry of the previous sections, but a further specialization of it. The introduction of the concept of measurement takes us beyond those properties of geometric elements which remain invariant under topological or projective transformation—e.g., the definition of inclusion or of straightness derived earlier—and into the competing metric geometries, whose different congruence definitions, derived from further specifications of the properties of straight lines, present rival options to the measurer. All are internally self-consistent. Which metric geometry is the appropriate one to use can only be determined pragmatically, in terms of its "power of elucidating observed facts" (PR 503), i.e., in terms of further empirical observation. Therefore, there are as many congruence theorems as there are rival metric geometries—in our cosmic epoch, at least three: parabolic, hyperbolic, and elliptical. Congruence in its most general sense consists in "a certain analogy [between the functions of two segments] in a systematic pattern of straight lines, which includes both of them" (PR 505). The further definition of that analogy is performed by the dominant society in a cosmic epoch, and hence, on Whitehead's assumption, is discoverable in nature through presentational immediacy. With the dominant congruence definition established, physical measurement is possible to the scientist.[26]

[26] Whitehead's further explication of measurement procedure is more relevant to the philosophy of science than to metaphysics, since it involves his own version of relativity theory; hence it will not be developed here. For a full development, see PRel.

6

GOD AND THE WORLD

(PR, Part V)

AFTER THE INTRICACIES of Parts III and IV, through which the specifics of a process metaphysics are elaborated, Whitehead returns in a moment of generalization to what has been the underlying theme of PR: the reconciliation of the primordial oppositions given in and for experience—the one and the many, order and creativity, permanence and change, now as subsumed in the foundational dialectic of God and the world. It is no longer necessary to plumb the obscurities of the text, for Whitehead speaks lyrically and directly, pulling aside the curtain for a moment to enable the reader to catch a glimpse of the massive simplicity of his cosmological vision. It is indeed only a glimpse—a return to romance—the preface to the theological counterpart of process cosmology, a beginning not an end. The details are not worked out; the language is more evocative than precise; more is concealed than is revealed. Yet the revelation in and not despite its poetry gives process philosophy a scope paralleled only by the synoptic vision of a Hegel or an Aquinas.

The text is more appropriate for meditation than for critical analysis; hence what follows will concentrate neither on systematic rigor nor on the divergencies in post-Whiteheadian process philosophy which the text has spawned, but on the vision which Whitehead strove to incarnate in words, and on what for me are the implications of that vision. To elaborate those implications fully would require volumes, would entail the construction of a Whiteheadian theology, and consequently would violate the intent of this work. However, to gloss over the richness of Whitehead's suggestions would be equally inappropriate. I have therefore attempted an intermediate approach, one which follows Whitehead in its use of the more romantic, less metaphysically precise methodology and manner of expression, one which broods over Whitehead's suggestions in a meditative manner and which itself suggests further avenues for systematic development in other volumes.

The vision to which Whitehead gives expression is a vision of the ultimate contrast in terms of which the creativity finds its fulfillment: God and the world. Neither pole is autonomous and yet, in a qualified sense, both are; neither pole is contingent, yet both are. Each transcends the other, is immanent in the other, creates and is created by, perfects and is perfected by, the other. Each resolves the tragedy latent in the nature of the other by supplying what is lacking in the other. In a genuinely Hegelian sense, each is the truth of the other, passing over into the other in a manner reinforcing Whitehead's affirmation of the influence of Hegelian thought on his own (ESP 115–16).

The tragedy underlying the cosmological doctrine is the tragedy of loss, of the perishing of subjectivity, with its inherent unity of feeling, into objectivity, with its plurality of modal afterlives: the immortalization yet fragmentation of value achieved.

> The ultimate evil in the temporal world . . . lies in the fact that the past fades, that time is a "perpetual perishing." Objectification involves elimination. The present fact has not the past fact with it in any full immediacy [PR 517].

No finite beauty can survive in its pristine unity. It can shape all process consequent upon itself only at the price of its own self-functioning and unique individuality, because individuality *qua* individuality is obstructive and must be sacrificed to newly emergent creation. Every creature receives its ideal of itself from God through the mediacy of its actual world, weaves the content of that world into an immediacy, a concrete value patterned by the ideal, and perishes—leaving behind its power and its memories in its manifold objectifications but not its inner subjective unity. In becoming a value for the others it loses its value for itself. In Whitehead's words, "There is a unison of becoming among things in the present. Why should there not be novelty without loss of this direct unison of immediacy among things?" (PR 517).

The tragedy hidden in the theological doctrine is the tragedy of divine aloneness. God, under the abstraction of his primordial nature, is totally isolated from finite process, despite his essentiality to the speculative scheme. Granted: he functions as the "principle of concretion" (PR 523), creating the conditions for the possibility of finite particularity, providing the source of all finite beauty and order and structure through his primordial valuation of the eternal objects. But under this aspect he is utterly indifferent to creatures in their concrete individuality, despite the fact that he is their "initial 'object of desire' " (PR 522). He is merely the "unlimited conceptual realization of the absolute wealth of potentiality" (PR 521), unloving, unhating, unconscious, oblivious of actuality: eternal beauty, the source of all exemplifications but unexemplified itself. In a word, God under the abstraction of his primordial nature is deficient in actuality. He is merely thought thinking thought. As Hegel expressed it, "this content shows forth God as he is in his eternal essence before the creation of Nature and of a Finite Spirit."[1] He is devoid of physical experience and hence "bodiless," locked in his conceptual aloneness as the first creature of the creativity.

Yet the infinite beauty of his conceptual structure is the immortal appetition of the universe, actively luring finite creatures up the ladder of love. Beauty diffuses itself, not through acts of efficient creation but through its infinite evocation of novel instances of itself: universes of creatures stirred by the creativity to become God-like by temporalizing the eternal togetherness of primordially ordered form in their concrete immediacy; universes of self-creating creatures whose response to the divine seduction is the incarnation of beauty. With poignant sensitivity to the overwhelming dignity and worth of the individual creature, Whitehead's "unmoved mover" sacrifices the efficient creative force exercised by a traditional omni*potent* deity in favor of the autonomy of the *self-creative* creature. Whitehead's God "thinks" the Word; he does not create the world. He orders the possibles; he does not command the actual. The latter activity is reserved to finite creatures, whose hearing of that Word as it echoes through an actual world straining for new births and whose acceptance of it in a creaturely *fiat* initiate the self-creative process in which the abstract Word is modified and particularized until it comes to term as a drop of fully determinate existence fully responsible for what it is. The transcendent Word becomes flesh in the speech of every concrescence, acquiring concreteness and full determinateness by drawing the many onward into ever new unities in which "the temporality of mere fact [acquires] the immortality of value" (ESP 84).

But again the tragedy of loss intervenes, a tragedy which God's primordial functioning cannot resolve, any more than it can overcome the divine isolation it creates. The immortality achieved in world process is objective, fragmentary, and public—subjectivity, privacy, and undivided unity having perished with the closing up of each drop of creaturely process. The limited victory which personal threads win over time is the partial stabilization and propagation of incarnate value through increasing intensities of memory and anticipation. Character endures and develops, canalizing the creative urge, reiterating past value, and reaching out to future embodiments. But the victory is only partial, and the ultimate evil —the loss of immediacy, the fading of the past—ultimately triumphs. When the value achieved, the subjectivity attained, is trivial in intensity, the loss is merely part of the profligacy of a universe which strews its shores with death because its depths teem with life. But when that value is significant, when that subjectivity attains rational consciousness, its

[1] *Hegel's Science of Logic*, trans. W. H. Johnson and L. G. Struthers, 2 vols. (New York: Humanities Press, 1966), I 60.

loss, its perishing, brings despair to the human spirit. The perfect moment, the culmination of expectation, passes; and in its passing becomes more and more an object to be viewed in a memory impotent to revive its subjective immediacy. It becomes merely "the time when . . .," a fact still efficacious in the present, still objectively immortal, but incapable of being re-experienced in its overwhelming beauty. The most acute form of the evil of perishing lies in the ultimate disappearance from the world of fact of the most profound beauty finite process has created: the human individual. Here the cry is not simply "Why must the perfect moment perish?" but "Why must *I* perish?" "Is my life, with its beauty and ugliness, its exaltation and degradation, merely to end as an unfinished painting, left behind as an historical curiosity without an ultimate unity, without the final brush stroke which would transform its ongoing incompleteness into aesthetic unity?"

The universal hunger of humanity is for redemption: redemption from loss, from partiality, from temporal limitation, from finitude; redemption through an activity which somehow weaves the threads of life into an immortal tapestry immortally self-conscious. The world itself pleads for such a redeemer, for it too, from its less to its more personalized elements, self-destroys as it self-creates, attains only limited harmonizations of the many, partializes, negatively prehends, decides *against* because it decides *for*. Even in its totality, the world of fact is essentially incomplete and transitory, merely a voyage between the deaths of cosmic epochs. Without a redeemer, one who feels the totality of finite process into himself and gives it the immortal and perfect unity attainable only from an infinite atemporal perspective, world process, conscious process, human life, are absurd. Without love as the primordial orientation of the redeemer and the redeemed, a love which draws rather than coerces creatures into harmony because it reverences their autonomy, that redemption is impossible.

These longings find expression in the deepest religious experiences of mankind and manifest a fundamental finite need and aspiration for immortality, self-perfection, and self-transcendence: for redemption through love. For Whitehead, the need and aspiration contained in them reflect the incoherence of the speculative scheme as thus far constructed. The speculative circle is not closed; finite process is left essentially disjointed and alienated. Despite finite efforts to weave the many into one, the creativity is essentially unsatisfied. Nature needs more than eternally ordered form to become and to remain *in solido*; it needs a final, redemptive synthesis to overcome the tragedy inherent in the endless partiality of selective objectification, loss, and perishing. If redemption is the wishful thinking of visionaries and old men, then God himself as presented in the scheme is an abstraction suitable only for mathematical study—a complex pattern of valued possibilities and not an actual entity, *not determinate.* To be actual, God must take on a "body" and in so doing, redeem: i.e., he must have physical feelings of the totality of each and all finite achievements, integrating them into the ongoing unity of his consequent nature. He thus creates himself out of the world by accomplishing its final integration, as the world creates itself out of him by concretizing the divine ideas.

What follows from the exigencies of this ultimate integration marks out God as significantly different from other actual entities. (*a*) If he is to overcome the partiality which characterizes world process, he cannot selectively objectify the data of his physical feelings. He must feel the totality, the subjective *unity*, the immediacy, of each spatio-temporal creature into himself. (*b*) He must therefore *become* both each creature and the togetherness of all creatures. Therefore his feelings cannot take place within the confines of *a* spatio-temporal perspective or of a *private*, exclusive, idiosyncratic subjective aim. (*c*) In consequence, he must be atemporal, immediately connected with each creature's actual world, contemporaneous with every creaturely concrescence. The concrete, determinate, individuality (satisfaction) he aims at must be such that in it all finite satisfactions, despite the disparate and obstructive character of their individuality, can be united without losing their immediacy. His subjective aim must therefore be general enough to subsume all less general subjective aims as specifications of itself and hence as harmonizable.

However, to make such assertions about the divine actual entity seems to be exempting him in an ad hoc manner from the rules of metaphysics in order to salvage the coherence of the metaphysical scheme. Is this really the case? I think not, at least not with regard to the wider issues concerned. Whitehead has consistently underlined the fact that each actual entity becomes its own creative appropriation of its actual world, that no concrescence can outgrow its actual world. With respect to God, the relevant problems are: (*a*) What is the divine actual world? and (*b*) What is the nature of the divine subjective aim? With respect to (*a*), some Whiteheadian scholars, notably Charles Hartshorne, have rejected Whitehead's assertion that God is "always in concrescence and never in the past" (PR 47) and replaced it with an interpretation of God as a personal order of divine occasions. Under this rubric, the divine actual world would grow with the creative advance of the universe, as "The many become one, and are increased by one" (PR 32), and God would be compelled to perform *successive* redemptive acts. In consequence, there would be many "arrests" of divine existence, many episodes of divine redemption linked in the unity of a personally ordered society by a divine defining characteristic. By the principle of relativity, each of these episodes would be superjected to the world, would become part of the objective datum for future creaturely process, would become *fact*, stubbornly insistent, incapable of being negatively prehended. In other words, an enduring creature would be confronted willy-nilly with the fact of its past redemption and compelled to accept it, to integrate it as part of its present determinateness in the same way as it must appropriate any other fact in its actual world. Whitehead might be interpreted as lending support to this view when he states that "the perfected actuality passes back into the temporal world, and qualifies this world so that each temporal actuality includes it as an immediate fact of relevant experience" (PR 532). However, that he calls it "*immediate* fact," that in virtue of his redemptive activity God is termed "the great companion—the fellow-sufferer who understands" (PR 532), point to an alternative interpretation in which a *single* redeeming act is contemporaneous with all finite immediacies, such that it can be grasped only indirectly—i.e., presentationally objectified in an act of faith through which the creature gives free assent to its own redemption, freely incorporating it as an ingredient in its definiteness. To make redemption an historical series of acts rather than one overarching process takes it out of the realm of "faith" and into the realm of objective, inescapable fact. To remove the element of faith, even well-founded faith, from human religious life *and* from the vital process of any actual entity, to excise presentational objectification and its implied interest in the present, is to bind the present irrevocably to the past, to sacrifice spontaneity and autonomy at the altar of necessity.

It seems closer to Whitehead's intentions, therefore, to infer that the divine actual world includes all actual worlds simultaneously and all spatio-temporal drops emerging from those actual worlds in unison of becoming. From the divine perspective, time becomes space in the sense that all "times" are co-present in divine feelings, although retaining, and related by, the various forms of extensive connection. However, we cannot assume that God *directly* feels each creaturely "becoming," that creaturely immediacies are immediately present to and felt into the divine concrescence, for this would involve a violation of the causal independence of contemporary occasions. Therefore, each creaturely immediacy must be presentationally objectified in God (indirectly felt) on the basis of the real potential for that immediacy contained in the creaturely past as causally objectified in divine physical feelings. Inasmuch as the graded eternal objects which structure that real potentiality are the divine conceptual functioning, God grasps them in their fullness by *being* them and hence has a full, albeit indirect, feeling of each creature's present. At the same time, he feels that present as past vis-à-vis a future concrescence in the same thread, since he feels all creatures in unison of becoming. He therefore both directly and indirectly feels each item in his actual world: his indirect feelings "creating" the concrescent item by supplying it with its subjective aim; his direct feelings experiencing the efficient causality of the item's satisfaction. His comparative feelings contrast the generality of his gift with the particularity of the creature's free particularization and in that ultimate affirmation–negation contrast, bring God to consciousness. In his final synthetic feeling—the divine satisfaction—the importance of the contrast and all other such contrasts in the particular thread of finite existence as well as in all other such threads are adjusted so that the totality has the unity, immediacy, and concrete value of the one divine experience without losing or eliminating the unity, immediacy, and concrete value of the many creaturely experiences.[2]

However, as a noted Whiteheadian scholar once remarked, "Is it that God has a marvelous memory and will eternally enjoy thinking about me?" Is it that the immortality which creaturely immediacy gains in the divine consequent nature is merely objective (i.e., factual) immortality and not the subjective immortality which humans crave? Two strains of thought suggest themselves. First, in virtue of the unique nature of the divine concrescence, the entire life history of a person would be redeemed and transfigured in the divine synthesis, the many nows unified in the one, divine, overarching now. Since God overcomes the obstructive character of the now, all the many nows retain their full determinateness—i.e., conscious unity—in God. The historic ego becomes ahistorical and speaks one "I" which sums up the completeness of its conscious life. But while this satisfies the human craving for immortality, it does not quench the human thirst for eternal *life*, for never-ending development, for continuance of the ongoing process of experience which constitutes finite reality. Thus the second thread must be developed as well; an account must be given of "afterlife" which is not at the same time inconsistent with the metaphysics of life. Two answers might be explored. Just as the complexity of the bodily society makes life and conscious life possible, so the complex structure of the consequent nature of God could become the "body" for the individual soul, the structured society in whose interstices the soul would "lurk." Given the reciprocal paradoxes which haunt Whiteheadian thought, this is a solution not to be rejected out of hand but to be explored for its metaphysical consistency. An alternative solution would postulate that, in its union with the divine immediacy, the human "soul" overcomes the obstructiveness and limitations of its finite perspective and shares the divine perspective, becoming God without losing its own individuality. Thus the ongoingness of its life would be-

---

[2] It would be naïve to suggest that there are not as many problems with this interpretation as there are with "divine personal order" interpretations; and, indeed, in order to resolve its latent inconsistencies, God must be granted certain exemptions from the rules of metaphysics. But at least the spirit of Whiteheadian thought is retained.

come identified with the ongoingness of the divine concrescence: it would "participate" in the divine Life with its ongoing novelty in the "I live, now not I; but Christ liveth in me" (Ga 2:20) manner described by St. Paul and a host of other Western (and Eastern) mystics. Both alternatives need and deserve further explication and examination. For our purposes, they demonstrate that the religious longings for an afterlife need not be ruled out *a priori* as inconsistent with Whiteheadian metaphysics.

The second problem alluded to earlier—the nature of the divine subjective aim—is as thorny as the question of the divine actual world. If God is to reach satisfaction, his subjective aim cannot be so abstract (general) as to be unconcretizable—it must define a perspective (albeit divine) —and yet at the same time it must be general enough to harmonize both all finite subjective aims and their concrete realization no matter how incompatible and mutually obstructive they may be. The key to a solution lies in Chapters 10 and 11 of SMW, wherein Whitehead elaborates the inner structure of the world of eternal objects, and the divine activity of ordering that world. A detailed exposition is not in order here, but certain general indications can be made about the directions an attempt at solution might take. The central issue has to do with the character of the divine activity which orders the forms in such ways that their isolation in status relations becomes a realized togetherness vis-à-vis each possible creaturely perspective. As was detailed earlier, the general abstract relevance of form to actuality becomes in the divine primordial nature a real relevance to potential actualities, to possible perspectival unifications of actual worlds. This aspect of the ordering of the forms constitutes the irrational element introduced by the divine activity, an irrationality whose reason cannot be given since it is the source of all rationality. The divine conceptual activity structures the forms into a world of mutually implicated, mutually relational possibilities. God conceptually *realizes*—overcomes the disjunctive diversity of—the forms, thereby becoming the principle of concretion. Only "after" the divine action of "thinking together" the forms as they could relate to each and all possible finite perspectives can talk of a "world of forms" have any meaning. It is the "worldliness" of this world, the general structure reflected in the structure of each particular form, which constitutes the primordial irrationality as the condition for the possibility of rationality. God's conceptual activity "at once exemplifies and establishes the categoreal conditions" (PR 522). The task of the metaphysician, however vaguely and metaphorically that task can be accomplished, is to grasp and to express that irrationality. In a very real sense, metaphysics (at least Platonic metaphysics) has the divine subjective aim as its principal object, since that aim establishes the intelligibility of the cosmos. But what is the divine subjective aim?

If one were to take as an explanatory framework a Platonic interpretation of Whitehead (or a Whiteheadian interpretation of Plato, since the two are correlative), the question translates as: What is the nature and function of the Form of the Good? In the Allegory of the Cave (in Book VII of the *Republic*), it becomes clear that the relation of imaging which holds between shadows, artificial objects, reflections, and natural objects, drops out as soon as Plato begins to talk about the Sun, which is both the condition for the possibility of visibility *and* a visible phenomenon itself, though "hardly seen" (*Republic* 517B). Both aspects of the Form of the Good must be held in mind if it is to be interpreted properly: (*a*) it is the source of all intelligibility; (*b*) it is in itself intelligible, albeit irrational (i.e., inaccessible to discursive thought, hence unjustifiable). With respect to (*a*), we must ask: What is the relation of this grounding condition to particular intelligibilities? Of this primordial form to all other forms? Is it the case that the world of forms is to be conceived as a pyramid of ascending degrees of abstractness with the Good at the apex? If this is the case, then the movement of dialectics would consist in a progressive withdrawal from, abandoning, and leaving behind of the concrete in the reach for the more abstract. If the vision of the Good is construed as a vision of the ultimate abstraction, it would be impossible for the return to the Cave to occur, for philosophers to become kings, for wisdom to be the ability to rule well. Granted: the philosopher must be dragged into the throne room; nevertheless his vision has prepared him for the task from which he shrinks. The vision must therefore be a vision of a form which is most concrete, not most abstract, of a form which structures together the totality of forms in its unity, of a form which relates to each form as its form-ness, as its "soul," its inner depths, its coherence, and relates each form to all others in an organic fashion.[3]

If the divine subjective aim is taken to be the Form of the Good, the divinely realized unity of all eternal objects which makes finite realization possible, the ultimate obstructiveness of subjectivity and immediacy and the lesser obstructiveness of evil cease to be a problem vis-à-vis the divine physical synthesis. The divine perspective is a perspective in that the divine ordering is *this* rather than other, and yet is a perspective broad enough to prehend physically all other concretized perspectives into itself without eliminations and negative prehensions, inasmuch as all other perspectives and the subjective aims luring their concretization are already ideally realized (i.e., together) in it and for it. Divine physical feelings merely realize actually what is already ideally realized in the divine conceptual order. Immediacy is only obstructive in the context of finite perspectives and finite subjective aims. Hence when a finite subject–superject is felt into a subsequent finite process, the immediate unity of the subject

---

[3] See Whitehead's discussion of the types of abstraction (SMW 166ff.), and Chapter 1, note 35, above.

is fragmented into its many potential objectifications. In God, however, the multiplicity of objectifications superjected by a finite entity and separately seized by subsequent entities can be grasped in their subjective unity by divine physical feeling and in their contrast with the entity's subjective aim as originally received from God. All other oppositions and inhibitions among finite entities can be overcome through adjustments of importance lured on by the divine subjective aim—the καλὸν κἀγαθόν. In such wise, the secondary evil of the world, the aesthetico-moral evil of incompatibility, is overcome. As aesthetic, the evil is the mutual obstructiveness of immediacies—"that those elements with individual weight, by their discord, impose upon vivid immediacy the obligation that it fade into night. 'He giveth his beloved—sleep' " (PR 517–18). As moral, it is the victory of the lesser value over the greater value—natural disaster, human "sin." In the divine consequent nature, nothing is allowed to perish, neither the sparrow which falls from heaven nor the hair numbered on a human head. Neither the good nor the evil is lost in this final transformation into concrete beauty. The sparrow, the hair, the good, the evil—all have their place as background or foreground or contrast term. "God saw all the things that he had made, and they were very good" (Gn 1:31).

In that divine glance, God attains consciousness. Prior to his physical feelings, prior to the impact of the world upon him, God is "infinite, devoid of all negative prehensions," "free, complete, primordial, eternal, actually deficient, and unconscious" (PR 524), an unmoved mover luring incarnations but oblivious of them. In taking up the world into his consequent nature, he loses the "freedom" of indetermination, becoming "determined, incomplete, consequent, 'everlasting,' fully actual, and conscious" (PR 524). He is determined in the sense that the world in providing him with a content to be structured allows him to attain definiteness, i.e., actuality. But from the standpoint of the world, that definiteness is never "finished"—God is "always in concrescence and never in the past" (PR 47). He emerges as with each creature and with all creatures "all days, even to the consummation of the world" (Mt 28:20). This "withness" of God's concrescence, its simultaneity with that of all finite occasions, is the creature's guarantee of finite freedom and at the same time the keystone of creaturely faith and hope. All creatures, all spaces, and all times, past, present, and future, are everlastingly knit together in beauty in the divine consciousness. That consciousness in its subjectivity is not directly accessible to finite occasions, any more than the consciousness of any finite occasion is open to scrutiny, but insofar as any finite occasion shares a portion of both God's presented locus and God's actual world, the creature can make the symbolic reference, grounded in the act of faith, that its past and future have been redeemed by the divine vision in the goodness which has no opposite. The creaturely sense of this is the creature's presentational objectification of God, the ultimate application of the principle of relativity—God's superject nature. But, as stressed earlier, the superjection is not to be construed in the same terms as a finite superject, functioning objectively as efficient cause of futures, for the divine concrescence is never in the past of any occasion. It is a superjection graspable only through faith: tenderly leading through inspiration, gently redeeming through a love whose effect must be freely seized by the creature, which thus becomes its own co-redeemer, divinized through its willing absorption into the divine.

> God's rôle is not the combat of productive force with productive force, of destructive force with destructive force; it lies in the patient operation of the overpowering rationality of his conceptual harmonization. He does not create the world, he saves it: or, more accurately, he is the poet of the world, with tender patience leading it by his vision of truth, beauty, and goodness [PR 525–26].

The eternally present poem, the never-to-be-completed yet always complete epic of world process, is the ultimate marriage of primordial valuation and finite achievement, creaturely words wedded in the everlasting meter, rhyme, and structures of beauty. "In this way God is completed by the individual, fluent satisfactions of finite fact, and the temporal occasions are completed by their everlasting union with their transformed selves, purged into conformation with the eternal order which is the final absolute 'wisdom' " (PR 527). The vague sense of that order, coupled with its affirmation and responding love, is human religious experience.

II · CONCLUDING MEDITATIONS

In a final hymn to the ultimate opposites, Whitehead presents the great litany which closes PR, a litany expressing the ultimate complementarity of the cosmological and theological perspectives, the ultimate orchestration of the classic themes of metaphysics: the one and the many, permanence and change, immanence and transcendence, freedom and divine causality.

a. **It is as true to say that God is permanent and the World fluent, as that the World is permanent and God is fluent [PR 528].**

In the former sense, the emphasis is laid upon the primordial, atemporal valuation of eternal objects which renders world process possible: in micro-process, providing the initial lure of subjective aim, private subjective forms, and the mutual relevance of forms which grounds conceptual reversions, contrasts, propositions, and more complex modalities of mental life; in macro-process, providing the interconnectedness of form which keeps objectification from being murder by dissection, thereby effecting genuine transition from past fact to present immediacy. Thus, divine permanence, the eternal atemporality of the primordial nature, grounds the shifting character of the creativity in its surge for novel expression. When the emphasis is shifted, however, the world in its character of objective immortality, achieved fact, becomes the exemplification of permanence and the divine consequent nature acquires fluency as it ever expands in its ongoing absorption of finite achievement.

b.　　**It is as true to say that God is one and the World many, as that the World is one and God many** [PR 528].

The divine unity is the absolute oneness of God's primordial valuation, which stands opposed to the multiplicity of realized values in the world, a manifold transformed into the unity of a perspectival realization by the process internal to every actual occasion, a process by which "The many become one, and are increased by one" (PR 32). As the many become one, the One becomes many. The primordial valuation radiates itself as creaturely subjective aims relevant to unique actual worlds, evoking novel satisfactions to be felt into the divine consequent, which thereby embraces the discordant multiplicity and structures it into unity through its interfusion with the primordial One. God's conceptual feeling is one but abstract; his physical feelings many but concrete. His hybrid feelings synthesize abstract unity and concrete multiplicity into determinate, concrete, and everlasting value—"the complete adjustment of the immediacy of joy and suffering . . . the final end of creation" (PR 530). The consequent nature is thus Emmanuel—"God with us"—"the kingdom of heaven" (PR 531).

The paradoxical nature of the kingdom is that it is always complete yet always growing. However, the metaphysics of the divine has always yielded "this incredible fact—that what cannot be, yet is" (PR 531). The paradox results from the incapacity of the human mind to conceive nontemporal sequence, an incapacity which renders adequate expression of the phasic succession within the micro-process of even a finite entity almost impossible. The sequence in the divine entity is further complicated by the fact that divine physical feelings, as atemporal, feel the totality of finite causality, past, present, and future, in immediate unison, and yet as ordered in causal sequences. The paradox can be resolved by abandoning the finite perspective from which growth must be postulated as a necessary characteristic of God's appropriation of a world in process and assuming the atemporal perspective of God[4] in which the bi-directionally infinite series of creaturely immediacies is grasped in the unity of one datum.

---

[4] Whitehead does not assume this perspective, since the orientation of PR is expressly cosmological; hence the work is written from within one pole of the ultimate God–world opposition.

Thus, from the divine vantage point, the endless fruitions of the creativity are simultaneously co-present in the immediacies of their self-creative activities. The divine concrescence *quoad se* is complete insofar as past and future are not relevant terms. In eternity, *interminabilis vitae tota simul et perfecta possessio* (Boethius, *De consolatione Philosophiae*, V.6); God's physical feeling IS complete. *Quoad nos*, however, it is incomplete, in that the future from any finite perspective is not yet actual and is perpetually actualizing itself.

c. **It is as true to say that, in comparison with the World, God is actual eminently, as that, in comparison with God, the World is actual eminently [PR 528].**

From the creaturely vantage point, God, viewed in the abstraction of his primordial nature, is deficient in actuality, whereas the creature in its fully determinate concreteness attains the fullness of actuality. From the divine perspective, on the other hand, the creature achieves actuality in and through a selective concrescence from its actual world, one involving negative prehensions excluding the totality of both creaturely and divine accomplishment in the decisions which admit a relevant set of objectifications. This partiality in the creature's inclusion of actuality and potentiality in its self-creative process, renders the creature deficient in actuality when contrasted with the non-exclusive feelings of the divine consequent nature. The infinite actuality of God[5] entails that the divine subjective aim is such that it can encompass all less general aims, resolving their antinomies and mutual obstructiveness. It must thus be a complex eternal object so general that all other eternal objects are unified in it despite their contrareity—in a word, the divine subjective aim can have no opposite, no contrast term. It must be the supreme genus, the sun of the world of forms, the Platonic Form of the Good. World redemption is therefore the becoming determinate of the Form of the Good through its ingression into the divine process of feeling the world into fully determinate unity and hence eminent actuality.

d. **It is as true to say that the World is immanent in God, as that God is immanent in the World.**
It is as true to say that God transcends the World, as that the World transcends God [PR 528].

In the opposition between God and the world, the strain between transcendence and immanence which is a universal theological problem is overcome in a duality of contrasted relations. Each pole of the opposition both transcends and is immanent in the other. It is critical that the rela-

---

[5] And it must be recognized that in a Whiteheadian context "infinite" and "actuality" can only be conjoined in mystery, for "infinite" denotes "unlimited" and hence "indeterminate," and "actuality" means "determinate" and hence "finite."

tions be carefully explored, for, as is the case with any terms in a dialectical relation, to devalue or to diminish the absolute character of one pole is to do the same to the other. Both God and the world can be immanent in each other only to the extent that they transcend each other. To weaken one relation is to weaken the other.

From the standpoint of God, transcendence is absolute to a degree unimaginable by the most ardent deist. In his primordial nature, God is so indifferent to the world that he is not even aware of its existence. As has been said before in a different context, he is, to use Peirce's evocative language, "totus, teres, atque rotundus, . . . solitary, celibate, a dweller in the desert,"⁶ totally disconnected from finite reality, an Aristotelian unmoved mover. Contrasted with this absolute transcendence is the absolute immanence of the world in the consequent nature, which takes up all finite accomplishment in its "tender care that nothing be lost" (PR 525), in its "judgment of a wisdom which uses what in the temporal world is mere wreckage" (PR 525). Good and evil, joy and sorrow, find their niche in the divinely perfected world, which quite literally becomes the Body of God. To speak of redemption without realizing that it means Transsubstantiation is to miss the point entirely. The creature is redeemed by having its factuality and its immediacy transformed as an aspect of the determinacy of the divine actual entity. The creature, be it regnant monad in a man or a puff of existence in empty space, becomes consubstantial with God, everlastingly sharing the divinity, the infinite beauty of divine fruition. For the conscious creature, particularly one attaining the intensity of human consciousness, this implies that in a very Spinozistic sense, redeemed human consciousness is a modality of divine consciousness. Following the lead of Hegel: since no entity, God included, can be immediately self-conscious, it might be said that human consciousness as fragmented through time and space *is* God's consciousness of the content of his own concrescence, that human religious consciousness *is* God's self-awareness diffused through the eyes and ears and mind of humanity and reunited in the redemptive act. Might it be said that in redeeming the world from partiality God also redeems himself from self-alienation? Be that as it may, God's absolute transcendence and the world's absolute immanence render both poles fully actual, fully determinate.

From the standpoint of the world, every entity transcends God in that God gives himself as both conceptual and physical datum to be woven into the finite superject. This is the absolute humility of God—that he consents to become man, mountain, or molecule, giving to each without reserve or exception both its subjective aim and its transformed, redeemed self. God is thus an element in the satisfaction of every finite occasion, immanent in it as luring form and everlasting value. The creature transcends

⁶ *Collected Papers*, edd. Hartshorne and Weiss, 6.235–36.

the Creator as whole transcends part; the Creator is immanent in the creature as having his infinite primordial valuation finitized in a limited subjective aim, as having limited the infinitude of his consequent unity to be datum for a perspectival grasp.

Throughout the perishing occasions in the life of each temporal Creature, the inward source of distaste or of refreshment, the judge arising out of the very nature of things, redeemer or goddess of mischief, is the transformation of Itself, everlasting in the Being of God. In this way, the insistent craving is justified—the insistent craving that zest for existence be refreshed by the ever-present, unfading importance of our immediate actions, which perish and yet live for evermore [PR 533].

Thus, in fine,

e. **It is as true to say that God creates the World, as that the World creates God** [PR 528].

God creates the way beauty creates—by the evocation, unification, and self-donation of intensities of feeling. The love of Creator for creature is found in the awesome aloneness of the self-creation of beauty, in the poetic tenderness which shapes the world epic out of the scattered, obstructive incomplete phrases of world-process, and in the revelation of that redemption for the free appropriation of the redeemed. The love of creature for Creator is manifest in attunement to beauty, in openness to creative ideals realizable in the present, and in concern (in the sense of *Sorge*) for the future as implicated in every present decision. As overtly religious, this love is a continual surrender to the hierarchy of values, a constant endeavor to actualize the greatest value in each occasion of existence, and an unshakable confidence that all one's failures and inadequacies will be re-created in beauty.

The world creates God in the way in which any fact creates the future consequent upon it—by limiting the creativity to be a manifold of novel creations superjected as data for creative transition. By providing the data for divine physical feeling, the world brings about the concreteness of God, ransoming him from his abstract conceptual solitude, giving him matter to be woven into divine Flesh, objects to be illumined in divine consciousness, values to be purified by divine redemption. God is what the world makes him to be; the world is what God lures and redeems it to be. "Either of them . . . is the instrument of novelty for the other" (PR 529); "each is all in all" (PR 529), the all-ness of physical enjoyment everlastingly unified with the all-ness of conceptual appetition, thus perpetually satisfying the endless yearning of the creativity: "that all may be one." "For the kingdom of heaven is with us today" (PR 532).

BIBLIOGRAPHY

Collected Papers of Charles Sanders Peirce. Edd. Charles Hartshorne and Paul Weiss. 6 vols. Cambridge: Harvard University Press, 1931–1935.

Ford, Lewis S. "Whitehead's First Metaphysical Synthesis." *International Philosophical Quarterly,* 17 (1977), 251–64.

Hegel's Science of Logic. Trans. W. H. Johnson and L. G. Struthers. 2 vols. New York: Humanities Press, 1966.

Kline, Morris. "Projective Geometry." In *The World of Mathematics,* ed. James R. Newman. 4 vols. New York: Simon & Schuster, 1956. I 622–41.

Gottfried Wilhelm Leibniz: Philosophical Papers and Letters. Trans. Leroy E. Leomker. 2 vols. Chicago: The University of Chicago Press, 1956.

Lowe, Victor. "Ford's Discovery About Whitehead." *International Philosophical Quarterly,* 18 (1978), 223–26.

The Philosophical Works of Descartes. Trans. Elizabeth S. Haldane and G. R. T. Ross. 2 vols. New York: Dover, 1955.

Rock, Irvin, and Harris, Charles S. "Vision and Touch." *Scientific American,* 216, No. 5 (May 1967), 96–104.

Russell, Bertrand. *The Principles of Mathematics.* London: Allen & Unwin, 1937.

Skinner, B. F. *Beyond Freedom and Dignity.* New York: Bantam, 1972.

INDICES

INDEX NOMINUM

Aquinas, Thomas, 1, 159
Aristotle, 1, 13, 30n1, 41, 82, 97, 172

Bacon, Francis, 17–18
Bergson, Henri, 5, 6, 15, 23, 81n27, 128, 128n1, 129n4
Berkeley, George, 19
Bradley, F. H., 34

Cayley, Arthur, 143

Desargues, Gérard, 143
Descartes, René, 1, 13, 36, 76, 82, 132

Einstein, Albert, 3, 135
Euclid, 134, 140, 142, 144, 148

Ford, Lewis, 12n2

Hartshorne, Charles, 163
Hegel, G. W. F., xi, 46, 91, 159, 160, 172
Heidegger, Martin, 6
Heraclitus, 1
Hume, David, 16, 20, 70, 77, 79, 82, 83, 86

James, William, xii, 14

Kant, Immanuel, xi, 59, 70, 76, 82, 86

Leibniz, G. W. von, 2, 15, 18, 52, 58, 132
Locke, John, 1, 76
Lowe, Victor, 12n2

Maxwell, J. C., 151
Milton, John, 6, 9
Molière, 96

Newton, Isaac, 12, 15, 15n5, 59, 129, 135, 154

Peirce, C. S., 16n6, 92n39, 96n41, 149, 172
Plato, 30n24, 41, 47, 109, 114, 133, 150, 167
Plotinus, 37

Reimann, Georg, 145
Russell, Bertrand, 15, 142

Shelley, Percy Bysshe, 26, 27
Skinner, B. F., 132, 133n9
Spinoza, Baruch, 1, 172
Staudt, Karl G. C. von, 143

Wordsworth, William, 26–27, 75

Zeno, 14, 16, 22, 25, 135, 150

INDEX RERUM

Sections covering major discussions of a term are indicated in **bold-face.**

Abruptness, 36

Abstraction, 35, 35n34, 41, 43, 104, 109, 111, 127

Abstractive set, 23–24, 139–40, 147 (*see also* Set)

Actual entity(ies), 9, 23, 46, 52, 60, 62, 69, 72, 73, 88, 89, 91, 92, 104, 113, 115, 117, 123, 132, 150, 155, 163; as final actuality, 2; as perishing, 2; as act of experience, 20, 70; as self-realizing, 20, 70; as space–time quantum, **21–26**; as prehensive unity, 21, 22, 28, 31, 48, 49, 56, 97, 98; as governed by subjective aim, 49, 107; as subject–superject, 49–50, 101, 103, 105; as mutually immanent, 50–51; as fully definite, 40, 55; Real essence of, 55; as self-functioning, 55; as objectified, 56, 93, 105, 149; as satisfied, 58; as social, 62, 63, 64; as concrescent, 70; as logical subjects of propositions, 91, 93, 113–15, 121–22, 130; as arising from its actual world, 114, 124; as element in a contrast, 117–19, 130; Coordinate analysis of, **127–58**; Genetic analysis of, **101–26**, 127, 129; as "at rest," 59, 154; as perspective on the world, 26 (*see also* Actual occasion)

Actual occasion(s), 38, 40, 59, 66, 68, 91, 102, 104, 126, 153, 154, 157; as act of experience, 20, 77, 87, 98; as prehensive unity, 20, 36; as space–time quantum, **12–26**, 59, 60, 127; as related to eternal objects, 32–33, 35, 57; as self-creative, 37; as social, 39, 92; as perishing, 53; as free, 55; as rupturing the extensive continuum, 60; as housing and pervading all space-times, 60; as arising from its actual world, 61, 62, 135; as propositional (logical) subjects, 91; as concrescent, 98; Genetic analysis of, **101–26**; Co-

ordinate analysis of, 101, **127–58**; as divisible yet undivided, 101–102; as objectified, 105; as extensively connected, 150; as actualizing a strain, 150–51, 154; as "at rest," 154; as a perspective, 26 (*see also* Actual entity)

Actual world, 60, 66, 104, 105, 108, 110, 111, 113, 117, 123, 130, 135, 150, 163, 166, 168, 171; as relative to subjective aim, 48–49, 106–107, 160; as orderly, 61, 62, 117, 124; as disorderly, 61; as unique to each actual entity, 62, 114, 135, 163, 170; of a percipient occasion, 69; as subordinate nexus, 104, 135; as a unity of objective datum, 104–105, 114; as real potential for an actual entity, 106; as interrelated, 114, 131, 134; as a medium, 128, 135, 149–50; as geometrized via strain feelings, 151–53; of the divine actual entity, 163–65; of a "separated" soul, 165–66

Actuality, 34, 40, 56, 59–60, 63, 119, 160–61, 168, 171

Actualization, 85, 127, 149

Adequacy, 45

Adversion, 112, 125

Aesthetic character, 117

Aesthetic complex, 105

Aesthetic decision, 39

Aesthetic experience, 110–11, 126

Aesthetic intensity, 112

Aesthetic phase, 83 (*see also* Aesthetic supplement, Supplemental phase)

Aesthetic supplement, 71, 72, 88, 99, 112 (*see also* Supplemental phase)

Aesthetic unity, 61, 110, 162

Aesthetic value, 61–62 (*see also* Value)

Affirmation, 87–88 (*see also* Affirmation–negation contrast)

Affirmation–negation contrast, 88, 119–25

Animal body, 65–69

Anticipation, 36, 50, 161
Appearance, 95
Appetition, 47n4, 109, 173
Association, 140
Authentic feeling, 116, 120
Autonomy, 49n8, 65, 112
Aversion, 112, 125

Beauty, 161–62, 168–69, 172–73
Becoming, 1–3, 23, 28, 154
Being, 1–3, 28
Bifurcation, 82, 87, 132
Boundary, 134, 136–37

Canalization, 68
Categoreal Obligation: of Conceptual Reversion, 47, 125; of Conceptual Valuation, 110, 110n5, 115, 121; of Objective Diversity, 48, 107, 107n4, 121; of Objective Identity, 48, 107, 107n4, 119; of Subjective Harmony, 112, 112n7, 114, 124; of Subjective Intensity, 50, 125; of Subjective Unity, 48, 67, 106, 106n3, 107, 112, 124; of Transmutation, 48, 73, 73n8, 125
Categoreal scheme, xii, 45, 46–53
Category(ies) of Existence: (iii) 51
Category(ies) of Explanation: (ii) 48, (iv) 47, (ix) 49, (xii) 47, (xiii) 48, (xviii) 48n6, (xxi) 50
Causal feeling, 86, 153
Causal independence, 154
Causal objectification, 77, 101 (see also Causal feeling, Perception in the mode of causal efficacy)
Causal perception, 72–73 (see also Causal feeling, Perception in the mode of causal efficacy)
Causal relation, 16, 39
Causal transference, 132
Causality, 16, 32n29, 36, 70, 83, 84, 85, 86, 105, 109, 119, 120, 132, 133, 150, 154, 169, 170 (see also Efficient causality, Final causality)
Change, 1, 15n5, 21, 27, 65, 159, 169 (see also Becoming)
Coherence, 45
Comparative feeling, 120, 124, 126, 127, 133 (see also Intellectual feeling, Intellectual supplement)
Comparison, 120, 128

Complete locus, 126n20
Complexity, 66
Conceptual prehension(s) (feeling), 47n3, 109, 115, 132; as feeling of eternal objects, 46–47, 109, 132; as appetition, 47, 109; as interwoven with physical prehensions, 47–48, 110, 111, 112; in reverted feelings, 67; in transmuted feelings, 89, 111, 116; subjective form of, 109; as initiated by physical prehension, 110, 115; as introducing purpose, 110; as adjusting importance of physical prehensions, 112; in suspense judgments, 123; in physical purposes, 125, 153; no discrete multiplicity of, 129–30; and geometric elements, 151; and the divine actual entity, 170
Conceptual (mental) pole, 57, 123
Conceptual registration, 115, 117, 122
Conceptual reversion, 110, 115, 116, 126
Conceptual valuation, 107, 109, 110, 112, 126, 160
Concrescence, 36, 46, 50, 53, 56, 60, 69, 70n16, 78, 79, 81, 82, 85, 88, 91, 94, 95, 97, 98, 127, 130, 135, 149, 161, 163; Definition of, 3; as guided by subjective aim, 48, 61, 72; as phasic, 59, 70, 71, 94, 98; as limited by its actual world, 61, 163; Genetic analysis of, 70; as resolving indeterminations in data, 71; Conformal phase of, 71–72, 83, 99; Supplemental phase of, 72, 83, 99; as "closing up," 99; Structure of, 101–26; as presupposing its space-time region, 127, 128; as determined and free, 129; as actualizing a space-time region, 130; as spatializing its world, 150–51; of initial percipient, 153; of final percipient, 153, 156; of the divine actual entity, 164–65, 166, 168, 170; as selective, 171
Concrescent subject, 10, 26, 32, 46, 48, 49, 50, 53, 56, 94, 95, 98, 109, 111, 112, 113, 114, 115, 116, 117, 123, 125, 127, 130, 133, 136, 143, 149
Concreteness, 59
Conformal feeling, 86, 94 (see also Causal feeling, Primary feelings, Vector feeling)
Conformal phase, 71, 72, 83, 105 (see also Primary phase, Receptive phase)

Conformation, 71, 74

Congruence, 156, 157

Connection, 60, 132, 134, 136, 137, 138, 139, 143 (see also Extensive connection)

Conscious experience, 70

Conscious feeling, 151 (see also Comparative feeling, Conscious experience, Consciousness, Intellectual feeling)

Conscious perception, 20 (see also Perception in the mode of presentational immediacy, Perception in the mode of symbolic reference)

Consciousness, 116, 124; of bodily inheritance, 69; Human, 76, 161, 172; as subjective form of affirmation–negation contrast, 88, 90, 119–20; and propositions, 94; and transmuted feelings, 111; and environmental order, 112; of the divine actual entity, 165, 168, 172, 173

Consequent nature of God: as synthesis of physical fact, 51–52, 163, 168; and objective immortality, 165; and subjective immortality, 165–66; as fluent, 170; as non-exclusive, 171; Immanence of world in, 172

Contemporaneity, 77, 154

Contiguity, 24

Continuity, 24, 68

Continuum, 23–24 (see also Extensive continuum)

Contrast, 66n10, 88, 110, 117, 119–20, 123, 125–26, 130, 159, 165, 169 (see also Affirmation–negation contrast, Comparative feeling)

Convergence, 139, 140, 141, 147, 148

Converging tail, 140, 141, 147, 148

Coordinate analysis (division), 70, 101, 103, **127–33**, 134, 135, 136

Corpuscular society, 64

Cosmic epoch, 31, 60, 62, 63, 64, 97, 98, 129, 133, 139, 147, 151, 156, 157, 162

Cover, 23, 24, 140, 147, 148

Creation, 40, 160, 163, 164, 170

Creativity, **36–38**, 55, 99, 108, 132, 161, 170, 171, 173 (see also Substantial activity, Underlying activity)

Creator, 114, 173

Creature, 40, 169, 172, 173

Curvature, 139, 145, 148

Decision, 9, 10, 19, 20, 32, 39, 55, 56, 61, 70, 102, 104, 105, 112, 113, 129, 162, 173

Defining characteristic, 62, 64, 89

Definiteness, 50, 57, 66, 106, 113, 115, 116, 124, 149, 164, 168 (see also Determinateness)

Derivative judgment, 95–98

Determinateness, 22n18, 104, 114, 161, 164 (see also Definiteness)

Determination, 112, 124, 169

Determinism, xi, 31

Direct authentic feeling, 235–36, 238

Disharmony, 106

Disorder, 61, 64, 65, 66, 67

Division, 103, 105, 114 (see also Coordinate division, Genetic division)

Dogmatic fallacy, 46

Duration, 23, 24, 25, 27, 85, 127, 154, 155 (see also Time)

Efficient causality, 3, 29, 50, 65, 101, 105, 108, 112, 130, 165, 169

Elimination, 103, 104, 106, 108, 115, 130, 149, 160, 167 (see also Objectification)

Elliptical geometry, 145, 157

Elliptical space, 145

Emotion, 9

Endurance, 25, 63, 64

Enduring object, 21, 22, 24, 64, 69, 128, 156

Energy, 32, 68, 73

Energy transfer, 109, 135

Enjoyment, 9, 10, 50, 94

Entertainment, 94, 116

Entity, 5, 14, 47

Environment, 63, 64, 65, 66, 112, 116

Epochal theory of time, 23–26

Equivalence, 140, 141, 143, 147–48

Error, 81, 82, 95

Eternal object(s), 32n29, 36, 37, 38n37, 42, 66, 95, 109, 113, 117, 130; Analysis of, **29–36**; Individual essence of, 38; Relational essence of, 38; as complex, 38; as a realm, 38; as related to actuality, 38; as isolated, 38; Need for aboriginal limitation of, 38–39; as limited (valued, ordered, ideally realized) by God, 39–40, 49, 51, 56, 57, 58, 59, 90, 98, 103, 107, 110, 114, 160,

164, 166, 167, 169; as objects of pure conceptual prehension, 47, 99, 109, 123; as objects of impure prehension, 48; as propositional predicates, 48, 51, 88–89, 90, 113, 115; as "together" ideally, 57; as objectifications, 57, 71, 82; as subjective forms, 57–58, 71; as subjective aims, 58, 106–107, 114; as defining characteristics, 63, 64; as supplementing the given, 72; as datively functioning, 72, 108–109; as sensa, 72, 78, 79, 82–83; as simple, 73; and transmutation, 73, 111, 116; as geometric (spatio-temporal) relations, 78, 79, 85, 153; as relational between perceiver and perceived, 79; Two-way functioning of, in symbolic reference, 82–84; in physical purposes, 88, 99, 124, 126, 153; and the affirmation–negation contrast, 90; and indicative systems, 91–92; as tied to the datum, 99, 124–25; and the real potentiality, 107; as valued, 109, 110; as derived from physical feelings, 109–10; as lures, 110; and conceptual reversion, 66–67, 110, 126; and conceptual registration, 110, 115; and physical recognition, 114; and conceptual valuation, 115; and contrasts, 118–19, 122; and judgment, 121; Two-way functioning of, in intuitive judgment, 122; and suspended judgment, 123; Two-way functioning of, in physical purposes, 125; and intensity of experience, 126; as public and private, 132–33; objective species of, 132–33; as Platonic forms, 133; Subjective species of, 132–33, 136; and the divine subjective aim, 171 (*see also* Form)

Event, 31, 80

Evil, 106, 160, 161, 162, 168, 172

Exactness, 156–57

Exemplification, 33, 45, 61, 88, 90, 111, 120, 122, 123, 124

Existence, 2

Experience, 2, 12n1, 22, 30, 44, 70, 86, 87, 93, 97, 152, 164; as synthesis, 10, 87, 105; as basis of philosophy of organism, 11–12, 42–43, 44, 45; and the actual entity, 20, 70, 99, 102; Scientific, 26; as concrete, 26, 43; as abstract, 43, 77; as already interpreted, 43; Provincialism of, 44; as private, 57; as enjoyed, 58, 78; Physical, 66; Perceptual, 69–70, 78, 82–83, 86, 120; as self-realizing process, 70; as conscious, 70, 76–77, 120; of pure causal efficacy, 76; Manageable elements in, 79; Togetherness in, 87, 94; and judgment, 95; and geometric structures, 133–34, 136, 149, 150; and the primordial opposites, 159; and the divine actual entity, 165

Explanation, 42

Extension, 59, 134, 135, 141, 150, 155

Extension over, 134, 139

Extensity, 60, 63n7, 78, 83, 85, 128, 129, 131, 135, 155, 156

Extensive connection, 78, 132, **133–41**, 145, 150, 156, 164

Extensive continuum, **58–60**, 77, 78, 85, 101, 104, 127, 131, 149, 150, 151, 153, 155

Extensive region, 152

Extensive relation, 77, 136, 150, 152, 153

External connection, 138, 146, 148, 150

External relation, 128, 150

Fact, 3, 27, 29, 36, 45, 46, 48, 50, 57, 115, 116, 150, 157, 164, 170

Facticity, 2, 170

Faith, 164, 169

Fallacy of Misplaced Concreteness, 1, 46, 70, 76

Fallacy of Simple Location, **12–16**, 18, 21

Fallacy of the Perfect Dictionary, 6, 8

Falsity, 87, 94, 112n13, 113, 117, 122, 130

Feeling, 6n1, 135, 173; Language of, **9–10**; as feeling the feeling in another, 32, 133; Vector character of, 46; as separable yet inseparate, 114; Propositional, 115–16, 153; Conscious, 119–20; and genetic analysis, 127–28; Subject as unity of, 127, 160; Subjective form of, 133; Divine, 163 (*see also* Causal feeling, Comparative feeling, Conceptual feeling, Conformal feeling, Hybrid feeling, Imaginative feeling, Indicative feeling, Intellectual feeling, Perceptive feeling, Physical

feeling, Predicative feeling, Presentational feeling, Propositional feeling, Reverted feeling, Strain feeling, Transmuted feeling)
Final causality, 3, 44, 47, 48, 65, 101, 112
Flat, 142, 151 (*see also* Flat locus, Flatness)
Flat locus, **141–49**, 150, 154
Flatness, 142, 144
Focal region, 151, 152, 153
Force, 120
Form, 29, 30, 36, 45, 47, 48, 50, 62, 166, 167, 169 (*see also* Eternal object)
Freedom, 9, 55, 65, 81, 103, 112, 168, 169 (*see also* Autonomy)

Generalization, 44, 111, 132
Genetic analysis (division), 70, **101–102**, **102–108**, 113, 123*n*3, 127, 129, 132
Geometric element, 140, 141, 142, 146, 147, 148, 155, 156, 157
Geometric inclusion, 134, 136, 137, 138, 139, 140, 141, 144, 150
Geometry, 30, 78, 85, 131, 133, 134, 136*n*12, 138, 142, 143, 149, 150, 151, 153, 155, 157 (*see also* Elliptical geometry, Metric geometry, Parabolic geometry, Projective geometry)
Givenness, **55–58**, 61, 70, 90
God, 132; Nature of, **38–40**; and finite subjective aims, 49; The primordial nature of, 49, 51, 57–58, 59, 90, 109, 114; as alone with himself, 51; as an actual entity, 51; Consequent nature of, 52; Superject nature of, 52; as source of subjective aims, 105, 107, 114, 127; as creator, 114, 128; and the world, **159–73** (*see also* Primordial nature of God, Consequent nature of God, Superject nature of God, Principle of concretion)
Good, 106, 168, 169, 172

Harmony, 31, 69, 162, 169
Hope, 168
Hybrid entity, 48, 51, 88, 90
Hybrid prehension (feeling), 89, 170
Hybrid physical prehension (feeling), 114, 115, 116, 125, 153
Hyperbolic geometry, 157

Identity, 32, 61, 110 (*see also* Defining characteristic)
Imagination, 36, 123–24
Imaginative judgment (feeling), 116–17, 121, 123
Immanence, 127, 160, 169, 171, 172, 173
Immediacy, 3, 11, 20, 46, 50, 160, 161, 162, 163, 164, 165, 167, 168, 170, 171, 172 (*see also* Subjective immediacy)
Immortality, *see* Objective immortality, Subjective immortality
Importance, 33, 61, 63, 73, 80, 99, 111, 112, 150, 151, 153 (*see also* Significance, Value, Worth)
Impure prehension, 48–49 (*see also* Hybrid prehension)
Inauthentic feeling, 120, 122
Incidence, 141, 142, 143
Incident element, 140, 141
Inclusion, 33 (*see also* Geometric inclusion)
Incompatibility, 115, 117, 168
Indicative feeling, 114, 115, 116, 119, 120, 121, 122
Indicative system, 92, 93, 115
Individualization, 40
Indirect authentic feeling, 116
Induction, **17–20**, 96, 97, 98
Infinitesimal, 15*n*5, 16*n*6
Ingression, 32, 33, 34, 35, 36, 39, 58, 66, 72, 107, 123, 125
Inheritance, 64, 65, 67, 68, 69
Initial aim, 50 (*see also* Subjective aim)
Initial datum (data), 71, 103, 104, 105, 106, 108, 114, 115, 124, 130
Insistence, 120
Integration, 66, 107, 117, 120, 121, 124, 125, 128
Intellectual feeling, 119, 124 (*see also* Comparative feeling)
Intellectual supplement, 71, 72, 88, 99 (*see also* Supplemental phase)
Intelligence, 81
Intelligibility, 31, 36, 167
Intensification, 99
Intensity, 61, 62, 64, 65, 78, 106, 108, 111, 112, 117, 125, 133, 161
Interest, 90
Internal relation, 16, 34, 38, 131, 150

Interpretation, 42–43
Intersect, 137–38, 144, 145, 146, 148
Intuition of suitability, 98, 156–57
Intuitive judgment (feeling), 95, 121–24

Judgment, 77, 81, 82, 87, 88, **94–98**, 103, 121–24, 125 (*see also* Derivative judgment, Intuitive judgment)

Knowledge, 41

Language, **5–10**, 12, 43
Laws of nature, 97, 117
Life, 65–68
Limit, 141, 146, 148
Limitation, 34, 39
Line, 133, 134, 135, 136, 139, 140, 141, 142, 144, 145, 147, 151 (*see also* Straight line)
Linear stretch, 141–42, 146, 148
Literature, 12, **26–29**, 81
Living person, 68
Locus, 154
Locus of points, 148
Loss, 160
Love, 162, 169, 173
Lure, 32, 49, 58, 102, 110, 169, 172–73 (*see also* Subjective aim)

Mathematical relation, 155–56
Mathematics, 12, 13, 15, 15n5, 29, 30, 30n23, 31n26
Matter, 20, 21
Meaning, 80, 82, 93, 136
Measurement, 135, 141, 145, 149, **154–57**
Mechanical causality, 14
Mechanics, 13
Mediate connection, 137, 150
Memory, 17, 20, 36, 50, 128, 129, 129n4, 162
Mental (conceptual) pole, 57, 123
Meta-geometry, 134
Metaphysical proposition, 93–94
Metric geometry, 142–43, 156, 157
Mind, 69
Motion, 14–15, 154
Multiplicity, 38, 177

Nature, 4, 12–13, 14, 17, 26, 27, 28, 29, 162
Necessity, 45

Negation, 120, 122, 124 (*see also* Affirmation–negation contrast)
Negative judgment, 123
Negative prehension, 65–66, 113n8, 162; of irrelevant or contrary eternal objects, 47; as positive exclusion, 55, 58; and environmental disorder, 66, 112; of inconsistent elements in the data, 104, 108, 114, 126, 171; as directed by subjective aim, 107; and elimination, 115; and objectification, 114; in intuitive judgments, 121–22; in negative judgments, 122–23; in imaginative judgments, 123; in coordinate analysis, 130, 133, 135; in the divine actual entity, 167, 168
Nexus, 74, 86, 88, 95, 113; as public matter of fact, 51; as most general form of togetherness among actual entities, 51, 115, 132; as propositional subject, 51, 58, 88–89, 90, 94, 113; Actual world as subordinate, 52–53; of eternal objects, 57; and actual world, 60, 104; and society, 62, 64; as non-social (living), 65–66; as entirely living, 67; and transmuted feelings, 89, 111, 115, 152; and indicative systems, 92, 93; and reverted feelings, 111; and perceptive feelings, 111, 116; and reverted feelings, 111; and imaginative feelings, 117; as common element grounding a contrast, 117–19; and conscious perception, 120, 124; and intuitive judgment, 121, 122; and the "yes" form of judgment, 122; and truth, 123; and physical purposes, 125; and strains, 150; as structured by systematic relations, 156; and measurement, 156, 157
"No" form of judgment, 122
Novelty, 3, 11, 51, 65, 66, 66n9, 67, 68, 74, 89, 90, 98, 107, 110, 116, 125, 160

Object, 10, 60, 109, 115, 130, 133 (*see also* Enduring object, Eternal object)
Object of judgment, 94
Object of primary feelings, 108
Objectification(s), 70–71, 74, 91, 106, 113, 150; Nature of, 50; as selective (elimination), 53, 57, 99, 114, 149, 162, 163, 171; as functioning of past

in present, 53, 56–57, 105, 136; as potential, 59, 93; and the eternal objects, 59; and social order, 63, 106; as structured by eternal objects, 71, 133; Chains of, 74, 83, 128–29, 150–51; of organ region, 83–84; Indirect, 86; and propositions, 93; as decided by past actual entity, 104; of the divine actual entity, 107; and subjective forms, 107–108; and physical feeling, 109; and conceptual feeling, 109; and subjective unity, 112; and conceptual valuation, 115; immediate, 149; and sensa, 153; and the divine actual entity (see also Causal objectification, Presentational objectification)

Objective datum, 71–72, 103, 104, 105, 106, 108, 110, 114, 123, 151, 164

Objective immortality, 3, 29, 50, 53, 59, 161–62, 165, 170

Objectivity, 3, 28, 75, 94, 98, 99, 103, 105, 107, 136, 160

Ontological principle, 48, 51n9

Order, 40, 61, 62, 63, 64, 90, 111, 151, 159, 160, 166, 167 (see also Personal order, Serial order, Social order)

Organic structure, 17

Organic universe, 17, 18, 26, 27

Oval region, 145, 148

Oval surface, 147

Oval volume, 147

Ovate, 144–45

Ovate abstractive set, 145–48, 149

Overlap, 52, 78, 137, 138, 145, 150

Parabolic geometry, 157

Participation, 166

Particle, 14 (see also Matter)

Pattern, 56, 67, 239, 251, 264, 268 (see also Eternal object)

Perception, 19, 58n2, 81n27, 152n24; in CN and PNK, 3–5, 31; in Bacon, 17–18; Modal theory of, 69–77; Basis of 74; Human, 81, 87; as abstract, 86; Reception and display of nexus in, 111; Bergson on, 119–20; as an integration of feelings, 120; Conscious, 120, 122; of extensity, 155 (see also Perception in the mode of causal efficacy, Perception in the mode of pres-

entational immediacy, Perception in the mode of symbolic reference)

Perception in the mode of causal efficacy: Analysis of, 72–76; as integrated with presentational immediacy, 76, 80; as concerned with past world, 77, 111; as indistinct, 79, 85; as infallible, 81; in symbolic reference, 82, 84; Sense data given by, 82; as indirect feeling of the presented locus, 85; as primary, 86 (see also Causal feeling, Causal objectification, Causal perception)

Perception in the mode of presentational immediacy, 135n11, 156; Analysis of, 152–60; as infallible, 81; Source and function of sensa in, 82, 83; Illustration (display) of regions in, 85–86; as a pure phenomenology of appearances, 86; and the presented locus, 86; and transmutation, 111; and consciousness, 120; and measurement, 135–36, 155, 157; and strain feelings, 151–52; as exhibiting systematic, mathematical relations, 156; Objectivity of, 156; as display of contemporary environment, 157 (see also Presentational feeling, Presentational objectification)

Perception in the mode of symbolic reference, 77n20; as ordinary mode of human consciousness, 76; Analysis of, 80–87; and transmutation, 111–12; as synthesis of was and could be, 120; Objectivity of, 134, 136; and strain feelings, 151–52; and measurement, 154–55

Perceptive feeling, 116, 120, 121, 124

Perceptual quality, 79

Perishing, 53, 160, 162, 168, 173

Permanence, 1, 2, 3, 28, 157, 159, 169–70 (see also Being)

Personal order, 64, 65, 68, 126, 128, 156, 163 (see also Personal thread)

Personal thread, 154 (see also Personal order)

Personality, 68

Perspective, 18n10, 19nn11&12, 114, 131, 143

Phenomenon–noumenon, 77, 82

Philosophy, 12, 42, 42n2 (see also Speculative philosophy, Speculative scheme)

Philosophy of organism, xii, 2, 5, 18, 87, 143, 149

Physical field, 150

Physical pole, 115, 128, 129

Physical prehension(s) (feeling): as feeling causal agency, 46, 109; as never negative when pure, 46, 113n8; as basic element in concrescence, 47, 111; Divine, 52, 163, 164, 167–68; as dominating primary phase, 108; Subjective forms of, 108–109; as vector feeling, 108–109; as alien, 108–109; as objectifying element, 109; as energy transfer, 109; as source of conceptual feelings, 109–10, 112, 115, 123; as valued, 110, 112; as integrated with conceptual feelings, 111; of nexuses through transmuted feelings, 111, 115; as indicative feelings, 114; and propositional feelings, 117; and judgment, 121; and suspended judgment, 123; and physical purposes, 125, 153; and the unity of the superject, 127; as the basis of coordinate division, 129–30; as almost independent entities, 130, 131; as public and private, 132; in immediate objectification, 149; in remote objectification, 149–50; and strain feelings, 150, 151, 157

Physical purpose, 48, 88, 124–26, 153

Physical recognition, 114–15, 116, 120, 121, 122

Physics, 7, 20, 31n25, 64 (see also Relativity physics)

Plane, 133, 141, 142, 145, 151, 153

Poetic insight, 26

Point, 133, 134, 139, 140–41, 142, 144, 146, 147, 148, 149, 150, 155

Position indicator, 91–93

Possibility, 37, 93, 119, 123 (see also Potentiality)

Potentiality, 93, 120, 122, 160, 164, 171 (see also Possibility)

Power, 76, 96

Predicate, 48, 88, 89, 90, 91, 94, 115, 116, 121, 122, 123, 130 (see also Predicative feeling, Predicative pattern, Predicative relation)

Predication, 2, 5, 93, 97

Predicative feeling, 115, 116, 119, 121

Predicative pattern, 93, 115, 117, 119, 122

Predicative relation, 91

Prehension(s), 21, 35, 36, 37, 47, 80, 84, 98, 105; Analysis of, 17–20; as patterned unification, 21–22, 49, 103; as emotional grasp, 26; as feeling the feeling in another, 32, 133; as a concrete fact of relatedness, 46; Kinds of, 46–47; of subjective aim, 49; Actual entity as concrescence of, 50; Propositional, 51, 56, 87, 113; in physical purposes, 88; and genetic analysis, 100; as incomplete, 102; as a proper entity, 102; as separable but not separated, 102; as public and private, 132; Subjective forms of, 133; of a region, 152 (see also Feeling, Conceptual prehension, Hybrid prehension, Hybrid physical feeling, Physical prehension, Negative prehension)

Prehensive unification, 19

Presentational feeling, 86, 87

Presentational objectification, 78, 84, 152, 153, 154, 155, 164, 169

Presented duration, 87

Presented locus, 79–80, 85, 86, 168

Presiding occasion, 69 (see also Regnant monad)

Primary feelings, 108–12 (see also Conformal feeling)

Primary phase, 108 (see also Conformal phase, Receptive phase)

Prime, 141n15, 147, 149

Primordial envisagement, 109 (see also Primordial nature of God)

Primordial nature of God, 73n17, 110n6; as principle of concretion, 40; as protean ordering (limitation) of eternal objects, 49, 51; as appropriated by the world, 51; as ideal realization of eternal objects, 56–57, 90; as undergirding the solidarity of the world, 58; as irrational ordering of eternal objects, 166; as atemporal, 170; as deficient in actuality, 171; as transcending the world, 172 (see also Primordial order, Primordial valuation, Principle of concretion)

Primordial order, 90, 107

Primordial valuation, 114

Principle of concretion, 39, 40, 160, 166
Principle of relativity, 30–31, 47, 51, 113, 163, 169
Privacy, 2
Private aim, 61
Probability, 95–98
Process, 2, 3, 25, 49, 55, 59, 102, 160, 162, 163, 167, 169, 170, 171; as atomic, 1, 161; as ongoing and creative, 5; of subjectification, 50; as different from reality, 53; Schema of, 71; and novelty, 90–91; Overview of, **98–99**; Modes of, 101; Phasic succession in, 102; as organic, 136; as initiated by subjective aim, 161; as needing "redemption," 62; Functioning of the primordial nature of God in, 169, 170 (*see also* Concrescence, Transition)
Process philosophy, xii, 159
Progress, 44, 123–24
Projection, 143, 144, 151 152, 153, 155
Projective geometry, 143, 145, 151, 153
Projective space, 145
Projector, 151, 152, 155
Proper entity, 102n1
Proposition(s), 48n5, 87n33, 117, 121, 153, 169; as partially indeterminate, 8; as verbal, 8; Subjective aim as, 48, 58, 102; as togetherness of nexus and eternal object, 51; as lure for feeling, 51; as interesting, 81; Analysis of, **87–94**; and judgment, 94–95; and consciousness, 94; "Entertainment" as ordinary subjective form of, 94; as true or false, 51, 89, 94, 122–23; Genetic analysis of, **112–17**; as a contrast, 117; Role of, in coordinate division, 130 (*see also* Metaphysical proposition, Propositional feeling)
Propositional feeler, 90
Propositional feeling(s) (prehension), 99; as impure (hybrid) prehensions, 47–48, 89, 90; and judgment, 87, 94, 95; Object of, 89; as synthetic feelings, 89, 115; and conscious feelings, 94, 119–20; Genesis of, 114; Initial data of, 115; and indicative systems, 115; Subjective forms of, 115–16; Truth or falsity of, 116; Source of data for, 120; and conceptual valuation, 124; and eternal objects, 132–33; and strain

feelings, 152–53 (*see also* Proposition)
Propositional (logical) subject, 87, 88, 89, 90, 91, 92, 93, 94, 113, 115, 116, 117, 121, 130
Purpose, 9, 48, 110 (*see also* Physical purpose)

Qualia, 31, 32, 36
Quality, 2
Quantity, 2
Quantum mechanics, 21

Rationalism, 6, 13, 14
Reality, 4, 53, 131, 165
Realization, 20, 27, 32, 37, 56, 166, 167, 170
Reason, 31, 81, 82, 86
Receptive phase, 73 (*see also* Conformal phase, Primary phase)
Receptivity, 99
Redemption, 162, 163, 164, 171, 172, 173
Region, 127, 128, 131, 133, 134, 135, 135n10, 136, 137, 138, 139, 141, 143, 148, 150, 151, 152, 153, 155
Regnant monad, 68–69
Relatedness, 46
Relation, 2, 3–5, 16, 29, 30–31, 35, 77, 93, 132, 156 (*see also* Extensive relation, External relation, Internal relation)
Relational essence, 34–35, 38
Relativity physics, 21, 59, 77, 154
Relevance, 47, 90, 114, 115, 152
Religion, xi, 12, 43, 81
Religious experience, 162, 169
Responsibility, 106, 112
Rest, 154
Reversion, 74, 75, 79, 83, 115, 116, 120, 122, 125, 126, 169 (*see also* Categoreal Obligation, Conceptual reversion, Reverted conceptual feeling)
Reverted conceptual feeling, 47, 57, 66, 66n10, 110, 111, 112, 116, 126
Romance, 11

Satisfaction, 9, 70, 70n16, 102, 153, 165; as fully determinate, 10, 46, 55, 56, 127, 163; as a unitary feeling, 56, 71; as exclusive, 58, 103; as a synthesis, 59; Intensity in, 60–61, 62, 63, 64–65,

68, 106, 111, 117, 124, 125; Subjective form of, 61, 107–108; Aesthetic structure of, 61, 62, 126; and social order, 61–62, 64–65; and living occasions, 65–66, 68; Novelty in, 78; in low-grade occasions, 99; in high-grade occasions, 99, 124; as divisible but undivided, 101, 105, 128; as objectified, 103–104; as actualizing a strain, 150; of the divine actual entity, 166

Science, 12, 13, 16, 16n7, 43, 155, 156, 157

Scientific materialism, **12–16**

Scientific Revolution, 12

Section, 143, 144, 151

Segment, 141–42, 148, 157

Self-congruence, 156

Self-reference, 7, 45, 103, 129n3

Self-value, 28 (*see also* Value)

Sense, 18

Sense data, 82, 136

Sense perception, 75, 76, 87 (*see also* Perception in the mode of symbolic reference)

Sense projection, 84 (*see also* Perception in the mode of presentational immediacy)

Sense qualia, 73 (*see also* Qualia, Sensum)

Sense reception, 72, 86n31 (*see also* Perception in the mode of causal efficacy)

Sensum, 73, 74, 78, 82–84, 86, 111, 120, 151, 152, 153, 155

Serial order, 22, 144, 145

Set, 139, 140, 141, 142, 146, 147, 148, 154 (*see also* Abstractive set)

Significance, 3, 50 (*see also* Importance, Relevance, Value, Worth)

Simple location, 14, 15, 16, 45, 63, 113, 114 (*see also* Fallacy of Simple Location)

Sin, 168

Social institution, 43

Social occasion, 85

Social order, 62, 97, 98, 156 (*see also* Society)

Social past, 66

Social relation, 17

Social structure, 12

Society, 39, 62–66, 69, 97–98, 106, 151, 156, 165

Solipsism, 28, 79

Soul, 69, 165

Space, 19, 21, 22, 129, 131, 134, 149, 164, 168, 172

Space–time, 22n18, 26, 30, 52, 59, 60, 101, 102, 131, 135, 142, 150

Space–time region, 128

Spatial intuition, 142

Spatial region, 127

Speculative philosophy, **41–46**

Speculative reason, 31

Speculative scheme, 38, 41, 43, 44, 45, 160, 162

Spontaneity, 164 (*see also* Freedom)

Spread, 136

Statistics, 97, 98

Straight, 139, 142, 148, 149 (*see also* Flat)

Straight line, 80, 142, 144, 146, 147, 148, 149, 150, 153, 155, 157

Straightness, 142, 143, 144, 147, 148 (*see also* Flatness)

Strain(s), **149–54**, 155, 157

Strain feeling, 79, 150, 151, 152, 155, 157

Strain locus, 153, 154, 155

Strain seat, 150, 151, 152, 153, 155

Structured society, 65, 66, 67

Stubborn fact, 13

Subject, *see* Concrescent subject, Propositional (logical) subject

Subject–superject, 103, 104, 107, 114, 127, 135 (*see also* Concrescent subject, Superject)

Subjectification, 28, 50, 105, 114, 127

Subjective aim, 49, 57, 61, 74, 78, 114, 123, 124, 125, 127; as final causality luring the concrescence, 48, 49, 107, 108; as a proposition, 48, 102; grounded in the primordial nature of God, 49, 58, 106–107, 114, 165, 169, 170, 172; and creaturely initiative, 49; as determining subjective forms, 58, 109, 129; as immanent in all phases of the concrescence, 101–102; as a possibility-for-a-subject, 106; as aim at intensity of feeling, 125–26; and conceptual feelings, 129; Negative prehension of, in coordinate division, 130; of the divine actual entity, 163, 166–68, 171 (*see also* Initial aim)

Subjective autonomy, 267

Subjective form(s), 26n21; as emotional-purposive, 19, 48, 72, 99; as how an actual entity feels its data, 48, 56, 71, 107, 108; as "sympathetic," 48, 49, 57; as structuring feelings, 56, 83; as eternal objects, 57–58, 71, 132–33; of negative prehensions, 58, 66, 122; as determined by the subjective aim, 58, 108; of the satisfaction, 61; as seat of novelty, 66–67, 107–108; and consciousness, 69, 72, 90, 112, 116, 119, 124; as re-enactive, 72, 73, 109, 110; as supplementary, 72; and geometric eternal objects, 85; of judgmental feelings, 94; as embodying the genesis of the feeling, 107; as private and pragmatic, 107; of conceptual feelings, 109; as valuations, 110, 112; of propositional feelings, 115–16; of "yes" form of judgment, 122; of "no" form of judgment, 122; in genetic analysis, 128; in coordinate analysis, 133

Subjective immediacy, 2, 71, 73, 78, 98, 162

Subjective immortality, 165

Subjective unity, 160, 163, 167

Subjectivity, 3, 10, 103, 105, 109, 161, 162

Substance, 1, 2, 37

Substantial activity, 37–38 (see also Creativity)

Succession, 102, 127

Suitability, 98

Superject, 10, 50, 53, 55, 56, 56n1, 67, 70, 101, 127, 128, 128n2, 169, 171

Superject nature of God, 52, 169

Superjection, 56n1, 104, 125, 156, 163, 168, 173

Supplemental phase, 71, 99 (see also Aesthetic supplement, Intellectual supplement)

Supplementary feeling, 72

Surface, 133, 136, 141, 144, 147

Suspense form of judgment, 123

Symbol, 80, 82, 87

Temporalization, 24–25

Theology, 159

Thought, 5, 36

Time, 14, 21, 22, 24, 25, 27, 128, 129, 131, 154, 162, 164, 168, 172 (see also Duration, Epochal theory of time)

Togetherness, 30, 33, 34, 51, 52, 57, 87, 88, 89, 91, 94, 117, 153, 161, 163

Topology, 143, 144

Transcendence, 32, 160, 169, 171, 172, 173

Transition, 25, 101, 103, 104, 105, 169

Transmission, 129, 149, 150, 152

Transmutation, 74, 75, 82, 89, 111, 112, 115, 116, 152 (see also Categoreal Obligation, Transmuted feeling)

Transmuted feeling, 111, 112

Truth, 81, 82, 87–88, 94, 95, 96, 105, 112n13, 113, 117, 120, 122, 123, 169

Uncertainty principle, 7, 8, 155

Underlying activity, 36–38 (see also Creativity)

Understanding, 41–42

Unity, 117, 119, 165

Valuation, 109, 110, 112, 122, 125, 126, 160

Value, 3, 10, 14, 29, 37, 49, 102, 124, 168, 173; as permanent (immortal), 3, 27, 32, 160, 161; in nature, 29; as aesthetic achievement, 28, 39, 61, 62; Trivalent nature of, 28, 33, 50, 61, 160; as pattern aimed at, 29; as pattern achieved, 29, 56; as concrete, 29, 58, 61, 160, 161, 170; as abstract, 29, 58; as outcome of process, 39; as trivial, 61; in the satisfaction, 65; Adjustment of, 87; Function of the divine actual entity with respect to, 170, 172 (see also Importance, Significance, Worth)

Vector feeling, 20, 46, 73, 74, 75, 78, 83, 84, 99, 128, 128n2, 129, 136, 150, 151 (see also Conformal feeling, Physical feeling, Primary feelings)

Verification, 42, 44

Vivacity, 120

Volume, 133, 141, 142, 144, 147, 150, 155

World, 26, 159–60, 161, 164, 166, 168, 169–73

Worth, 28

"Yes" form of judgment, 122